HOME, JAYNE!

Frances McCaffrey

Copyright © 2019, FRANCES McCAFFREY

All rights reserved. No part of this publication may be reproduced, distributed or transmitted in any form or by any means without permission of the publisher, except in the case of brief quotations referencing the body of work and in accordance with copyright law.

Registered with the Library of Congress

ISBN: 978-1-913479-07-7 (paperback)
ISBN: 978-1-913479-08-4 (ebook)

Cover Image by Michael Webb
Book Design by Michael Maloney

First edition published in 2019

That Guy's House
20-22 Wenlock Road
London
England
N1 7GU

www.ThatGuysHouse.com

That Guy's House

Praise for *HOME, JAYNE!*

In this gutsy book Frances McCaffrey shares with humor and simplicity an unusual and fascinating life. Your artistry is a gift. This book shows how to unwrap your gift.

Life coach/Author/Motivational Speaker, **Mary Manin Morrissey**

There is a magical reality to HOME, JAYNE! Frances bets on herself while reaching for the stars. Her unshakable belief in the basic goodness of life triumphs over bad betrayals and setbacks. This is the poignant, often hilarious adventures of an indomitable spirit.

Indie filmmaker, **Charlene Brinkman**

Frances is a gutsy, vivacious and passionate woman who knows how to create with magic! Travel with her from East to West – from Woodstock to Hollywood – and enjoy the sexy, exhilarating ride! From success to losing it all- she rides with beauty, love and adventure. I say "go home with Jayne!"

RN, MS, MFCC, **Joyce Lechuga**

Frances McCaffrey is a bold, vivid, engaging writer! She has a knack of giving you a "one-two knock-out punch" while still maintaining her feminine grace. I adored working with her on her autobiographical solo play. Frances is an audience favorite!

Award Winning Theatre Writer/Director, **Debra De Liso**

ACKNOWLEDGMENTS

I gratefully acknowledge my siblings—Nancy, Lee, Mark, Russell and Billy—for giving me their unconditional love and meaningful support while writing this book. I also wish to express immense gratitude to my nephews, Holden and Justin, who always show up to help me through challenges, be they legal, creative, or medical. To my other three nephews—Skyler, Ryan and Kevin—thank you for your unwavering love from afar. Following the demise of my "ATM business," I'm sure it would have been less worrisome to all of you had I chosen the more practical path of finding a new job. So, thank you for being there with your love, brilliance, and humor when life has brought me to my knees. I love you beyond. This book is for you.

I thank my dad, William McCaffrey, who instilled in me the importance of personal integrity and a generosity of spirit. Though no longer on this physical plane, I sometimes get to say "hello" to him in my dreams, and I know that when my time comes he'll be there to greet me with a glass of heavenly water.

I thank my amazing mother, Edna, my close confidant still at age ninety-eight, for bringing me into this world and supporting me in everything I've tried to accomplish. She has encouraged me to believe in myself and to be bold enough to go for my dreams. Having her love and prayers supporting me through all my ups and downs has meant more to me than words can say.

I thank my dear and longtime friends, Brinke Stevens and Jeanine Anderson, for willingly reading multiple drafts and kindly offering encouragement and corrections. I thank Guy Guilbert for his assistance and expertise with the photographs, as well as for his influence on the cover design. I am so blessed for these and all of my precious friendships. I trust you know who you are.

I profoundly thank my dear friend, Toby Rafelson, for her generous interest in, and attention to, my manuscript throughout its various stages of development. Her expertise upped my writing game and moved me forward.

I am grateful to the editors that I have had the honor of working with: Amanda Rooker, Anita Clayton, and Clare Coombes. Each of these talented women encouraged me, while at the same time requiring me to grow as a writer. I respect your special role in this process enormously and look forward to working together again.

Charles Hope—I don't know where he is, or even if he still lives on this Earth, but I extend a heartfelt thanks to him for being my angel that fateful August day in 1976 in New York City. His unorthodox generosity came at a time when I needed it badly, and it enabled me to go for a great adventure—one that allowed me to transport my weary self to the west coast, where I happily reside still.

I want to profoundly thank Bob Rafelson for his belief in me and his willingness to do something about it.

In a general sense, I wish to express gratitude to all of the celebrities mentioned in this book, some of whom I was privileged to chauffeur around in a limousine. Thank you for the rich stories you've given me.

I wish to extend my deepest gratitude to Reverend Michael Bernard Beckwith, founder of the Agape Spiritual Center in Los Angeles, who has provided guidance and support to me and countless others for the past twenty plus years. Not surprisingly, it was through this beloved community that I found Sean Patrick Parker, publisher and founder of That Guy's House. Sean's enthusiasm to bring *Home, Jayne!* forth into the world has transformed what might have been an arduous process into a joyous one. I thank his team members for their support and specifically Michael Maloney for his talent and patience as he guided me through the cover and interior design process.

Contents

PART ONE

WOODSTOCK, 1969 .... *1*

WHO AM I? *7*

CANNES FILM FESTIVAL *15*

A MILE RUNNER ON A QUARTER TRACK *31*

THE BIG APPLE *39*

ROBERT ALTMAN *47*

SPIDERS AND RAINBOWS *53*

FROG LEGS & RAZOR BLADES, 1975 .... *59*

SHOCK & DELIGHT *65*

AMERICA *73*

EATING CAKE *87*

HIT & MISS *93*

GOIN' SOUTH *97*

FRANCINE AT THE WHEEL *103*

FLEETWOOD MAC	*109*
CARRYING MY WEIGHT	*113*
ROYAL ROLLS, 1978/79	*115*
THE SAUDI CONNECTION	*123*
MICKEY MANTLE & BILLY MARTIN	*131*
TO BE OR NOT TO BE—*REAL*	*137*
WOLFMAN JACK	*141*
WHEN SHAME PAYS 1979	*147*
TONY BENNETT	*161*
PLATO'S RETREAT	*167*
MAKING WAVES	*173*
BOB RAFELSON	*181*

PART TWO

THE MANUSCRIPT	*195*
CHERRY 2000	*201*
KEEPER OF THE FLAME, 1986	*205*
ALICE IN BUSINESSLAND	*213*

BREAKING A MILL...221

MY BABY'S BEEN KIDNAPPED!......................................227

TO HEED OR NOT TO HEED—ADVICE......................235

MATTERS OF THE HEART...245

THE SKY IS FALLING..255

THE LAST LUNCH...265

BURNING THE SCANDAL AT BOTH ENDS................271

JUDGEMENT DAY..279

WHAT WISDOM GARNERED?..283

INTRODUCTION

In 2014 I was stunned to learn that the company that I had invested my life savings with, and had proudly represented to family and friends for over seventeen years, was discovered to be nothing more than a Ponzi scheme—and I was at the very heart of it, being scrutinized by the FBI, the Security Exchange Commission, and several fellow victims. As a means of coming to grips with how I wound up in this unimaginable nightmare, I turned back the clock and revisited my life's journey. This memoir is the result of that process.

PART ONE

WOODSTOCK, 1969

I was seventeen years old, living in Birmingham, Michigan, and was about to board a plane that would take me from Detroit to Rochester, New York. My parents thought I was going to Lansing to visit my older sister, Nancy, for the weekend, but I actually had a hot date who was taking me to Woodstock. It was August, 1969.

Getting settled into my seat as the plane boarded, I was shocked to find myself looking at a familiar face and quickly turned my head away toward the window. *Oh my God! That was Mr. Jenson, and he saw me. Oh, what a bummer. And he'll tell Dad. Of course he will—they're golfing buddies. Shoot! I hated having to lie to them. I was going to tell them about it afterwards, once I was home safe. Then they'd be okay with it. It's for their own good that I spare them. That way they don't have to worry about me unnecessarily. Hell, they wouldn't let me do half the stuff I do if they knew about it.*

Anyway, I'm making my own money. I did well in school, doing great at my sales job, and pretty good at this modeling thing. Besides, I'm very mature for my age. Yeah, I think I've got good karma and can handle myself well out in the world. I'm actually quite excited about my future. Not sure what it looks like yet but I'm excited about it. I wonder if it will include Randy.

The plane rose up into the heavy dark clouds. *I've never been to an outdoor concert before and now it's supposed to rain. I don't want to think about that or I'll dread it. I just want to think about Randy and his welcoming arms around me when I see him.*

I had met Randy ten months earlier in Boston while attending a college open-house with a friend. I'll always remember the first time I laid eyes on him. Tall with dark wavy hair and broad shoulders, he had these gorgeous green eyes with super thick eyelashes and his cheeks were chiseled looking, giving a depth of character to his face. I said to myself, "That is the best-looking guy I have ever seen." I couldn't help but smile at him as we left the building, never dreaming it would lead to anything.

To tell you the truth, I knew I was cute—in a pixie sort of way, had a great smile and a "world-class ass," as Nancy loved to say. But I also knew that I was no great beauty. But regardless, before meeting Randy, I believed that no guy was ever going to find me sexually attractive. The reason being because I was what many referred to as "flat chested." God, I hate that phrase, and I don't mind admitting that it led to a double-D size complex. So, let's just say, I was lacking big-time in the boob department, which was a tough pill to swallow, especially since both my sisters developed decent ones. *But no! I had to draw the Old Maid card and take after my mother!* Anyway, I knew there were more important things in life, so I tried to accept my bum luck and follow my grandmother's advice, "Franny, what God has forgotten—fill it with cotton."

At twenty-three, Randy was six years my senior—two years older than my big sister Nancy, the oldest of six. Besides being a Dartmouth graduate going for a master's degree at the University of Rochester, Randy was also kind, respectful, and fun-loving. He was my dream-come-true first boyfriend, the epitome of what most people would think of as a "great catch."

Though I was somewhat experienced socially, I was grossly uninformed about sex, and clung to my virginity like a child might to their favorite blanket. Ten years of Catholic schooling was not lost on me. Just to give you one example of my naiveté—a few months into our relationship, Randy invited me to Long Island to meet his mother. There we slept in separate bedrooms but snuggled for hours in the family-room before saying goodnight. Trying to hold the line at petting, I kept the guy in a constant state of frustration and one night he lost it, so to speak. He stifled his orgasm so well that I had no idea it had even occurred. But there was one thing I knew to be true in that moment. "Hey, I smell lobster," I said. He looked at me blankly. "No, really, I smell lobster!" And on and on, until finally he had to explain that he had ejaculated in his pants—and that semen can smell a little fishy. Oh, dear.

Upon exiting the plane, I felt reassured when I saw him there ready to sweep me into a warm embrace. I could only hope that Mr. Jenson wasn't watching. After a delicious, minty kiss, he took my bag and guided me out to the curb where a couple of his friends awaited us. Then we set sail out into the stormy night.

Our excitement mounted as we listened to radio reports about unprecedented crowds and epic traffic jams. The authorities urged everyone to turn around and go home. When we finally got as close as possible, a police officer told us that we had an eighteen-mile walk. That was a bit daunting, so Randy and his buddy consulted a map and drove around the state, approaching from a different angle. A few hours later, we got it down to four-miles.

The rain subsided as the sun's rays brought the morning to light. Pungent manure steam rose from the saturated farmland, mixing with wafts of incense, sage and marijuana. Slowly, we trekked through the mud amid a maze of happy faces. "Look!" I said, pointing to a police car parked on the side of the road, covered with flowers and peace signs. "There will be no governing here," I added with a laugh. Smiling strangers offered us pieces of fruit and drags off of joints. Randy and I weren't smokers, so we refused. We were straight arrows—an oddity at Woodstock.

A mile or so along the way, we bore witness to a scene where a couple of guys were having a heated exchange. Everyone around them stopped and looked at them, channeling a vibration of peace. It was the order of the day and could be no other way. The hostility dissolved, the clenched fist morphed into a peace sign, and harmony once again prevailed. Just then, a voice bellowed out over a megaphone, "The Woodstock Festival has been declared a nation unto itself. The whole world is watching!" A thrill swept through the crowd as we all realized that we were a major happening, the likes of which the world had never seen. *Oh, my God! I can't wait for my brothers and sisters to hear that I was at Woodstock.*

Once we claimed our tiny patch of real-estate high up on the hill, Randy and I went exploring. After a while, we came upon a scene of naked adults, sliding and tumbling together in the mud. I played it cool but couldn't bring myself to look directly at Randy. Nudity was not something I was comfortable with, and certainly not with such abandonment. Still, it was a sight to behold. *How can they be so free?* Sheepishly, I felt ridiculous in my padded bra and false eyelashes.

Richie Havens saved me from my discomfort when he took the stage and rendered his epic version of "Freedom." As my body began to echo the music, my personal insecurities were forgotten and replaced with an intense feeling of connectedness to everyone present, a feeling infused with purpose. I found myself thinking, *Wow, I want to be a part of this. I want to take a stand for peace, for love, for freedom.*

Later that evening, after Creedence Clearwater Revival rocked the night with "Green River," "Bad Moon Rising," and more, Randy and I slipped into a snooze. The next thing I knew, I was rising to my feet as if being called to attention by a god—or goddess. *Who is behind this voice?* I had to know. There, at the center of the stage, looking about as big as my little finger, stood the one and only, Janis Joplin.

My older brother, Mark, had recently turned the family on to Janis's Cheap Thrills album, but I had only heard a lot of screeching at the time. Now she was slaying me with "Bobby McGee." The thing that tipped the scale, however, was when she stilled the musicians and sang acapella. Her power, her passion—it was beyond human. Goose bumps rose up my legs and spine and my heart opened, as I looked around at the sea of people, all gathered under the stars, united by music. I could barely contain myself—I was ecstatic.

Randy? Not so much. He was still snoozing. He'd been complaining a lot about the discomforts and lack of conveniences. Of course, the bathrooms were an unsanitary joke and the lines crazy long. In fact, it was so bad that I refrained from peeing for the entire thirty-six hours we were there. Still, I was deeply troubled that we weren't on the same page with the experience.

Randy was looking to take us to the next level, but the vision of a future where I lived in the same house, day after day, year after year, being referred to as someone's wife, or God-forbid someone's mother, struck a chord of sheer dread in me. *I am not going to become my mother. I want to be happy. And I don't want to ever blame someone else if I'm not. I will take full responsibility for all of my decisions and will regard my own happiness as a top priority.* The seed of doubt had been sewn, and I knew that Randy and I were not going to make the long run. When the time came, almost a year later, Cat Stevens provided the break-up song: "Wild World."

Little did I know how wild it would be, or how often I would long for the love and security that Randy had offered. But I treasured my freedom—and that has its own rewards.

WHO AM I?

As a young girl, I was disappointed that my mother wasn't more like her mother, who actually enjoyed being a home-maker. For instance, my grandmother had a pot specifically designed for poaching eggs and she took pride in delivering the perfect little works of art every time. Together with a slice of buttered toast and a glass of orange juice, you were on your way to a great day. In the afternoons, if she wasn't peeling potatoes or trimming green beans, she was likely cooking. She also did a good deal of mending and making garments from scratch and was rarely in a sour mood.

Not only was my mother a little less than stellar in the kitchen but she didn't seem to be into the whole mothering thing really—beyond getting us here—which, granted, was huge. The first three kids, Nancy, Lee, and Mark, were just one year apart. Dad used to say that all he had to do was hang his trousers on the bedpost and she'd get pregnant. Mercifully, she had a year off before I came along, (all ten pounds & seven ounces of me), and then a three-year break before Russell, and another three before Billy. Her doctor put an end to things at that point by insisting she have a hysterectomy.

It's understandable that the best she could do was to keep us fed, clothed, and delivered to school. Forget about nurturing mother/daughter time. That was not a priority, nor was it her nature. Her happiness kicked in when she was getting ready to step out for the evening. I resented her for that, and one day, I boldly addressed her by her first name, Edna. To my amazement, she allowed it. And though it wasn't the reaction I expected, it marked a shift in our relationship. From then forward, I made a conscious effort to relate to her more as a peer than as a mother. Interestingly enough, we did begin to bond like girlfriends. I could pretty much tell her anything.

The women's liberation movement was gaining momentum when I was a teenager. Women were claiming their territory in what had traditionally been male-dominated fields, including sports (Billy Jean King), the military, and business. The invention of the birth control pill was making it possible for them to have premarital sex, and for the first time maybe ever, not be judged harshly for it.

One day, while soaking up some Florida sunshine with my mother and grandmother, they started commiserating about their missed opportunities in life. "What if's" ranging from matters of education to employment to unexplored romances, lingered in their minds as they passed the metaphorical baton to me. "Go out there and do everything we couldn't, Franny," Mom Heneks said. My mother concurred and they enjoyed a good laugh. I took their statement to heart, and from that moment forward, operated with the belief that I had their blessing for any bold choices I might make in life.

Myself, Mom Heneks & Mother

My father was a formidable six-feet, two-inches tall, Irish/Italian, capable of demonstrating quite a temper if provoked. My earliest memory of him is when I was just two years old sitting in the highchair at the dinner table wanting more mashed potatoes. "Pass the potatoes," I asked, but chaos persisted and I was ignored. "Pass the potatoes," I said again, but again nothing. I knew I was clearly understood because Mark translated my baby-talk. It was my dad that had access to the coveted potatoes but he continued to ignore me. Finally, when I'd had enough, I grabbed my fork and threw it at him, barely missing his eye. The bickering instantly ceased and I braced myself for the flare-up that was sure to follow. But something quite different occurred. His eyes welled up with tears, and for the first time in my young life, I felt something along the lines of love. That night in the den, I climbed onto his lap and became Daddy's Sweetheart forevermore.

The sales manager of a steel-hauling company, he serviced the Midwestern and eastern states. His job kept him on the road much of the time, and when he did come home, he'd often go straight to the golf course. Understandably, that would raise any woman's ire, but because my mother never refrained from expressing her resentments, I always saw him as the sympathetic one.

He wanted college for all of us but especially for the boys. Money was tight but he did finance Nancy at Michigan State—at least until she came home pregnant after the first semester. He didn't know I was watching when, after he got the news, he sat in the living room, hunched forward with his head heavy in his hands. Seeing him so disappointed hit me hard, so I slipped upstairs and vowed never to be the cause of such pain.

I came into this world with a feeling that I was extraordinary and didn't understand why my family didn't recognize it. In fact, the first conscious thought I remember having was, "A terrible mistake has been made. I've been born into the wrong family."

I searched for ways to win their admiration. For instance, at six I thought I might become a great singer and attempted to impress my first-grade class by singing my favorite song, "Que Sera Sera." The shrill sound that came out of my mouth was far from the one in my head, and I was humiliated and saddened to realize that singing was not my talent. Then, I dreamed of being a martyr and dying for my faith, like the saints in my picture bible. But I soon realized that martyring was a thing of the past and set my sights on gymnastics instead.

At ten, after learning how to do all kinds of cool tricks on the trampoline, I felt ready to do a one-and-a-half off the high-dive. My entire family, along with several other club members, gathered to watch. Confidently, I climbed the tall steel ladder, but as I walked out onto the board my knees started to shake like leaves. A deep breath, then step-jump-spring, and my skinny little form propelled high into the air. Tucked tight, I spun around and then opened my eyes, shocked to see the water coming at me way too fast. I couldn't get my legs up in time. It was over. It felt like I'd landed on glass. As embarrassed as I was hurt, I managed to get out of the pool and put one foot in front of the other until I was inside the locker room. There, I let go and cried like a baby, concluding that gymnastics wasn't my special talent after all. "Just a skinny kid with no special anything," seemed to be what the world was telling me, but I wasn't buying it.

When I asked my dad for a ride to Kay Baum's because I'd been hired to work there as a stock-girl, I expected him to be proud that I had secured a job. I didn't understand the pathos he'd feel seeing his fourteen-year-old daughter go off to work. After all, it was from him that I learned the importance of making money, and how it was the very key to one's freedom. That day marked the beginning of my financial independence.

Two years later, I'd be one of the store's top sales people. Finally, something I excelled at.

When I was fifteen, Nancy, Lee, and I were invited to participate in a fashion event that marked the opening of Paraphernalia, a popular and very trendy store based in London. The fashion supervisor gave me an orange-and-purple, sequined, micro-mini dress to wear. It was brazenly short, barely covering my butt. Once made up and dressed, I was told to go stand in the front window with a happy face and dance. Cringing, but wanting to please, I stepped into the window box. After a few minutes of dancing to songs in my head, I ducked out and went begging for a radio. I don't know what was worse, dancing to "People" by Barbara Streisand or to nothing but the song in my head, but when the media arrived and pointed their cameras at me, I put forth my best boogie.

That evening, my dad and brothers were watching the local news when the coverage of Paraphernalia came on. The camera focused on a pair of dancing feet and slowly panned up the legs to a scandalously clad body, ultimately landing on my smiling face. Later, Mark said that it was my dad's face you should've seen.

From that experience the head of a Detroit modeling agency offered to help me get started in the business. Enthusiastically, I gave it a go. I was able to juggle my job, the modeling work, and school, with ease because I belonged to a club that gave credit to working students. I only had to attend high school for half a day. I soon learned that I was a natural in front of the camera, and at sixteen I had two promising careers, a killer wardrobe, and a healthy savings account.

In March, 1969, I won first-place for the state of Michigan in a sales competition sponsored by DECA, the company that supported us working students. Consequently, I went to Atlantic

City for the national competition where, after making it into the finals, the judges decided to disqualify me for holding an unfair advantage over the competition, all of whom were boys selling cutlery and such. They told me it was because I was wearing some of the clothes that I was selling. "But that's what we do at Kay Baum's," I pleaded, but to no avail. It was done. I was out and that was that.

Perhaps if there had been an adult present to stand up for me, things might have been different, but I was on my own and could only suffer the shaft. *"You chauvinistic bastards! What a crock! I don't need your stupid scholarship anyway,"* is what I would've said to them if I'd spoken my mind. Instead, I accentuated my unfair advantage by wearing a short, loosely crocheted dress over a flowered body suit to the awards dinner. *Their loss*, I told myself, as I sashayed through the room, and then jetted off to rendezvous with my boyfriend.

On July 20th, 1969, I was headed home from one of my Rochester trips when the pilot announced over the loudspeaker. "Ladies and gentlemen, if you look out the windows on the left side of the aircraft you can see the moon. I think you all might want to take a look out there for, in a minute, Neil Armstrong will be walking on it." Having secured a window seat but on the wrong side of the plane, I hurried across the aisle to peer over someone's shoulder. And there it was: the biggest, most brilliant moon ever. As I took the historic moment in, my heart flooded with love for all humanity. I thought about my family, gathered in front of the TV back home, and hoped that they missed me. *Someday, I'll be able to show them how much I love them.*

One Spring day in 1970, I got a phone call from my modeling agent. "Franny, you have an audition tomorrow for *Playboy* magazine."

"You're kidding!" I replied.

"No, I'm not. They're seeing girls for a full-page ad: 'What Kind of Man Reads *Playboy*.'"

"But *Playboy* would never hire me!" I exclaimed, laughing at the ludicrousness of the idea. "They're only interested in big boobs. And I don't have any!"

She laughed and went on to explain, "Your character will be wrapped in a towel, so breast size doesn't matter. There's going to be another model in the shot and she will be topless. You'll be in the background, standing in the doorway to the sauna. The producers are coming to Detroit to shoot it and will pay triple rate."

"Wow. Okay, then—when and where?"

At the audition they asked me to behave sensually toward a couple of executives sitting around the room. Having developed pretty good flirting skills by then, I slinked around, finally draping myself across the arm of the couch. The next day I got the call that I had booked the job. Flat-chested Franny is going to be in *Playboy* magazine! I thought it was hysterical.

WHAT SORT OF MAN READS PLAYBOY?

CANNES FILM FESTIVAL

At the age of nineteen, while working on an industrial film, I struck up a conversation about college choices with the producer, Brent. He was thirty-six years old, dressed in a traditional suit but sporting a Beatles hairdo and pointed boots. Though not exactly attracted to him, I found him interesting, especially when he shared with me that he was about to open a production company called Cinema Club.

"We're going to make documentaries and industrials," he said, "but the long-term goal is to make feature films. Patrick Cragin is going to work with us, too."

"Really?" I responded, impressed. "I've heard that he's like the best cinematographer in the Midwest."

"Yes, he's genius. It's going to be something like Detroit has never seen," he said with supreme confidence. "You're a smart young woman, capable of doing anything you want, a gem in the rough. Why don't you come and get in on the ground floor? I'd give you full access to all of our projects. You could learn any aspect of the business you're interested in."

I loved the idea of a career in film, and I thought that perhaps his offer was my answer. Still, I didn't want to be naïve, and knew that he might be working an angle. After all, what did I really bring to the table? Was it stupid of me to believe him when he said that he thought I could do anything I wanted? Or was it stupid not to? I happened to agree with him that I was a gem in the rough. My God, how I craved such recognition!

I inquired about his personal life and learned that he was a newlywed, which made me feel more secure about his intentions. So, after a couple more in-depth conversations, I decided to enroll at Wayne State University downtown, and spend my spare time at Cinema Club.

Soon I found myself working as a "go-fer", doing everything from making sandwiches and going on coffee runs, to chauffeuring "talent" to and from sets. I loved being part of a team working toward a common goal and was eager to learn every aspect of the business. My resourcefulness, combined with my youthful enthusiasm, made me well-suited for the job. *This is where I belong.*

When Brent told me, a year and a half later, that they were doing a documentary on the Cannes Film Festival, my heart leapt for joy—for one brief second. It plummeted just as fast when he added that he was sorry but there wasn't enough of a budget to include me. It would be only him, his partner, Tom, Cragin, and Flavio on sound.

As big as my desire was to be a part of it, I knew that my contribution wasn't enough to justify the expense—but oh, what a disappointment it was. Brent then pulled me into a hug and assured me that there would be other, equally wonderful, opportunities. I knew he was only trying to be kind but it irked me that he would even say such a thing. What could possibly be more fabulous than going to the Cannes Film Festival as part of a documentary crew? "Nothing" was the answer to that one— and we both knew it.

If I could make it so that I didn't cost them anything, then they'd welcome my help. What if I surprised them and just showed up— offering my assistance free of charge? Yeah, that's the ticket! The wheels turned as I looked for my way in.

Since my breakup with Randy, I had dated several different guys, leading mostly to disappointment. Somehow, Brent always had the time and interest to hear my stories of woe and would inevitably respond by assuring me that I was beautiful, powerful, and lucky to be free from whomever. Though not always convinced, I soaked up his bolstering encouragement, and came to think of him as my closest confidant.

Soon it came time to put the trip together, but because I

no longer held the Kay Baum's job, and was financing my own education, my savings had dwindled. So, I entrusted my secret to my brother, Russell, who had been saving money from odd jobs for years. True to his generous nature, he offered to loan me two hundred and fifty dollars. That, combined with five hundred of my own, would be enough to cover my flight and some kind of lodging. Then, at the last minute, I decided to tag on a three-day jaunt to Madrid to see Mark who was studying at the university there.

Brent, Tom, and the others left Detroit for Cannes by way of London for a few days. I played my role as the sad but good sport, wishing them a successful adventure. To Brent, specifically, I said, "Think of me whenever you see a yellow rose." I didn't know why but the yellow rose would be significant.

While selecting some items from my closet, the doorbell rang. My mother hollered, "Franny! Come down here!" I went down the stairs and saw a fellow standing in the foyer.

"I have your passport, Miss. Please sign here," he said. My mother, bewildered, held my passport in her hand. I figured it was time to come clean.

"You see, Mom, there's this flight to Paris tomorrow, and I'm planning to be on it. I'm going to be a production assistant on a documentary about the Cannes Film Festival. The reason I haven't said anything to you is because my going has to be kept top secret." Concerned, she led me into the living room where we sat, side by side, on the gold velour sofa.

"You see, the truth is that Cinema Club didn't actually invite me to go. And the reason for that is because there isn't enough money in the budget to include me, which I understand. However, when Brent first asked me to come on board, he promised that I would have access to all of the company's opportunities, that I would be a core member. And now, when they land their biggest deal ever, I'm expected to stay home! No way. So, that's why I came up with a plan that resolves their budget issue, while allowing me to have the experience. The most important thing though, is that word cannot get out that I am in Cannes, for that would cause serious problems for the guys with their wives, none of whom are going."

She listened intently. "You see, I figure, if I'm already there when they arrive, and offer to work for free, they'll be grateful for my help. I know they're going to need it. And if by some chance I'm wrong, and they say 'no'—well, at least I will have called Brent on his bluff." A hint of worry came into her eyes, so I quickly added, "Plus, I've scheduled a visit with Mark in Madrid before returning home." That pleased her, and I felt it was safe to get on to a serious wardrobe matter. "I was hoping I could borrow your gold pleated gown, and maybe your black silk suit."

With a little girlish excitement of her own, she responded, "Do you want my black high heels, as well?" I never loved her more than in that moment.

Later that evening, I heard my dad's angry voice coming from their bedroom. He was fearful that these men were taking advantage of me. He didn't trust the situation at all, especially since they were nearly twice my age and married. Edna did her best to persuade him that I knew what I was doing. After all, I was twenty years old and had been living an independent life for quite some time. Mom prevailed, and I was off to France.

While changing planes in Paris, I learned that there's a Caen, France, as well as a Cannes. To my ears the pronunciation was the same. You can imagine how relieved I was when a woman standing behind me in line realized that I thought I was going to *Cannes* but was actually about to board a plane to *Caen* and explained to me the difference. Disaster averted, I managed to arrive at the correct airport. Unfortunately, my suitcase did not.

I hung around for hours before giving up and catching a shuttle into town. The thought of never seeing my suitcase again gave rise to near panic. Everything would be ruined if that happened. *Oh, well—it'll show up. It's got to,* I assured myself.

The weather was heavenly, and though I was distraught over my lost luggage, it was a relief to be able to stroll freely. My impulse was to walk along the crowded "Croisette" that bordered the beach, so as to be closer to the sparkling blue ocean. But my first order of business needed tending to: I had to find a room.

Stopping people to ask questions was mostly futile, as I spoke no French. Nonetheless, ask I did, and eventually an English-speaking hotel clerk gave me the address of a place exclusively for women. I went there and, to my utter amazement, was able to secure a room for three dollars and fifty cents a night; an unbelievable deal, even back then.

The owner led me up five flights of stairs, pointing out the communal bathroom as we approached my room. It was a decent size with a double bed and a few basic furnishings. Its outstanding feature was a large window overlooking the street below. As he opened the white wooden shutters, a beautiful light flooded in.

The bed was cushy and most inviting with white embroidered linens. I was exhausted and eager to crash, but the gentleman had one more thing to tell me—he pointed out the button on the wall just above the headboard. Though he didn't speak English, I was able to understand that I should push that button in the morning when I was ready for breakfast. *Three dollars and fifty cents a night—and breakfast is included? Far out!*

After a long, deep sleep, I woke up ravenous, wasting no time in pushing the black button. Twenty minutes later there was a knock. I opened the door and there he was, standing in the hallway with my tray. "Bonjour, mademoiselle," the tall man said cheerfully, as he gracefully moved into the room and placed the tray on a nearby table.

I broke off a section of the hot croissant, buttered it and added the marmalade, and then took a bite. I'd never had sweet butter before and I'd never been too keen on orange marmalade, but those combined tastes created a symphony of flavor in my mouth. The croissant was out of this world!

Then there was the espresso coffee with steamed milk. *Oh, my God! So, this is what coffee is supposed to taste like!* And, to top it all off, there was a large glass of fresh-squeezed orange juice, one of my favorite treats in life. No, there would be no turning back—not once I'd had café au lait.

I had a full day to try to recover my luggage before the guys arrived. Figuring out which hotel they were at…well, I was leaving that up to chance. I took a bus to the airport and haggled with officials there, and finally left with only the hope of trying again the following day.

Each night's premier was going to require formal attire, even for film crews. I had planned to wear the shimmering gold, thinly pleated, floor length gown, each and every night. It was a unique, low maintenance garment that could be rolled into a ball and easily packed. Without it, I was sunk. Meanwhile, the outfit that I'd traveled in—black bell-bottoms made out of a shiny, stretchy fabric with a white tank top and matching jacket—was working out exceptionally well.

That evening, as I was dining alone at one of the many beckoning restaurants on the strip, the maître d' came over and said, "Madam, there is a gentleman who would like to join you." He then pointed to a heavy-set, well-dressed man, who appeared to be in his fifties. I was longing for someone to talk to, and since he didn't look scary, I said, "Alright."

He was a French lawyer who spoke fluent English, so naturally I told him about my lost luggage. "I can get your suitcase back for you," he said. "It'll just take a phone call. But it'll have to wait till tomorrow." Even though I couldn't fathom how he could know that, his certainty offered me hope. So, when he invited me to accompany him to a local nightclub, I agreed.

He was well-known at the popular dance club and before

long we were part of a good-sized group. Since he was not a dancing kind of guy, I enjoyed sitting back quietly and observing. I saw several couples where the man was decades older than his date. I knew that's what it looked like with me and him, as well, but I didn't mind. Feeling confident of my social skills, I was friendly and warm toward him, while maintaining a distance. When he walked me back to my hotel, the owner was there to greet us, pointing to a sign that said in French "No Men Allowed Past the Lobby." Happily spared an awkward moment, I said good-night and went upstairs. I would ring him up at his hotel in the morning.

The Carlton was situated in the midst of the action and was the place to stay in Cannes. I stood a little taller when I walked into the magnificent lobby, pausing to appreciate the scene. I made note of such things as the big white columns and the fabulous artwork placed throughout. A little nervous, I rang my new pal from a house phone. He gave me his room number and told me to come up. I didn't argue because I knew that was where the telephone was, and he would need me nearby for the call. So, to his room I went.

Without delay, he made the call, motioning for me to sit next to him on the bed. Smiling, I shook my head "no" and remained standing. Speaking in a commanding tone in French, he succeeded in causing my bag to be located. Though I contained it, I was ecstatic. Then, when he hung up, he sweetened the deal by offering to drive me to the airport to pick it up. Feeling blessed, I accepted.

He gathered his things, and as we were about to walk out, he grabbed and kissed me with a powerful passion. It took my full strength to push him off, and as soon as I did, I opened the door and made a mad dash out of there. As I was running to the elevator, he called out, "Never mind, Francoise! Never mind!" I looked back to see him holding his hands up in the air in a gesture of surrender. "Don't worry. I'll take you to the airport."

He's just a typical bad boy, I thought, and accepted his offer.

A white Jaguar convertible awaited us at valet. As we were making our way out of the circular driveway, Brent and Tom were suddenly right there, walking toward us. I slid all the way down in my seat and tucked my face away. This was not how I wanted to be discovered, in some strange Frenchman's Jaguar. No, I'd been conjuring up a special scenario for that moment, and this was not it. What was perfect was that I then knew: first, that they were in town, and second, that they were likely staying at the Carlton. I breathed a sigh of relief, as we cruised on out in his pearly white convertible.

After securing the suitcase and delivering me back to my hotel, my association with the lawyer came to a polite close. I was all too happy to wrap that one up.

Around 4 p.m. I slipped into my mother's black dress-suit. The pencil straight skirt showed off my nicely rounded derriere, while the top that zipped up the back and cinched at the waist, created a slight flare. It was a stunning little number. I wore a large, antique, black velvet hat, adorned with a black ostrich feather that draped down over one eye. I detailed the outfit with a pair of short, black, fishnet gloves, dark seamed stockings, my mother's high heels, and my Jackie Kennedy sunglasses. My fantasy was that the guys (especially Brent) would see me and mistake me for a French woman of great intrigue, one that they'd find so mysterious and compelling that they'd simply have to approach her. Then I'd say, "Bienvenue en France, monsieurs," and take off my glasses, letting them see it was me. Then, having blown their minds, and thereby gained their respect, I'd explain myself. Exactly where I'd run into them and how it would actually unfold was in the hands of the gods.

When I was completely put together, I uttered a prayer for magic and walked out onto the lively street below. The warmth of the sun still strong, butterflies fluttered in my gut. Not far down the road, I spotted a rose bush with a beautiful yellow bloom beckoning me—ah, the final touch. Breaking off easily in my hands, as roses rarely do, I secured it to my suit with the hatpin I'd brought along for just that purpose.

As I walked along the Croisette, I could see people turning their heads to check me out. And though extremely self-conscious, I told myself that with such a plentitude of starlets in town, I couldn't be all that much of a rarity. Anyway, it mattered not, for I was on a mission.

Nearing the Carlton Hotel, I saw the guys about a hundred feet ahead of me. For a second, I froze, but then lunged over to a nearby palm tree, hiding behind its scrawny trunk, (I'm sure my hat's rim extended well beyond its parameters). People were definitely tripped out now but I couldn't afford to care. Then, to my great relief, the guys crossed the street and went into the hotel.

What next, I deliberated? *I'll go settle into one of the lounge areas in the lobby.* But as I approached the entrance, I saw an empty café just off to the right. Ah, perfect! I took a small table in the center of the patio and ordered an ice cream sundae. My nervousness was no joke, and the last thing on my mind was food, but I tell you truly, it was the ice cream sundae of a lifetime. My butterflies literally dissolved into the delectable deliciousness, and I was born again.

Then, in a flash, there they were—like the three musketeers, crossing the patio in my direction. With my sunglasses on, I looked at Brent who was in the lead. He walked on by. Then Tom, who looked directly at me but also, kept walking. *Oh, dear. Maybe this isn't going to go so great.* Then Flavio took one look at me and hollered, "Holy shit!" He stopped in his tracks, set down his case, and grabbed his camera to capture the moment. Meanwhile, Tom and Brent began retracing their steps toward my table, trying to figure out what was up. When the perfect moment arose, I took my shades off, and said with a smile, "Bienvenue en France, monsieurs!"

Once over their shock, the three men took a seat and listened as I explained myself. "I get that there's no room in the budget to pay me, but nonetheless, I am offering my assistance to you, free of charge. No one back home knows I'm here, and I promise you that I'll do all I can to make sure they never will. I believe that I deserve this opportunity, as you (looking specifically at Brent) initially invited me to be a core member of this company. So, don't ask me to play the game and then sit out when the pot is gold. So, that's it—I'm ready, willing, and eager to work. What do you say?"

Brent mouthed silently, and for my eyes only, "I love you."

Pat Cragin arrived the following day and requested that I be his script girl. I would announce the name of every person being interviewed and the number of each take. Then I'd smack down the wooden hinge and "get the hell out of frame." The big burly Irishman would teach me a tremendous amount over the next couple of weeks, and we would become long-time friends. Standing over six feet tall and weighing around three hundred pounds, he always wore dungarees with red suspenders, sported a full beard and long hair, and threw out a bellowing laugh when he was amused. He also had a wicked wit of his own and used it to get people to open up on camera. I was thrilled to be his assistant.

I also became the person that would do anything the others preferred not to. For instance, when Flavio spotted Ravi Shankar walking down the street, Brent asked me to run over and confirm that he was, in fact, Ravi Shankar—and if so, to ask him if he would give us an interview. Not familiar with the name, I asked Flavio to say it again, so I wouldn't mess up.

"Excuse me, are you Rabbi Shankar?" The Indian man chuckled heartily before correcting me. "It's Ra*vi*, dear—not Ra*bb*i." My embarrassment was a small price to pay, for not only did we get our interview but we also were invited to a surprise screening of his and George Harrison's movie, *The Concert for*

Bangladesh. The next day, Ravi and George paused so Cragin could get a nice shot of them together as they walked into the movie theater. *How cool is this?* I had to pinch myself.

Another time Robert Redford was spotted walking along the strip. I ran up, tapped him on the arm, and with my most charming smile, asked if we could have a brief interview. He seemed rather annoyed, which I took personally. I could not get that handsome guy to smile at me, nor were my charms able to secure an interview. *What is wrong with him*, I wondered? The movie he was there supporting was *Jeremiah Johnson*, which wasn't my favorite, but I guess he did go on to have a pretty decent career.

Patrick spotted Robert Altman, a very hot director at the time, and one of my personal favorites, and managed to engage him in a spontaneous interview. I had to smack that script-board in front of his face several times and, at one point, he addressed me, "What are you doing out here with all these men from Detroit?" I don't think he was really looking for an answer, but I was jazzed by his interest.

That night we all attended the screening of his movie, *Images,* and loved it. The buzz was that it was going to win the Best Picture award. On that fateful final evening when the awards were announced, his lead actress, Susannah York, took "Best Actress," but the prize he was hoping for went to *Slaughterhouse-Five,* another great film that I got to see while there. Afterwards, I peeked into the room where he had planned to host a celebration and happened to catch his eye. He motioned me over and said, "Why don't you and your crew join us on my yacht for a small party?" That invitation garnered me near heroic status with the guys. Happily, we accepted his offer and ended up spending a couple hours on the boat with Mr. Altman, his wife, Kathryn, and several others of his inner circle.

He wondered aloud again, as to what my story was, so this time I told him. "I'm learning the ropes of the business, working with the Cinema Club, while studying filmmaking at Wayne State University." Then I added, "I wrote last semester's term paper on you—specifically on *McCabe and Mrs. Miller*." It was at that point that Kathryn said I reminded her of the actress in that film that comes running out of a tent in a rage, wielding a knife. Altman agreed.

My greatest triumph at Cannes, however, had to be when I, single-handedly, secured an interview with Anthony Burgess, author of *A Clockwork Orange*. Our crew spent three hours in his suite with him and his wife, Liana. Normally, in these circumstances, I tried to be "seen but not heard" as my uncle used to say. But, because l had been blown away by the movie version, which inspired me to read the book and then write a review of the film—one that got published in the university's paper—I was able to make a few intelligent remarks about it. My comments elicited Mr. Burgess's interest and he engaged me in further dialogue. I told him that my brother, Mark, had taken a writing course with him in Majorca, and that Mark had shared with me some of his amazing stories. "Like what?" he asked.

"Well, he told me about how you became physically ill during the writing of *A Clockwork Orange* as a result of delving so deeply into the sick minds of your characters." He confirmed that was true and asked me if there were any other stories.

"Yes. He told me that you were diagnosed with terminal cancer many years ago and that, even though your dream had always been to be a writer for the opera, the terrible news caused you to begin writing feverishly—only not for opera."

"That's true," Liana said, smiling.

"And then, years later, it was discovered that you had been misdiagnosed and didn't have cancer at all! But you continued to write at the same pace, anyway." He chuckled and nodded affirmatively. "And now the whole world is blessed because you did," I added with a heartfelt smile. Brent was sitting across the room, beaming with pride.

Another day, we were scheduled to interview Groucho Marx in his suite at the Carlton. When we arrived, Groucho was locked out of his room in his underwear, and had everyone in a tizzy, trying to get his door opened. Patrick ordered me to run down and alert management. As I ran past Mr. Marx, he pointed at me and said, "Who's that slip of a girl?"

Later, when we were interviewing him, he took the award that was dangling around his neck and put it on me. It slipped right under my loose-fitting, midriff top, but no worries—he reached right down there and pulled it out. He loved the girls, that Groucho!

One afternoon, while we were mingling at a press event, Gregory Peck entered the room. His presence stilled the crowd. I couldn't take my eyes off of him: tall, handsome, and—my God, Gregory Peck! I found him to be the most charismatic star of all.

As I saw it, Cannes was like a crash course on readiness for the big leagues. Through all of these encounters, my confidence in my ability to move gracefully in and out of the various echelons of society was solidified. Also, I became aware that the more movies I watched, the more I identified with the emotional aspect of the characters. I began to imagine myself in certain roles, sometimes feeling that I could, perhaps, do even better than the actress on the screen. I knew I was photogenic and that I felt exceptionally free in front of a camera. *Could acting be my way in?* By the time I returned home, my decision was made.

I wish I could say that I managed to maintain my moral high ground with Brent, but that's not the case. Long work days with short turnaround times into formal evenings required that I have a place to change. My hotel was simply too far away from the action. Brent was happy to make his room available, and one night when we had worked well past midnight, I gave in to my desire to make love with him.

Three years earlier, I'd been safeguarding my virginity like the Holy Grail itself, saving the sacred event for true, committed love. Now, I had become the "other woman." How I managed to fall so far from grace was something that I couldn't afford to contemplate at the time. I figured we'd leave it behind us, once we returned home—but that's not how it went.

Brent put me on a pedestal and taught me that my femininity was powerful. I was a goddess before whom he was helpless. He purported to believe that we were destined to be together, to know true love, and to achieve great artistic heights. In time, he would work things out. Sometimes I bought into his fantasy, imagining that I would be to him like Liv Ullman was to Ingmar Bergman. Still, I hated living in a web of deceit. So, entrenched as I became, I did my best to keep one foot out of the water, one eye open.

Photo by "Flavio"

A MILE RUNNER ON A QUARTER TRACK

Shortly after deciding to pursue acting as a career path, an opportunity opened up in Detroit. *No Place to be Somebody* by Charles Gordone, which had won the Pulitzer-Prize in 1970, was playing to full houses at the Vest Pocket Theater. The New York company announced that they would hold auditions in Detroit for a few replacements before preparing for their next tour. I had just seen the play and was very moved by its powerful addressing of race issues and its cutting wit. I welcomed the challenge of putting myself out there to get the experience of a professional audition, never dreaming that I'd actually get hired.

Out of a mostly black cast there were two white female characters, both within my age range. The initial interview determined that I could read for the part of the college girl, Mary Lou Bolton. Mary Lou walks into Johnny's bar with her picketing sign that calls for the "Rights of Negros", and orders a Strawberry Daiquiri. She is not ready for the likes of Johnny.

My first audition went well enough to secure a callback for the director who was coming in from New York in five days. Meanwhile, Julian, one of the producers, granted me permission to come and observe as many performances as I wanted until that time. I attended every one of them and, in the process, became intrigued with the role of Dee, Johnny's girlfriend—a hooker with a drinking problem.

I was seated among dozens of others at the callback when word got around that the director would be staying in town for a couple of weeks to rehearse the new cast members. Dressed in a blue mini-skirt and matching top, I rose to my feet when my name was called and walked toward the mahogany door. *There's that nervousness wreaking havoc in my gut again*, I thought, as I reflected on the Cannes trip. I stepped into the small office and Julian made the introduction. "Frances, this is Nathan George." A tall, intense-looking, black man extended his hand and we exchanged a firm shake, as my parents had taught me to do.

An actor from the current production was standing nearby with a script in hand. "Wesley is going to read the scene with you," Mr. George said. "Take it from the top whenever you're ready." I jumped right into it, rendering the best Mary Lou I could. In a flash the scene was over. I looked to the director and after a considered moment he said, "I'd like to hear you read Dee." My heart skipped a beat, for I had played Dee many times over in my mind and had a good handle on her. I was prepared.

When I saw which scene he selected, I knew I'd barely need to glance at the page. *I have this. Now, give it everything you've got,* I told myself. Taking a moment, I invited the spirit of Dee in. Then we began the dramatic scene from a place of full intensity. Both my speech and body language transformed to reflect this broken, drunken woman. When we finished, the room was silent. I thanked them and took my leave.

One foot in front of the other, I walked to my car and just stood there. I took a few deep breaths and tried to ground myself. When I opened my eyes, I saw Julian hurriedly walking toward me. "You're not going to play the part of Dee!" he barked. "So, don't get your hopes up. You may have a chance for Mary Lou, but not Dee. So, don't get your hopes up."

"Okay, I hear you," I said, and drove home.

It would have been wonderful to catapult right to stardom in a hit play. *Oh, God! I could've been great as Dee.* My heart ached with the desire to do it but at the same time I was pleased about the quality of my first audition. But then, that very evening, I received a call from the executive producer's office, telling me that I had a callback for the part of Dee the following afternoon. *Oh, my God—maybe I'm going to get my miracle after all.*

When I entered the theater the next day, I found the current cast members sitting together in the first few rows. As I was about to take a seat off to the side, Nathan, who I soon learned had originated the role of Johnny at the Public Theater, called me to the stage. He would be directing me while also playing the part of Johnny. The rest of the cast would observe. For the next two hours, Nathan worked with me, taking me deeper and deeper into the complexity of the relationship between these two characters. At times, I believe he tried to intimidate me with his angry passion, and sexual overtures—but I never shrank.

At the end of the session, he shared with me that he was frustrated because I was so green. I didn't project very well and I looked way too young. Apparently, the 'Dees' of the past had been somewhat worn-looking, voluptuous and blonde. He said the voluptuousness, or lack of, wasn't an issue for him as long as I had it going on in my attitude. That was a relief.

"I can make myself look older—and I can project better too," I assured him. With that, he scheduled another audition/rehearsal for the following day. That same night, while watching the play, I saw that one of my action choices had been incorporated into the blocking. *Nice.*

With a brown 'fall' that added length and volume to my hair, and a heavy dose of eye make-up, I achieved a trashier look. I was fired up and ready to project. But after an hour or so of rehearsal, Nathan still had some trepidation about hiring me. Looking for a way to bring this situation to a victorious conclusion, I suggested that we step out for a drink. He agreed, and while sitting over a couple of cocktails, I said to him in my most sincere, heartfelt voice, "Nathan, if you take a chance on me, I promise I will give you one hundred and ten percent of my absolute, best effort. I will **not** disappoint you."

"Frances, you're a mile runner on a quarter track," he said. "Get your ass to New York!"

Later that evening, I got a call from the producer's office:

"You've been cast in the role of Dee. Rehearsals will start at 10 a.m. tomorrow."

Wow, I did it. This is my beginning. I have found my gift and now the world is going to see it, too. Thrilled beyond words, I shared my great news with family and friends. Then, ready to work hard and prove Nathan right, I arrived at the theater, and took my seat among the others. Julian walked in and came down the aisle to the row where I was seated. He walked over to me and said that he needed some paperwork signed. After handing me the papers, he cupped his hand around my head and moved in to plant a kiss on my mouth. I turned my face abruptly away. He froze for a second and then gave me a mean look, as he scurried away. Immediately, I regretted having brushed him off so harshly, humiliating him in front of everyone. Still, it was better than having allowed him to humiliate me.

Later, when we wrapped up the day's work, I was making my way out of the theater just as a blonde woman was walking in, carrying a suitcase. She asked me if I knew where she could find Julian. "I don't know," I said, wondering why she had a suitcase. I guess she saw my inquisitiveness and said, "I'm Sonia. Julian called me this morning and told me to catch the next flight—that I'd be taking over the part of Dee."

An hour later, Sonia and I sat alone in the theater, listening to Nathan and Julian holler at each other in an upstairs office. In the end, it turned out that Julian held most of the chips and was able to override Nathan. The carrot offered me was that I could have two matinee performances as Dee before the company left Detroit, and that I would play the role of Mary Lou on the upcoming tour.

It was a sunny Saturday in September, and I was leaving the house for my first matinee performance as Dee. Dad and Russell were outside tending to the lawn when something high up in a tree caught my eye. It appeared to be an apple, which was weird because the tree had never borne fruit before—or even blossomed. My father said it was an illusion caused by the way the light was hitting a particular leaf, but I wasn't convinced. It looked an awful lot like an apple to me. Finally, at my insistence, he retrieved the ladder from the garage and climbed up, rake in hand. To his amazement, he emancipated one perfect red/gold apple from the highest limb.

My dad, who thought he knew his trees, was stunned. I cackled with delight. I saw it as an omen of good fortune, arriving at the perfect time. I asked him and Russell to each hold it for a moment and bless it with their best wishes for my debut.

As I drove toward the city, I considered how I wanted to honor the golden apple. After the performance, I would take the first bite and then pass it around to each cast member to do the same—sort of like a peace pipe. When I got out of my car, the stage manager hollered out to me, "Frances! Ashton Springer wants to see you in his office." Ashton was the executive producer who had recently flown in from New York.

I entered the side door of the old brick building and went up a flight of stairs to his office. Following a friendly introduction, I took a seat opposite the extremely large man. "I'm afraid you won't be able to perform today due to a legal matter," he said, matter-of-factly. "One of the cast members has threatened to report me to the union if I allow you to go on stage." Seeing my spirit diminish, he added, "I'm truly sorry, but the good news is that you can perform tomorrow. One performance for a non-union member is allowed without penalty."

Because many of my friends were planning on coming that day, I felt deeply disappointed, and wondered who had it in for me. An audience member once again, I realized mid-play that I had left the apple in Ashton's office. As soon as the house lights went on, I hurried back over there to retrieve my lucky charm.

"Mr. Springer, I think I left a brown paper bag here. Did you see it?" He looked at me with a blank expression. "It had an apple in it." And with that, he sheepishly replied, "I'm sorry. I ate it."

Heading off to New York marked the end of my life at home and, while I was enthusiastic about launching my career, I was sentimental about leaving. I memorized every detail of my bedroom and of the tree that stood outside my window. I would miss its seasonal symphony of colors. I'd miss having meals with the family at our big round table and rocking myself to sleep in the living room while watching the boys play football in the yard. I'd miss coming home late at night, finding Russell and Billy partying and way too stoned. Yes, my family and the beautiful house we lived in was harder to leave than I would have guessed.

The other tug I felt was with Brent. I had sunk into a bad situation with him, and needed help freeing myself. The tour was my lifeline. I told him that I had to take advantage of the opportunity or I would never become all that I was capable of being, the very thing he so often said was his wish for me. He had no choice in the matter.

During the remainder of the run, I formed a friendship with David, a talented charismatic actor who played the role of "Gabe", a young man whose color was both black and white, and therefore not truly either. David and I spent many hours talking on the phone during the three months that preceded the tour. His nonjudgmental and sympathetic attitude toward my situation served to warm me up to him, which in turn helped me emotionally disengage from Brent. When rehearsals commenced in New York, David proved to be my only friend. It was both natural and necessary that we selected each other as roommates. The other two women were already hooked up, most notably Sonia with Julian.

On the road, several of the cast members referred to themselves as "clowns, freaks and *niggra* types." We were a colorful lot, to be sure. One day, while in Athens, Georgia, I ran up to David on a busy city street and hugged him. I thought it was a bit over-the-top when he urgently shrugged me off, paranoid about the demonstration of affection. I naively believed that racism, along with sexism was receding quickly into the past—that the peace movement was a done deal, and that love ruled the day. I was extremely proud to be part of an inter-racial group. In a way, that was my picket sign. I guess I was more like Mary Lou Bolton than I realized.

About one month into the truck-and-bus tour, we played at the University of Michigan. Waiting backstage, I noticed that my usual butterflies felt more like angry crows, and I realized that it was because I was afraid of facing Brent afterwards. He knew nothing of David and me. *Channel it into your performance*, I told myself. I received my cue and entered through the bar door.

As I made my entrance, the fingers on both hands quickly froze in position. A foreign tingling sensation moved rapidly up my arms, numbing them along the way. I felt close to panicking, without a clue of what to do. I looked at "Johnny" sitting across the room and hoped that he'd see the desperation in my eyes and would somehow save the day, but that wasn't happening. I knew that only I could save me.

I moved to the bar where I normally set my purse down and deftly used my right elbow to extract it from my grip. I expected this paralytic phenomenon to dissolve back into the nothingness from whence it came, but it was only getting worse. Managing somehow to continue speaking my lines, I nearly died when the tingling began to sweep across my lips and jaw. *I need a miracle and I need it now, or I'm going to pass out.*

In that instant, an idea struck, and I walked over to Johnny and started massaging his shoulders. Soon, the feeling came back into my fingers, then my hands, then up my arms, and finally back into my face. Disaster averted, the scene finished up fine, and the massage remained in the blocking from then on.

Having been only seconds away from succumbing to some kind of seizure, I thanked God for saving me, and delighted in the fact that a good bit of business came out of the ordeal.

The encounter with Brent afterwards was anticlimactic. With my parents present, he could only congratulate me and take his leave. That night, I wrote him a letter, telling him that I had moved on. A great sense of relief and freedom followed.

THE BIG APPLE

After three months on the road, I'd saved enough money to stay in New York for a while and put my new life together. David offered me his place to stay at until I got my bearings. On our first day back in town, he took me along to meet his agent, a middle-aged Jewish man, who was slumped over a cluttered desk in a small, dingy office. After they finished talking, the agent directed a few questions at me. With David's testimony to my talent, the man asked if I could supply him with some pictures and resumes. Then, just a few hours later, he called David to have him tell me that I had an audition for a SAG film the next day.

"Really?" I said, as I took the call.

"Yes, they just lost their lead actress and they're ready to start shooting in five days. They're looking for someone your age to play a gal who has recently moved to New York from the Midwest. Do you think you can pull that off?" he asked with a laugh.

At the designated office, I sat alongside several other women, studying the sides from *Seven Deadly Sins*. My reading went well enough that I was invited to stay and read again for the director. Following that success, he asked if I was okay doing nudity.

Shocked to find myself facing this question, I chose my words carefully. "There are some circumstances under which I would be alright with nudity—but not as a rule."

He then asked, "Did you see the movie, *The Fox?*"

"Yes, with Sandy Dennis?" I responded. He nodded affirmatively. "I thought it was an excellent film."

"I directed it. What did you think about the nudity in that one?"

Believing now that he was the real deal, I replied, "I thought it was handled very tastefully." And with that, I was asked to wait while he left the room. When he returned, he was accompanied by four other men, including the assistant director who I'd already done a scene with. Again, we read together.

Following that, the director asked, "Would you mind taking your clothes off— now?" *Oh, crap!* I thought, as he continued. "We can't afford to hire you and then have you freeze up on us on the set. We need to know that you really will be able to work with no clothes on."

Green as I was, I knew that a professional actress wouldn't take her clothes off at a first audition. And when she did take them off, if ever, it would be with the consent of her agent. With a feigned professionalism, I said, "I need to speak with my agent. If he agrees that it's necessary, then I'll do so at the callback."

"Normally, that would be our procedure, too," he responded. "But this *is* the callback and we start shooting in four days. We don't have time for normal protocol." *God darnit! Why does everything have to be so sketchy?*

One of the gentlemen who identified himself as the cinematographer then added, "And, frankly, we need to see your body to make sure that you don't have a beauty mark the size of a football or something on your thigh." That logic spoke to my Virgoan sensibilities. If I wanted this union job then I was going to have to step through my fears and bare my bones—on my first audition—on my second day in New York. I could hardly believe this was happening.

As it was a frigid day in February, I was wearing several layers of clothing: kelly-green, wool-knit slacks with a matching vest, a white turtle neck sweater, mid-calf leather boots with twenty-five laces each, pantyhose, white cotton bikini underwear, and a white push-up bra. Without a plan as how best to proceed, I removed the vest and then the turtleneck, only to panic at the notion of being topless while removing everything else. So, leaving my bra on, I changed course and started to remove my boots. With one leg hoisted up onto a chair, I started to undo the intricate lacing, soon realizing that I was rendering a very cheesy pose. I didn't want to drag out the process unnecessarily, and I figured that no one cared what my feet looked like, anyway. So, I abandoned the boot-removal and moved on to the knit slacks—but when I tried to slip them off, they got stuck around the top of the boots. *Oh dear.* Desperately wanting the ordeal to be over, I swiftly pulled down my pantyhose, bunching them up just above the pants, at knee level.

I was aware that I looked much like a kid about to sit on the toilet—and that the worst was yet to come. Matter-of-factly, I removed my bra and set it aside. Those poor little breasts of mine were now painfully exposed yet the moment of truth was still ahead of me. I had to take off, or rather pull down, my underpants. Sweat was dripping from my armpits. I desperately wanted to run and hide, but if I chickened out at that point then it would've been all for naught. I had to bring it home.

I took a breath, pulled down my underpants, and just stood there miserably in my nakedness. Then it occurred to me that they probably wanted to see me from the back too, so I shuffled my feet around in a circle for their viewing pleasure. When I faced them again, I made an effort to look directly at each one, and when I did so, it struck me as ironic that none of them were bold enough to look blatantly at my body. Suddenly, the cinematographer asked, "Are you nervous?"

I released a big laugh and said, "Yes, I'm nervous. I'm standing here, stark-naked, in front of five strange men—and you're all looking me right in the eye!"

The director laughed heartily and said, "You're beautiful. Put your clothes on."

Quickly, I pulled up my pants, all three layers at once, and slipped the turtle neck over my head without bothering with the bra. I was asked to go wait in the hall while they talked things through. On my way out, I requested, and was given, a copy of the script.

I settled into a tiny closet of a room and began to read. Not far into it, my heart began to sink, but I hung in there, hoping to arrive at some measure of appreciation. Sadly, it only got worse. My character was the last of seven victims of a serial killer who preyed on young, attractive women. I'd end up murdered, hanging upside down, naked, from a tree in Central Park. It was garbage—the worst kind of garbage, the kind where violence against women is sensationalized, ssomething I've always disdained.

Just then, my six-year-old nephew, Holden, popped into my mind and said with great sadness, "Aunt Franny, how could you let yourself be used like that?" That was all it took. If offered the part, I would turn it down. The Assistant Director then opened the door, threw his arms up and said, "You got the part!"

"I'm sorry. I can't accept it," and I handed him back the script.

The director then approached, "Congratulations!"

"She says she can't do it," said the A D.

"I'm sorry. I can't do it. It's too violent for me," I confirmed, and made my way out the door.

I called David from the nearest pay phone and arranged to meet up with him in an hour in Times Square. When he asked how it went, I spilled my story to him. He stopped in the middle of the street and hollered accusatorily, "You turned the part down?"

"Yes. It's garbage!" I screamed. "It's worse than garbage, David. It's…" and he cut me off.

"You turned down a lead role in a SAG film? Are you fucking kidding me?" His eyes were ablaze with condemnation, as he threw up his arms in disbelief. I shuddered under his tone and hurried across to the other side of the street. As he continued with his rant about what a fool I was, I saw the writing on the wall, if he couldn't support my values—we couldn't be together.

That night the director phoned and said that even though he was sorry to lose me, he respected my decision, assuring me that

I was very talented and would have many more opportunities. He sure didn't have to do that.

A year later the movie came out under the name, *Massage Parlor Murders*. I did not go see it. Oh…and it turned out that he had not directed *The Fox*. Go figure.

One-and-a-half years after my arrival in New York, my roommate and her boyfriend decided to move in together, which meant I had to find another living situation. I was just wrapping up a six-week run in a play directed by Nathan George. After seeing the show, Maggie, a highly-respected agent, asked me to come to her office to discuss representation. The meeting went well, and I expected to hear back from her shortly. I desperately needed a good agent who believed in me, for I was running out of steam on my own. After a week of hearing nothing, my optimism waned.

The vast concrete jungle of Manhattan was draining my spirit. Central Park was one of the only escapes into nature that the city offered, but I'd had more than one bad experience there, and by this time, avoided it altogether. I now fully appreciated that simply keeping one's self sheltered, fed, clothed, and mobile, was a tremendous accomplishment, especially with minimal resources. "If you can make it there, you'll make it anywhere," held new meaning for me. I, straight up, had to admit it—I couldn't hack it anymore. I wanted out. *I give up, New York. You win. I'm crying, "Uncle!"*

Relief came with letting go of the New York piece of the dream, for it had become more like a nightmare. Los Angeles had always been where I expected to end up, anyway. I just didn't know how I could financially manage the transition. So, I began the process of envisioning my move west.

Literally, a few hours following that decision, I received a call from Ed, an actor who had been in the most recent play with me, telling me he knew of an apartment available for seventy-five dollars a month. He told me that he, too, lived in the same west-side neighborhood and paid only fifty-five dollars a month. "In fact," he said, "there is a small group of us Hoosiers who have the inside track on several of these rent-controlled units. And, while it's true that they're in a less-than-desirable neighborhood, it's actually more desolate than it is dangerous."

"What neighborhood are you talking about," I asked.

"Hell's Kitchen," he replied. I figured I should at least check it out.

On my way to meet Ed, I stopped at a pay phone to check my answering service. Maggie had called and left a message that she wanted to represent me. *Wow! Could the signs be any more clear?*

A narrow, four-story building stood on the southwest corner of 52nd St and 11th Ave. DeWitt Clinton Park, host to many baseball games in the warmer months, sprawled out between 52nd and 54th, while a small Greek diner marked the southeast corner.

A funky bar, offering jugs of pickles and hard-boiled eggs, occupied the ground floor. Above were a total of six apartments, two per floor. Each one ran the entire length of the building, what they call a railroad flat. The available unit was on the top floor.

Ed and I arrived as the sun was about to set over the Hudson River, one block further west. Amber rays poured in through the singular westward window, casting a warm glow on the enormous kitchen with its hundred-year-old tin ceiling, and worn linoleum floor. I could imagine myself sitting there, writing in my journal, sipping a cup of tea.

There was a bathroom right off the kitchen that had a vintage, cast iron tub and from the perspective of sitting on the toilet, one could see all the way to the eastern wall of the apartment, the whole length of the building. That was quite a visual, as the floor and doorways were noticeably slanted in conflicting directions.

Two windows in the living room overlooked 52nd Street, while the nondescript bedroom bore a faded-blue carpet, which gave me a little sense of cozy. *I guess you're not through with me after all, New York!*

With the help of my new Hoosier neighbors, I moved in. Unfortunately, it didn't take long before the romance of the place faded, and I allowed myself to see the stark reality of my surroundings. The building was old, with decades of grime clinging to the ceiling, walls, and floors, not to mention the countless roaches roaming boldly about. I found strength in the assurance that this was only going to be a brief stop on the way to a better life—one that would come with my success, which was surely imminent. Plus, it would make for a good story someday, and that was always important to me.

Not long after signing me, I learned that Maggie had moved to the west coast. What the hell? When I called the agency, I was told that they would still represent me, which was good news until I met her partner. He had not seen me work and was unimpressed by my credits. Things were quickly becoming miserable again. *I don't get it, Lord! Are you just toying with me?*

The 11th Avenue location proved to be too scary for most of my scene partners. Cabs wouldn't even put on their availability lights until they were at least as far east as 9th Ave, two long blocks away. On more than one occasion, I entered the building, only to discover that the window above the doorknob of the interior door had been broken. Cautiously, I would proceed, sometimes seeing a bum slumped under the stairwell. Very scary.

My mother came to visit me that spring and saw how desolate my situation was. Together, we carried heavy bags of groceries for several blocks back to my flat. When we finally arrived, she noticed my friendly exchange with the bartender on the ground floor. "Make an arrangement with him where you alert him whenever you get home after dark. Ask him to call the police if he doesn't get a call from you within three minutes." I put her plan into place, which did provide me with a sense of security when I came home at night.

Before her visit, I had never cared for salad, but that night she made one with a new invention that had become quite popular, Ranch Dressing. Mixing a packet of powdered herbs with buttermilk, she created pure deliciousness—a salad that proved to be the portal through which I came to love my greens. Yes, Edna was proving to be a great chapter-two mother. Her eternal optimism and encouragement served to fortify my will to carry on. And, the little bit of financial support she was able to offer me (one or two twenties included with each letter), was always greatly appreciated. She had been a WAVE during World War Two, so she knew all about marching on. More than once, I've heard her say, "Just pick up your bucket of guts and keep going." *Nice, Mom.*

Photo by Guy Morrison

ROBERT ALTMAN

After receiving a letter containing a favorable review of my performance in an Off-Off Broadway production of *The Big Knife* by Clifford Odets, Patrick Cragin came to New York specifically to see the play. On the night he came—no one else did. I wanted to die, but what can you do? The cast, understanding my anguish, agreed to perform anyway, but the director was having none of it. Nope. His bar was set at "two or more." To make matters worse, he offered to perform my scene, singularly, for Patrick. *Oh my God! Can this get any more embarrassing?!!* And with that, I lost it.

While thoroughly humiliated, I also found the situation to be hysterical, and was overwhelmed with laughter. Patrick, a wise Irishman, took me to a nearby bar and ordered a few shots of tequila, which turned out to be the perfect remedy. Then, once I'd calmed down, and perhaps because he wanted to give me something new to think about, he told me that Robert Altman would be in town at the Sherry-Netherland Hotel the following week. How or why he had that information, I don't know, but he felt confident that Mr. Altman would remember me fondly, and that it couldn't hurt to touch base with him.

A few days later, I mustered up my nerve and made the call. He did remember me and was very friendly, inviting me to drop by his suite to say hello in person. It's tricky business going alone to visit a man in his hotel suite, but a suite is better than a regular room, so I took comfort in that. Additionally, it's really challenging to know how to strike the right note of casual when popping in on a world-renowned director, one who could change your life in the blink of an eye. *How do I walk that line where I manage to attract his interest while preventing myself from winding up in a compromising position?* I loved his movies. He was as well respected in the industry as anybody could possibly be. To end up in one of his films was a precious dream, perhaps one within reach.

Stepping inside the classy hotel gave me a good feeling. As I walked toward the elevators, I took notice of the massive floral arrangement in the center of the lobby. *Jeeze! You'd think they could afford real flowers.* Later, I'd learn that they were actual stalks of Birds of Paradise and Red Ginger, two species I had never seen before. I was still so green to this world.

"Bob", as he preferred to be called, welcomed me into the living room of his suite, where a few people were sitting around. Soon after my arrival, they all took their leave. I didn't know if it was because I had arrived or not, but I was nervous that he was going to come on to me. I had a little speech prepared, just in case; one that would clarify to him my sincere professional intentions and clear up any misinterpretation he might have about me. I was not some floozy starlet. When he sat next to me on the couch and put his hand on my knee, I figured the time was right.

"Um, I need for you to understand that I am a serious actress. That's why I moved to New York—to get some solid theater training. I'm in a production of *The Big Knife* right now. You could come see it." Though the fear of repeating the Patrick disaster was traumatic, I continued. "I have seen every one of your films and—" RING! And Bob excused himself to go answer the door.

A moment later, Faye Dunaway breezed into the room, toting several shopping bags. She took a seat in one of two velvet chairs and excitedly opened up a shoe box. She tried on her new pair of high heels and stretched her leg out for all to admire. *My God— what a stunning beauty.* I observed her graceful moves. Then, she reached into her purse and took out a razor, commencing to dry-shave her long, shapely legs. I began to feel a little weird and worried about overstaying my welcome. Then, the doorbell rang again, and a few more people arrived. I was just about to stand up to go when Bob approached me, putting his hand on my shoulder and guiding me to the door. "I'm afraid I'm going to have to ask you to leave now, Frances. It was great to see you. I'll let you know when I'm back in town." And off I went, my head held high—my tail between my legs.

To my utter shock, several weeks later, he did call. And I was taken off guard when he invited me to come over and "hang out" with him. I felt awkward about accepting for I knew what was likely motivating him, but still... *This is Robert Altman we're talking about! And he finds you interesting enough to want to hang out with you! You can prevent it from becoming sexual. He's not going to force you to do anything against your will. Hell, you'd be a fool not to go. Look at your pathetic life. How can you not go?*

Leonard Cohen songs filled the air, as did clouds of marijuana smoke. *Hmm, Bob and I have more in common than I realized.* Different folks came and went over the next couple of hours. With the influence of the music and the herb, I felt at ease, and while I enjoyed myself, I also remained vigilant about leaving at the right time. When I deemed it so, and said "good-bye" Bob invited me to join him and his entourage for dinner.

We went to Elaine's on the upper east-side where we lingered over scrumptious food, fine wine, and lively conversation. It seemed that Bob and I were developing a rapport. Then, when we walked out of the restaurant, I quickly hailed a cab and said goodnight. *Yeah! I did it! I had quality time with him, and we did not have sex. What next?* I wondered.

A couple days later, Bob called again, and said he missed me and wanted to spend more time together. *Oh, boy.* As I saw it, there were several reasons why having sex with this man was not a good idea. First and foremost, he was married. And though I had come to convince myself that it was strictly the man's sin if he chose to betray his vows, I never wanted to be the 'other woman' again.

Additionally, I knew that sleeping with him could backfire on me professionally, possibly even destroying the chance of ever working for him. On the other hand, I couldn't help but fantasize about what it might be like to be his object of desire. I imagined that with his artistic soul, he would recognize the same in me. He could be a great mentor. *Oh, God, why does sex always have to come up? I just want an opportunity to show what I can do. If I walk away, I risk losing the connection altogether.* Yes, this was tricky business.

By the time I arrived at his suite, I had pretty much opened myself to the idea. So, taking full responsibility, when he made the inevitable move, I let it happen. Soon, we were in the bedroom making out on the bed. We hadn't been there more than five minutes when the phone rang. Bob ignored it but it went on ringing for what seemed like a very long time. Finally, it stopped, and all was well until a few minutes later when it rang again. This time he was more annoyed and still didn't pick up. Then there came a knock at the door. Seriously agitated now, Bob threw his robe on and charged out to see who it was.

From the bedroom I could hear muffled laughter. It went on too long, and suddenly the notion that I might be the brunt of some good-old boy's joke hit me hard. I simply had to do something to turn the situation around—to reclaim my dignity. So, I grabbed Bob's shirt and slipped it on over my underwear. Hair mussed and mascara smeared, I straightened my spine and walked out. With a big smile, I extended my hand to the attractive and much younger man, standing with Bob. "Hi. I'm Frances McCaffrey."

"Hi. I'm Tom McGuane," he replied, as he shook my hand.

"I love champagne!" I exclaimed, referring to the bottle Tom had brought. Bob took the hint and popped the cork and poured three glasses. Tom, grinning from ear to ear, situated himself on the couch, while I graced the same velvet chair that Faye had. I've got to admit that in that moment, I was hot as a pistol, with both men riveted on me. I had turned their silly, humiliating game on its head. *But now what?* I wondered. *Should I finish my drink, get dressed and take my leave? No, because now he's starting to see me in my power. Now, he's more likely to recognize my worth.*

I soon learned that Tom was the author of a popular novel, *92 in the Shade*. Bob was interested in bringing it to the screen. The three of us actually got along very well together and I couldn't resist the opportunity to continue hanging out with them over the next few days. I loved how they appeared extremely interested in my point of view on movies. At one point, I told Bob, "Your soundtrack is like your trademark. It's where you offer clues to the plot and characters."

"I wish you could come along to my interviews," he responded.

Bob and I played and laid together over the next few days. There was one moment when we simultaneously said, "I love you." *Whew! This is for real.*

One afternoon, as the three of us were walking toward the elevator, Tom and Bob were having a disagreement about who should play the love interest in *92 In the Shade*. At one point, Tom actually said, "I want someone more like—like Frances to play the part." Tom then looked at me and said, "You're an actress, aren't you, Frances?"

"Yes, I am," I replied.

It was bold of him to put Bob on the spot like that. Still, awkward as it was, I was ready for it to be my big break. Bob looked at me and asked, "How old are you?"

"Twenty-three," I said.

"Oh" he said disappointed. "She's twenty-four," as if one year was a meaningful difference. He was going for a laugh, and though it was cruel, I gave it to him because it was kind of funny. Then the subject was dropped and soon it was time for my departure. When he said goodbye he told me that on his next trip to New York, just a couple of months away, he'd arrange a meeting for me with his casting director. That offer served to slightly soothe my hurt feelings.

It was a freezing day in January when his office called to set up my appointment. When I arrived at his suite, a young man greeted me and told me to have a seat in the living room. The casting director was in one of two adjoining bedrooms conducting an interview. When it was my turn, she took a look at my resume and chuckled. Compared to what she was used to seeing, I guess my three credits were rather pathetic. She wasn't even interested enough to have me read something. "You should keep building up your resume and come back in a few years," she said, with a grin. That was it. Done. Goodbye.

As I was walking toward the door, hoping Bob would appear and light up at the sight of me, I suddenly heard his voice coming from the other bedroom. I was able to discern something about "Bette Midler tonight." Then, I heard a female's voice squealing with delight. With that, my heart dropped into my boots and I closed the door behind me.

Every step down the hallway was one step further away from my cherished dream. I felt like a fish that had been caught, deemed unworthy, and tossed back to sea…with the hook still inside. By the time I reached the lobby and passed the flower arrangement that I'd come to love, my joy had morphed into a pit of disappointment and pain. I was hurt. I was angry. Yet, I knew from the start that sleeping with him could backfire. And now it had. I gambled and lost. There was no one to blame but myself. I walked out into the snowy night utterly dejected, wishing I was going to see Bette Midler.

The next day, I shared this saga with Ashton Springer, the executive producer of *No Place to be Somebody*, who had become a friend. After hearing the story, he offered this possibility, "You may have more nerve than you do talent." *Ouch!*

SPIDERS AND RAINBOWS

On a Friday afternoon in February, I arrived home to find my door busted wide open. Terrified, I ran down to the bar and asked the bartender to call the police. When the officers arrived, they went into the apartment to examine the situation. The perpetrator had gone through my dresser drawers and my jewelry but nothing was missing. Even the kitchen had been delved into but he/they didn't score there either. Whoever it was did leave a little something for me, however, all over the floor—urine.

The idea that some sicko had handled my panties, looked at my photographs, and knew where I lived, was very scary. Shaken, I sat across from the policeman in my living room to answer questions while he filled out a report. Fear gripped me when I spotted a bag of pot sitting on the coffee table between us. I did my best to keep eye contact with him, and to my great relief, he never noticed the stash.

A couple hours later, my Hoosier friends came by to offer their support. Not only did they clean the kitchen floor, God bless them, but they also brought me a large piece of plywood and nailed it to the damaged door, and then installed a police lock, which is basically a steel pole that leans from a wedge in the floor to another on the door. This added bit of security was intended to prevent someone from kicking it open, though we had to laugh because anyone could just kick right through the wall if they wanted to. The newly-reinforced door with its three heavy-duty locks was a sight to behold.

A couple days later, as the last of the sun's rays streamed in through the westward window, a surge of creativity moved through me, and I wanted to make art out of the plywood canvas. So, I lit up a joint and studied the door. Then, while gathering magic markers, scissors, and various photographs, I came across a psychedelic pill (mescaline) that I'd tucked away for a special occasion. I considered it, realizing that I had the whole weekend ahead of me and could afford to get a little messed up. *What the hell*, I thought, and ingested the little bugger.

Immediately upon popping it into my mouth, I entertained myself with the notion that I would play the part of a girl tripping. As I jumped into character, I started tracing the natural lines of the wood with a black marker until I'd created a big spider's web. Next, I began cutting away at my composites, gluing cut-outs of myself onto the wood, sticking an eye here, a pair of lips there, etc. High-spirited and dancing as I went along, I was fueled by both the drugs and some great tunes on the radio. Then, quite abruptly, a news flash came on: "A young woman found murdered on a rooftop…she had responded to an ad in Backstage…"

Striking too close to home, I tried to protect myself from the terrible story and get back on point, but it had an energy to it that seemed to boomerang around the room, ultimately returning back to me. Each time it did so, the gravity of the story sank in a little deeper until I felt the pain of her family. It was almost as if it were my story.

Hours later, lying in the fetal position on the kitchen floor, my tears finally subsided and I assessed my situation. Thanks to innumerable hours spent watching my acting teacher guide actors through deep emotional valleys, I surmised that I had just been through a primal therapy experience. I was also aware that I was in an altered state from the drug, and that my fears and insecurities were raw. I knew that what I needed to do was be my own best-possible parent and calm myself with loving kindness. But when I looked around, I saw such filth that it made me feel like giving up and wailing. I forced myself to draw a bath and make a cup of tea.

While pondering my artwork from the tub, I asked myself, *When did you abandon color? Back when you abandoned Catholicism,* my wiser self replied. I recalled how lovely it was to believe that an angel protected me 24/7— long before the many hypocrisies of the church caused me to walk away. I realized now that I had also left behind some aspects of Catholicism that had been beautiful to me: Jesus, the angels, and heavenly pastel colors. *But even if you wanted to go back to those days, the church probably wouldn't want you. You're not that perfectly pure girl anymore.* I did have some sketchy stories behind me by then, and what made it worse was that I couldn't be sure there weren't more ahead. Still, I was okay with who I was, and I believed that all was well between me and my creator. Yes, I still believed in God.

Feeling closer to my spiritual roots than I had in ages, I did my best to imagine an angelic presence around me. Then, with the utmost reverence, I promised that presence that if it would walk with me always, and keep me safe from harm, that I would do my best to do everything within my power to assist in the process. Somehow, that prayer passed beyond the realm of my imagination and rooted itself into my core belief system, (or maybe I should say re-rooted). A new sense of security and peace washed over me, freshly arming me for whatever dangers lay ahead. No longer would I feel so terribly alone.

When dawn broke, I ventured out and walked to the fountain at 59th and Fifth. I stood there, and through swollen eyes watched as the plump water droplets shot toward the sky and then fell back into the pool from whence they came, tiny rainbows reflected in each one. I soaked up the healing energy of the dancing water and saw color as if for the first time.

Feeling optimistic once again, I decided this would be the day that I would make a cold-call, one that had been a long time coming. My sister, Lee, had read in a showbiz magazine, many years earlier, that there was an agent in New York named William McCaffrey. He represented Art Carney, who co-starred in the *Jackie Gleason Show*, which was a staple in our growing-up years. Other than my relatives, I had never met another McCaffrey, much less one spelled the same way. On top of that, this McCaffrey had the same first name as my dad. So, with all that in common, I figured I'd be able to get in to see him, one way or another.

He was with ICM, a very exclusive agency that represented mostly big stars. I was going to have to be clever, charming, and ballsy, as there was no way I would be granted an appointment legitimately. With an air of absolute confidence, I walked into the lobby of the agency where a receptionist sat at a desk near the foot of a large spiral staircase.

"Hello," I said.

"Hello. May I help you?" she asked.

"Yes. I'm here to see William McCaffrey."

"Do you have an appointment?"

"No, I don't— but please tell him that Frances McCaffrey is here to see him."

"Oh…are you related?" she inquired.

"Well…that's what I'm here to find out," I said, as though I were holding a royal flush in my hands.

With a look as though she'd seen it all before and couldn't be bothered, she picked up the phone and rang the man up. "I have a young woman here at the front desk who wants to see you. She doesn't have an appointment. Her last name is McCaffrey and she says you might be related." She listened, then looked at me and said, "Mr. McCaffrey is very busy right now."

I said, "Tell him that my father's name is William."

Smirking now, she added, "And her father's name is William."

After a brief moment, she hung up defeated and said to me, "Go up these stairs and make a right. He's in the office at the far end." I gave her a special little smile as I sashayed up the spiral staircase.

On the floor above, a half-dozen people sat at desks lined up between the top of the stairs and the agent's door at the far end. As I made my way past them, they looked at me as though they were all in on the joke. Then, his door opened and a tall, ruddy, white-haired Irishman stepped out and stood strong with his arms crossed over his large belly. He reminded me of my dad. When I got closer, he said, "So, your last name is McCaffrey?"

"Yes, sir"

"And your dad's name is William?"

"Yes, sir"

"And what's your first name?"

"Frances," I said.

He opened his arms and said, "I'm William Francis McCaffrey. Please—come into my office."

While I was there, Art Carney called. William Francis had fun telling Art about how I came to be there. Everything was going swimmingly well and then it was time to wrap it up. Without offering anything further, he brought the meeting to a close. We shook hands and exchanged a quick hug, laughing once more at the coincidence. I left in high spirits.

Sometimes the story itself is the gift.

FROG LEGS & RAZOR BLADES
1975

Dorothy, the owner of a model agency in Detroit, referred me to a photographer in New York by the name of Chico. Even though I'm shorter at 5'6" than most New York models, she thought he might be able to offer me some work. I gave Chico a call.

I met with him at his office on the upper east-side. With dark curly hair, a small sturdy build and dark, intense eyes, he checked out my portfolio. Seeming unimpressed, he said he'd keep me in mind. Later that afternoon, I received a message to call him, as soon as possible. When I did, he told me that he'd had a cancellation for that same evening's shoot, a sample of some sort for Vogue Magazine.

"Sample" always means that there is no pay involved, at least not unless it's bought. But, considering that he'd been highly recommended and that he was doing this for Vogue Magazine—well, it was somewhat big-time. *Excellent! Things are rolling right along.*

The exclusive address turned out to be his personal residence. When I walked in, I was disappointed to realize that it was just the two of us. He asked me to select an item of clothing from a pile of garments in a large box. I rifled through the skimpy, negligee-type things until I came across a man's shirt in camouflage pattern that came nearly to my knees.

Because of Dorothy's high-standing in the business, I still harbored some trust and, in the privacy of a bedroom, I changed into the shirt, leaving my underwear on. When I came out, he asked me to pose on the top steps of the stairway. *Jeeze, is he really going for an under-shot?* I dreaded to think. Good thing I had enough length in that shirt to do what he asked, without giving him what he wanted—if what he wanted was a crotch-shot. Hugely relieved when he called it a wrap after one roll of film, I swiftly changed back into my clothes and was about to fly out the door when he invited me to join him for dinner. Grateful to get a meal out of the deal, I said, "okay."

It turned out that he was a revered regular at the upscale Italian restaurant located right across the street. A friendly maître d' escorted us to "Chico's booth" where photographs of him as a jockey lined the wall above. Soon after we'd been seated, the maître d' returned and said to Chico, "The chairman of the Doyle Dane Bernbach Agency is here and would like to meet you. Shall I send him over?"

"Yes, definitely," Chico replied.

A moment later, a distinguished, older gentleman arrived at our table and introduced himself. Chico invited him to join us, which he did, taking a seat to my right. They had quite a lot to talk about as Mr. Chairman was into horse-racing in a big way. When he learned that I was an actress, he handed me his card and said to give him a call. *Alright! Maybe this evening isn't a waste after all.* My horizons were brightening once again.

Following up with Mr. Chairman led to an invitation to come to his office and then to lunch. It felt good to dress up and step out with hope and purpose. The Chairman's office walls were populated with photographs of him with Elizabeth Taylor, Barbara Streisand and others. On the way out of his office, he told his secretary to set up an appointment for me with the casting director. I appreciated being treated with respect by his employees. I was on cloud nine as we walked to his favorite French restaurant.

He highly recommended the frog legs. The idea of it repulsed me but, out of some desire to impress, I ordered them. Some mighty big frogs were sacrificed for that meal and, even though they tasted like chicken, I could barely get them down.

Right out of the gate, Mr. Chairman steered the conversation to Chico. He shared with me that Chico had been at the center of a big scandal at the Aqueduct Race Track a few years earlier. I then confided in him that I had been very uncomfortable with Chico during the photo session. From there a variety of interesting stories flowed out of Mr. Chairman and time sailed by. When we left, he invited me to join him for lunch again in two weeks' time, same place. In the meantime, I met with his casting director and was assured that I'd be called in for something as soon as possible. *At last someone respects what I am about, and happily extends himself to try and be helpful.*

At the next lunch date, Mr. Chairman had some big news for me. Chico was in jail on murder charges. Yes, in the interim between our lunch dates, Chico had stabbed and burned the body of his ex-girlfriend's lover. My stomach knotted up at hearing this news and a meal was no longer possible. Mr. Chairman ordered me a Raspberry-Cognac Sparkler and French fries, while he chowed down on frog legs. From then on, he would claim credit for having saved me from certain death. I wasn't quite sure how he computed that but I didn't mind one iota.

Within a few days, I received a call from the casting director at the Doyle Dane Bernbach Agency, telling me that I had an audition for a national commercial for Proctor and Gamble. The product was White Cloud Toilet Paper. And though toilet paper wasn't exactly what I'd been dreaming of, it was a national spot for a major corporation, and that could mean big bucks. I was thrilled.

The audition went well and I was called back for a second round. Within hours of that meeting, I got the news that the job was mine. I would portray a young housewife who finally finds the toilet tissue she's been searching for. *Hallelujah! Praise the Lord!*

I sat at a table, feeling the two different brands, each with their identity hidden. I'd choose the softer one and then it would be revealed that it was the White Cloud product. With great delight, I'd say, "Mmm, White Cloud is softer!"

I treasured every moment on the set: having my makeup and hair done, working with the lighting technicians, and finally with the director. My only complaint was that it was over too quickly. I was in and out within four hours. I wanted it to be an everyday thing but, hey, it's a beginning. Payment for the day's work could not come soon enough but more exciting than that was the long-term potential. If it took off, it could garner tens of thousands of dollars. Mr. Chairman was an ace in my book.

In spite of the fact that connecting with men on the subway was a definite "NO" on my list of rules, I found myself laughing out loud at the comical commentary of a business man who was joyfully going about his day. Around my height, he was a black man with rather prominent buck teeth that added a playful quality to his moon-like face. We engaged in an exchange of our own, and when he asked if we could have lunch sometime, I agreed. His name was Charles Hope.

Charles worked for a community development project, was happily married, and lived in the Bronx. He was fascinated by my life and encouraging of my dreams. We started to get together for lunch once a month or so. One day, after meeting up in the financial district, we hopped a cab to go back uptown. When it dropped me at 52nd and 11th, something fell from the sky, striking me just above my left eye.

Charles witnessed the incident from the backseat, opened the door and rushed to my aid, telling the driver to wait. I looked down and saw three pointed razor blades. Blood began to flow into my eye. A moment later, the owner of the Greek diner on the corner came running out with a towel. As he patted my wound with the cold, damp cloth he said that he had seen the same thing happen earlier to the mailman. Acting on a hunch as to who the culprit was, he went running into the building next door. A few minutes later he returned with an eight-year old boy that he'd found on the rooftop.

Dragging the kid by the collar, he commanded, "Look what you've done! Look at her! You could have blinded this lady." The boy cowered, avoiding eye contact. Shaking him by the shoulders, the man insisted that the boy look at me and own his actions. By then I knew that my injury was superficial but nonetheless, I was traumatized. Finally, the small boy raised his eyes and looked at my bloodied face.

I wanted to believe that the moment penetrated him deeply, possibly altering the course of his life. At least that would provide a silver lining to the otherwise horrible experience. The nice man from the diner then took charge of the boy, while I assured Charles that I was fine and that he should continue on. I was eager to get home to my apartment.

Huddled on the bed, I shook as I thought about all the scary things that had happened to me since I'd moved to Hell's Kitchen—two-and-a-half long years earlier—and there were many more incidents than I've shared here. Yet, in every case, I came through unharmed. My spiritual armor was working, and for that I felt deep gratitude. Still, my spirits were waning, and I didn't want any more of it. I wanted to emancipate myself from my poverty-stricken life, from my roach-infested apartment, from New York altogether. I needed a break.

SHOCK & DELIGHT

It was mid-August, 1976, as I set out on a day of cold calls to production companies, producers, and casting directors. A lengthy list of such entities was published in Backstage Magazine, my weekly bible. On my way to midtown, where I planned to roll the dice that day, I found myself drawn to a street vendor selling a Little Red Riding Hood doll. The feature that most captured my interest was the doll's three characters in one.

First there was Little Red Riding Hood but when you turned her upside down you had Granny in her night cap. Then, when you took Granny's nightcap and turned it inside out and around, covering Granny's face, the Big Bad Wolf was revealed. It was very clever and cost only ten dollars. I thought about my sister Lee's soon-to-be-born daughter and decided to buy it. I also knew that it would make a good conversation piece as I made my rounds.

I approached one uninterested receptionist after another with a bright smile, pretending that all I wanted was to drop off a headshot. Usually there was a pile of them sitting on their desks. The real hope was that someone with influence would happen to be nearby and take notice, resulting in an interview. And so, it was that day, that a producer observed me from his open office as I showed off the three faces of my doll to his curious receptionist. He told her to send me in.

He was your classic cigar smoking, barrel chested producer type. Sometimes it wasn't easy to get clarity on exactly what such a person produced but he had an office and was listed in Backstage, so I assumed he was for real. I wasted no time communicating to him that I was a serious actress with no interest in sleaze. He said he understood and then offered me an opportunity to be seen for some print work. He set up a time and gave me an address. Optimistically, I went to the casting session the following day.

Several young women were sitting in the waiting area. I signed in, took a seat and soon got to talking with one of them who told me that the job was for the cover of a magazine. The image would be that of a scantily clad girl trying to escape up a ladder while being pursued by a man with a knife. I could not believe it! *How can this be showing up for me again?* I felt my ire rise but didn't want to let her see how disgusted I was lest she think that I was judging her. I pretended that I forgot something and got the hell out of there.

What part of "serious actress" did he not understand? I was so angry that I just couldn't let it lie, and spent the entire evening writing a highly expressive letter to "Mr. Producer." The following day, I hand-delivered it and, surprisingly, was invited into his office again. He listened as I vented my outrage and then apologized for having offended me. He said he wanted to make up for it, and that he knew a professional screenwriter who was working on a first-class project that I should meet. He made a call on the spot and arranged for me to meet Perry at 5 p. m. the following day.

With Earth, Wind and Fire's "Fantasy" blasting away as I put myself together, I considered carefully what I'd wear to the meeting. Judging by the address, I was pretty sure it would be an apartment situation. It was important to me that I project an image that, in no way, could cause one to mischaracterize what kind of an actress I was. I selected a printed, knee-length dress with three-quarter-length sleeves and a high neckline. As was always the case with me, I wore sensible shoes that I could comfortably walk in. Then, just as I was about to head out the door, a shiny piece of foil on top of my dresser caught my eye. I paused and considered its contents.

I went back, opened the foil and removed a dollar bill that had been folded into the size of a stick of Dentyne gum. I opened the bill and stared at the small pile of white powder. Alex, a friend that I had maintained contact with from my acting class, was one of the few actors from those days that had the hutzpah to come as far west as my place for rehearsals. We'd recently gone out for a meal together and when he saw me to my door, he insisted on giving me this little "gift." I told him that cocaine wasn't my thing, but he said to hang on to it anyway, that it might come in handy down the road. Now, for whatever reason, it had caught my eye.

Hmm, I wonder if I should take it with me. It's rampant on the film scene these days.

True, but..., and the opposing voice within me continued. *You certainly don't want to come off like a druggie. That's worse than coming across like a dummy.*

Yes, but wouldn't it be smart to have it, just in case? Suppose you're presented with a scenario where it turns out that it would be the perfect gift for the right person at the right time? The logic of that argument won out. It's not like I had to offer it, but best to be prepared. I folded the bill and slipped it where I felt it was safest, tucked inside my panties.

Perry greeted me at the door of his upper east-side apartment. His clothes were rumpled and he had dark circles under his eyes, as if he'd been up all night. I thought he looked like a writer should look and instinctively liked him. He ushered me into his spacious and comfortably furnished living room where he directed me to take a seat on a worn leather couch. He sat adjacent to me, as I relayed the story of how our appointment came about. From there it was the usual—highlights of my theater background supported by photos and reviews, while expressing my passion for film.

He told me that he was in the process of writing a script and that he'd keep me in mind when it got as far as casting. Satisfied that I had taken care of business, I deemed that it was time to leave and started to do just that when the buzzer rang. Perry went to the intercom had a brief exchange, and when he returned said, "You should stay a little longer and meet a friend of mine. He's coming up right now."

A moment later, a very big energy, in the form of a rather petite man, blew into the room. After they exchanged a warm greeting, Perry introduced me. "John, this is Frances McCaffrey, an actress." John's tan face gave way to a bright smile and we shook hands. "Frances, meet John Avildsen."

Following the introduction, John stepped over to the window, reached into his pocket and brought out a bag of marijuana. I was kind of digging his style as he stood there: shoulder-length hair, a sports jacket over a tee-shirt, and blue jeans. After dexterously rolling a joint, he took a seat on the chair to my left.

It was a rare occasion that a joint passed me by un-sampled, (though it was illegal, I didn't think of pot as a drug), and I saw no reason to make this an exception. So, as we sat there getting high, John spoke enthusiastically about the movie that he had just finished cutting. *Wow! He's got a movie in the can. Then, suddenly, I remembered my secret stash. If ever there was a perfect moment to offer the gift—this is it.*

"I have something that you guys might appreciate," I said sweetly.

They look puzzled, as I deftly slipped my hand under my dress and produced the folded bill. I removed the foil, unwrapped the bill and set it down on the coffee table, saying, "Please, help yourselves."

John broke into a huge grin, took out a twenty-dollar bill, rolled it into a straw and snorted up a dose. When he passed it to me, I said, "No thank you," and passed it on to Perry. They looked confused, so I added, "It's not my thing." Shock and delight. I was home with these guys.

After hearing fascinating tales about the making of his movie about a boxer, John extended an invitation to me to attend a screening the following night. I was feeling like I loved boxing movies at that moment, which is funny because I'd always hated them. John wrote down the necessary information and handed the slip of paper to me as I said my happy goodbyes. Heading out the door, I turned around and asked, "Hey, what's the name of your movie?"

"*Rocky,*" he said, with a smile.

Before the screening, I learned that John had also directed *Joe*, starring Peter Boyle as well as *Paper Tiger* which had received three Oscars. No doubt about it, John Avildsen was big-time.

The screening was an intimate affair for around twenty people, many of whom were distributors. Perry and his date sat near John in the back of the room, while I sat by myself up front. Let it suffice to say that I was blown away by the movie. When the credits rolled, I rose to my feet with tears streaming down my face, clapping enthusiastically. Everyone else seemed to have loved it, too, but nobody else stood up. It was hard to remain standing alone but I pushed through the discomfort, holding firm to my conviction that I had just seen a great movie, and that the director deserved the acknowledgment. Afterwards, when I congratulated him, John invited me to join his group of eight for dinner.

I sat to his left while he held focus at the head of the table. Perry sat directly opposite me next to his date. Every now and then, I'd catch someone looking at me, giving me the feeling that they were assuming that I was some new conquest for John. I did my best to let those thoughts pass on through, choosing to believe instead that I was being divinely guided, once again, toward the fulfillment of my dream. As I saw it, my job was to be fully present, to operate with integrity, and to be available to say "yes" when opportunity knocked. Meanwhile, I was planning to head home before he could hit on me, just in case that was what he had in mind. Nonetheless, I was aware that I was already responding to the aphrodisiac of the power he wielded. *Oh, boy…I don't want to mess this up.*

After dinner, John invited me to come along to a celebration at Sylvester Stallone's hotel suite. That sounded safe and fun, so I went. When he introduced me to "Sly" I shook his hand and said, "I loved the movie, man! You were awesome!" Flying high, he squeezed mine and responded, "Oh, from your mouth to God's ears! Thank you." What a future was in store for him!

That "odd one out" feeling soon swept over me, so I thanked John for the great night and exited the scene. While riding the crosstown bus, I reflected on the progression of events that had occurred since I stepped out to make cold calls a couple days earlier. None of this would have happened had I not purchased the doll, walked out of that sleazy audition, or vented my rage in that letter…and maybe, had I not brought along the little drug gift. Now, having just borne witness to the birth of someone else's dream, I was feeling encouraged, once again, about the possibilities for my own.

I thought about the tale of "Little Red Riding Hood." *Who is the Big Bad Wolf in this story? And, is he going to eat me? Oh, dear.*

The bus was nearly empty as it approached the last stop at 55th and 11th. "How far are you going, Miss?" the driver asked.

"To 52nd Street," I replied.

"You shouldn't be walking there alone at this hour. I'll take you." And he continued on to my corner. *If not for the kindness of strangers…* Feeling extremely blessed, I marveled at the goodness and magic in my life.

Several days later, John Avildsen called. He wanted to know if I'd like to join him for the weekend at his vacation home on Long Island. Gulp. I stalled and tried to absorb the decision that was facing me. I felt resentful that he was putting me in such a predicament. Wouldn't a dinner date have been more appropriate? *What's the matter with men?* Then I reminded myself that a different set of rules applies when one is actually making a movie. I froze in my dilemma, wanting desperately to successfully navigate the sketchy waters between personal integrity and professional goals. He filled the empty space with words of encouragement. "Come on, you'll love it here. The weather's gorgeous and you can relax for a few days. Wouldn't that be good for you?" He sure had me there.

"Okay," I finally said. "I'll come."

When I hung up the phone and turned to walk into my bedroom, the ironing board came crashing down in front of me like a guillotine. I felt it was a bad omen and knew that I should reconsider, but I ignored it, and got ready for a weekend at John Avildsen's beach house.

I was shocked when he greeted me with his two young sons in tow, ages four and seven. *Strange that he never mentioned them on the phone,* I thought. Hell, I didn't know anything about him other than he'd just directed a great movie. I hadn't even asked the basic questions. I simply made a lot of assumptions about him, based on his freedom to invite me to his home, his accomplishments, and the facts that he looked cool, smoked pot, and had long hair. Oh, well, I told myself, *it's kind of flattering that he thinks enough of me to bring me into his family fold—even though it seems a bit weird.*

Settled into the rustic cottage while the boys were playing outside, John retrieved a bunch of vegetables from the refrigerator and asked if I minded chopping. Happy to have a task, I stood there chopping while he pulled a dinner together. It felt like we were a couple that'd been doing this for years. A delicious stir-fry, topped off by a fine red wine, resulted. When dinner was over, I offered to do the dishes while John put the boys to bed. I was kind of warming up to him but I believed that a lady should always be in control and have her options. So, when he picked up my bag and invited me to follow him into his bedroom, I stopped him and asked if I could have my own room. He explained that it was a small cottage and there really wasn't another spare bedroom, so the answer was basically, "No."

I have to admit that I didn't hold my stance. Oh well, who knows…it might turn out really great, I thought. And being that I was in a sexually explorative phase of my life, I made the choice to proceed to the bedroom.

The next day, he and a friend that lived nearby, spearheaded a picnic for all of us at the beach. As it turned out, it was a bathing-suit-optional one, which didn't seem to faze them at all. Thankfully, they kept their suits on, but a couple of hours into the day I removed my top, which was surprising even to me. It was wonderful to feel free in my own skin, flawed as I was.

Relaxing on a blanket with various snacks and beverages, John pulled a script from his satchel. I sat back and listened while he told his friend the story that was slated to be his next picture. He was excited about the new young actor that was set to star in it—John Travolta. The movie was *Saturday Night Fever*.

It was surreal to be lying there, listening to a discussion about a movie that was in the works and slated to be directed by the man I had just slept with. I had to make a sincere effort to keep myself grounded. I did make sure, however, that at some point, I slipped in the mention of my recent toilet paper commercial, lest he should forget that I was an up-n-comer myself.

A second night of passion…okay, maybe not so much. A second night of sex, and then the weekend was over. It was Sunday, John had to be somewhere and it was time for me to take my leave, to return to my grim reality. John was cordial when he dropped me off at the train station, saying that we'd stay in touch. I wondered if that was true. *Anyway,* I told myself, *it's been fun. Yeah, it's all good.*

AMERICA

It was one week later, the last Sunday of August, 1976, the year of America's bicentennial. It was wickedly hot and humid in the city. Because I had less than twenty dollars to my name, I spent Friday and Saturday night alone in my miserable apartment. By Sunday, I was desperate to get out of there and go somewhere with air-conditioning. I decided to treat myself to a movie that John had raved about—*Taxi Driver*, starring another new actor on the scene, Robert DeNiro.

I was not prepared for the raw, human brutality portrayed in that movie. I covered my eyes through much of it but was blasted off-guard by the last scene. It was emblazoned on my brain before I knew what hit me. I felt as if it were my fingers blown off by the bullet. When credits rolled, I was immobile. Not until the house lights came on, did I stand up and, mindlessly, slip my arms into the baggy, teal-colored raincoat that I wore to camouflage my femininity. Slowly, I secured each fat plastic button, as I ventured back into the merciless, sweltering heat.

I took solace in the heavy flashlight that I kept in the deep, square pocket. Clutching it as I walked, I pretended it was a gun. Now and then, it would come in handy—like when I'd arrive home and find the hallway lights not working, which was often the case.

As I set out on the long trek back to my miserable apartment, the psychological armor that had been holding me together began melting away. My world, and the one depicted in the film, blurred into one-and-the-same. I walked westward along 48th Street, through the very neighborhoods that had served as the film's locations and began to crumble in the face of the awesome city that imprisoned me. It was hopeless to try and block the film's horrifying images from my mind, and with each passing minute my throat hurt more from trying to hold back the mounting sobs. A turning point—some sort of critical mass—had been reached, and an emotional volcano was soon to erupt. The best I could do was to make it home before it burst.

From the split second I stepped foot in my building, it was like the unraveling of the inside of a golf ball; every possible reason to feel miserable came flying to the surface. I was a goner. For the rest of the day, and well into the night, I sobbed and wailed like a dying dog, succumbing to the belief that I had been forgotten in this world. I fell into the great abyss of hopelessness.

Somewhere around 4 a. m., completely cried out, I sat rocking myself on the bed when suddenly the phone rang. Startled, I let it ring a few times before answering. "Hello."

A familiar female voice greeted me. "Did I wake you?" After a pause, I realized I was talking to Crystal, a friend from Detroit that I'd known through the Cinema Club.

"No, actually, you didn't."

"Great!" she replied. "I'm calling from a hotel in Montreal. I'm with a guy from the group, America. We're on tour and will be in Philadelphia tomorrow. I was hoping you could meet us there and come to the concert. We could pick you up at the train station."

Dazed and reeling from the shock, I stalled, asking her to remind me what songs America was known for. Then I added, "Crystal, you've called me in the middle of the darkest night of my life."

She said, "A Horse with No Name," and then asked, "Are you all right?"

Feeling a bit better already, I said, "Oh, my God—I love that song! What's another one?"

"Tin Man," she replied, and we sang a few bars together until we started laughing.

"Yes, I'll come meet you tomorrow," I said, as a rush of joy swept through me. "How is it that you're with them again?"

"I left Michigan around six months ago. I'm living in L.A. now and planning to bring the kids out as soon as I'm settled. I'll fill you in tomorrow. I'm so excited you're coming!"

"Me, too" I cried, as all the obstacles and concerns poured forth. "But wait! I only have eight dollars to my name. I can't even buy a train ticket with that. Also, what if they think I'm like some groupie or something? I can't handle that."

"No, they won't. I've already told them that you're an actress from Detroit and that I simply must see you while we're so close to New York. Isn't there someone you could borrow a few bucks from? A one-way ticket is only like fifteen dollars or something. We'll cover your return. Just get there."

With that, I remembered that I had a lunch date with Charles Hope that very day. I felt confident that he'd be happy to lend me twenty dollars. Poof—obstacle gone!

"Pack a bag in case you decide to spend the night," she added. "After the concert there'll be a party and you never know, you might want to wait a day before going back. Just bring some underwear and a toothbrush. And by the way, could you possibly bring some weed with you?"

"Oh, shoot, Crystal. I don't have any. And I don't know how I could score any in time. Plus, I don't have the money. I'm really sorry."

"All right, but if you do think of a way—it would be greatly appreciated. Okay then, there's a three o'clock train out of Grand Central. Catch that and we'll meet you at the Philadelphia station."

"Thank you, Crystal!" I said and hung up the phone. As I sat in the stillness, marveling at my transformation, I was humbled by what I deemed to be nothing less than divine intervention.

Charles and I met at noon that day at a deli where we shared an oversized Reuben sandwich. I wasted no time telling him what was up and before I could even ask, he offered to loan me some money if I needed it.

"Actually, if you could lend me twenty dollars…"

"No problem. I'll give it to you after lunch, back at your place, if that's okay. I have a birthday present I want to give you." Charles and I were both Virgos with birthdays just around the bend. So, following lunch, we hopped a cab to my apartment. We sat down in the living room where he took a joint out of his breast pocket and fired it up. I didn't even know he smoked, but I guess he figured I did. Pretty much everyone did in those days. I took a couple hits and was flying high in no time. As we sat there, enjoying the buzz, he pulled a quarter pound bag of the potent weed out of his pocket and set it down on the table. "Happy Birthday, Frances! I grew this myself in my back yard according to the most beneficial phases of the moon and everything. It's very special stuff," he said, with a wink.

"Thank you, Charles!!! Thank you so much! I can't believe this. I absolutely can't believe this!" I exclaimed. And truly, it seemed miraculous to me that the universe was providing me with the exact thing that I desired, and so immediately. The perfection of it humbled me.

Charles stood up to take his leave, and just as I wondered if I was going to have to remind him about the twenty dollars, he reached inside his jacket and retrieved a wad of hundred-dollar bills, peeling off three of them and handing them to me. "When's the last time you saw your family?" he asked.

"It's been a year," I said. "But, no! I can't take this, Charles," and handed them back. Ignoring me, he set the money down on the coffee table and made his way toward the door. I persisted, "Charles, I can't take it. I don't know when I can repay you."

"It's not a loan," he replied. "It's your birthday and Labor Day weekend coming up. Why don't you treat yourself to a trip home?" His generosity was blowing my mind. After one more attempt to resist, I relented. All of this behavior was atypical of our friendship: gifts, money—nothing like that had transpired before. He was simply being an angel.

With a full heart, I hugged my friend and said goodbye. From the living room window, I watched as he crossed the street. "Thank you, Charles!" I yelled out. He smiled and waved. Tears welled up in my tired swollen eyes, as I watched him walk away. In a daze, I packed a tiny overnight bag, locked up the apartment, and hailed a cab to Grand Central Station.

My excitement was slightly tempered by the shame I felt for having lost faith. The challenges I faced in New York as a result of my economic status, or lack thereof, were enormous, and what made it more difficult was being a single, attractive female. In addition to navigating those circumstances, I had to remain positive, open, and ambitious about achieving my goals. Considering all of that, it was easy to arrive at a place of self-forgiveness but even so, I swore that I would never fall prey to despair again—NEVER. With that fresh resolve and an overwhelming sense of gratitude, I thanked God and my angels for having saved me from despair. The train pulled into the station at 4 p.m.

As I rode the long escalator up, my eye was drawn to an image of Kokopelli, the Native American fertility deity that looks like a humpbacked flute player. It was embroidered on the back of a black jacket worn by a tall man with broad shoulders and long dark hair. I'd never been attracted to someone from the back before and I wanted to get a glimpse of his face. So, when I reached the main floor, I craned my neck in his direction, just as I heard Crystal call out my name. The blonde, green-eyed beauty welcomed me with open arms, and then introduced me to her friend. "Franny, this is 'Remy.'"

"Hello, Franny," he said.

"Hi Remy." We shook hands.

"Oh, and this," Crystal looked around and saw, yes, the Kokopelli man approaching, "this is Koko. He's the tour manager."

His dark intense eyes shone brilliantly as his strong hand shook my own. I could feel my face flush as the four of us made our way through the grand lobby, out the front doors, and into a black limousine that awaited us. Soon upon settling into our seats, I offered Crystal my bag of weed. All eyes lit up, and we had a most enjoyable ride to the hotel.

We hung out, along with the band and crew members in one of the musician's suites, snacking, drinking sodas and relaxing before the evening show. I learned that John Sebastian and Poco were also a part of this tour. It was a very cool scene.

Koko made sure that I had any food or beverage that I wanted, while Crystal and I busied ourselves, catching up and reminiscing about the people from Cinema Club. Suddenly my attention was pulled to the television by my own voice. "White Cloud is softer." Chuckling under my breath, I directed Crystal's attention to the screen but was mortified when she announced, "Hey, look, everyone! That's Franny on TV!" In an instant, I became the fecal point—oops—the focal point, of attention in the room.

Later that evening, it was surreal to find myself bopping in the wings next to Crystal, watching America play one great song after another. I'll never forget the moment when they played, "Ventura Highway" and how it spoke to my longing to move to California. Just then Koko approached from behind, put his hands on my shoulders, and massaged my tight muscles, sending shivers down my spine.

Following the show, we were all led out to a row of limousines and whisked off to the airport. The cars drove onto the tarmac and parked near a private jet. I knew Crystal wanted me to stay on with them but I said good-bye to her and Remy and was preparing to ask Koko if his driver would take me back to the station.

"Why don't you come with us to Syracuse?" he asked, as he

brushed a hair from my eye.

"Oh, um, wow. That's too much. How would I get back to New York?"

"I'll cover your return. No problem."

"Could I have my own room?" I had to ask.

"I'm afraid I can't do that. It's just not in the budget." *How many times am I going to hear that in my life?* I wondered. He then added, "I could get a room with two beds, if you wouldn't mind sharing, the room that is." He was charming, and at least he was giving me some sort of option. I nodded affirmatively.

"Yes...you *would* mind?" he asked, feigning confusion.

Appreciating the humor, I shook my head. "Great! Then, let's go!" He offered his hand and helped me out of the limousine. I stood awestruck for a moment, taking in the amazing visual: five, black stretched-out Cadillacs in crescent formation around a sleek, silver jet that glistened in the moonlight. Kokopelli man took my hand and pulled me forward. *Is it my Stairway to Heaven?* I wondered, as I ascended the steps.

In this instance, the chemistry was true and I did not hold back, (shocking, I know). The next morning, he ordered a breakfast feast and, in the midst of it, invited me to stay through to the next city, Burlington, Vermont. Happily, I accepted.

That afternoon was spent hanging out with Crystal and the band members. It was great fun being in their midst, privy to their joking around. They were rock stars, living incredible lives, making music that would carry on forever. Koko was occupied all day long, tending to business, happy that I was having fun. When bedtime came around, I was excited to be with him again.

The band rocked the house in Burlington and I was flying high, watching from the wings with Crystal. Koko came around and nuzzled me just often enough to assure me (and anyone else that may have had ideas) that our connection was tight. Another great overnight together and then, at breakfast, he asked me to stay on through Kansas City. I made sure that he'd still cover my return to New York and joyfully accepted.

Fortunately, it was summertime, as my overnight bag consisted of simply some underwear, a toothbrush, make-up, and a copy of *Seth Speaks* by Jane Roberts, my metaphysical bible at the time. When we got to Kansas City, I bought myself a bathing suit and a couple outfits, bringing my cash stash down by a third. Once the wardrobe issue was resolved, I lounged poolside with Crystal and the guys for the rest of the day. As I listened to their stories, I envied their lives in Los Angeles. Crystal, I learned, was currently renting a house with a few other women in West Hollywood. She encouraged me to make the move and offered me a couch to sleep on.

Ten years my senior, Crystal was genius-smart and had a complex life that included two ex-husbands and four children. She was cool to hang out with and was a magnet to artistic types. She had taken up guitar just a few months earlier and was already quite decent at it, but what impressed me most were her original songs and the sweet voice she sang them with. Somewhere around day three, I picked up on some weirdness going on with her. She may have been doing heavier drugs than I knew of, and I sensed that she was falling out of favor with Remy. She didn't confide in me why but, clearly, she was unhappy about something.

While in Kansas City, one of the lead singers came down with laryngitis. That night's concert was canceled. The next day, the other lead singer developed the same symptoms, causing a second show to be canceled. Then, on the third day, the rest of the tour was cancelled. I had so been looking forward to Colorado Springs for Labor Day weekend. I was bummed out big-time when I heard Koko order the jet to be readied for departure. They would be heading back to Los Angeles in a couple of hours.

Knowing it was time for me to return to New York, I mustered up my nerve and asked Koko, "Could I hitch a ride with you to Los Angeles? Crystal has offered me a place to stay for awhile."

With careful consideration, he responded, "That would be fine. And don't worry about your return to New York. I'll cover it." Then he added, "But I don't think it's a very good idea for you to stay at Crystal's. She seems a bit too scattered. You can stay at my house if you want, for a couple of weeks."

"That'd be great," I said, beaming.

It turned out that Crystal had to take a commercial flight home. When I asked Koko what happened, he was vague, implying that it had something to do with Remy not wanting to be seen with her on his home front. "Oh," I said, beginning to get the picture. Perhaps Remy had a girlfriend—or a wife, back home. In any case, it was strange and sad to me that Crystal was banished from the scene while I continued on.

Around midway through the cross-country flight, I got up and wandered down the aisle to where the roadies were playing poker. As I stood there, the guy nearest me won a big pot of money. He said, "Hey! You're good luck! Please, have a seat," and then handed me a twenty- dollar bill. "You can have ten percent of my take as long as you sit here." For the next hour or so, he continued to win. By the time we landed, I had "earned" three hundred dollars. *Ah, Life!*

It was September third, 1976, the eve of my twenty-fifth birthday. I could hardly believe that I was in Los Angeles, being escorted from a private jet to a limousine by the Kokopelli man. Hell's Kitchen was three thousand miles away. The thought that my time in New York might be over actually created new space in my lungs. Until Koko looked at me sideways, I remained unaware that I was continually releasing big sighs of relief. I'd been experiencing some powerful emotions all through this trip but had kept them under wraps. Koko was not a confidant on that level, and I wasn't sure if he ever would be. Time would tell if this relationship had wings.

Meanwhile, I had five hundred *smackaroos* in my wallet, and "Ventura Highway" playing in my head as we rode the considerable distance to Thousand Oaks. Then Koko said, "There's something I should tell you before we get to the house. I live with a woman…but she isn't my girlfriend. She's my assistant."

"Have you told her to expect me?" I asked hopefully.

"No, ah…I didn't." Then, he added assuredly, "But don't worry. She'll be fine with it."

It would've been so much better had he prepared her. Instead, I had to tolerate her lack of courtesy and obvious disapproval. The only moment she made eye contact with me was during our introduction. From then on, she ignored me. I knew that she was assuming he'd picked up some groupie. Oh well, I was too tired to give a crap.

A short while later, I laid my weary body down on his king size bed. Lights still on, he sat next to me reading. When she came into the room and plopped herself down near his feet, I opened my eyes and made an effort to be included, but she was adamant about making me invisible. Then, to add insult to injury, she started speaking in some kind of code language. Eventually, I reached my disgust quota, which was also towards him for indulging her in such rudeness and closed my eyes. As I lay there, I couldn't help but catch that she was talking about Crosby, Stills, Nash and Young. It turns out that they were another amazing group that Koko and his partner managed.

Then I was startled by a jarring sound. It must have been when she opened the bullet chamber of her new pistol. I opened my eyes to see her holding it proudly, as she showed it to him. He was obviously uncomfortable with me witnessing the exchange and gave her the eye. She promptly left the room with it, and I hoped that that would be it for the night, but no…she came back, sat at his feet again, and began a flirty dialogue that went something like this: "Do you know what tomorrow is?" Pause "September fourth…ring any bells?"

With uncertainty, he asked, "Is it your birthday?"

"Yes! It's my birthday!" she said.

Loving the serendipity, I took giggly pleasure in interjecting, "Oh, mine, too."

Koko, perhaps getting a kick out of it as well, said, "Well then, I guess I'm taking you both out to dinner tomorrow night." Pleased with myself, I finally dozed off.

We had a civil dining experience at a restaurant situated above a gift shop on the Sunset strip. Afterwards, Koko led us into the store, inviting us each to find a gift for ourselves. The shop was full of memorabilia, antiques and jewelry. Preferring any gift of jewelry to come from him directly, I settled on a photograph of a soulful little girl around three years of age. I was drawn to both the girl and the frame itself, which swiveled back and forth inside a stable base. I thought it was unusual and figured I'd eventually put some special photograph in it. Meanwhile, the picture within was obviously from long ago and the child looked like she knew too much of life's suffering. There was a handwritten signature that said, "To my Nurse… with Love". A few months later, I would look at that photograph and think of my newly born niece, Leta, who came into this world carrying the burden of a rare blood disease. It would be several years later when I would take the picture out of its frame and discover that the photographer's stamp on the back said, "Photograph by McCaffrey." There was an address on Sunset Blvd. I drove there to see if—who knows what? But when I reached the number, it was occupied by a dry-cleaner.

It was pretty cool, riding around Los Angeles that first day with Kokopelli in his Porsche—at least until I closed the door too hard. Then he snapped at me harshly. That was unpleasant, but then I remembered that some men have a sacred connection to their car and decided to cut him some slack.

Eager to plug into the acting scene in Los Angeles, I capitalized on every west coast connection I could think of. I called Mr. Chairman of the DDB Agency, Pat Cragin and John

Avildsen, all to let them know that I was in L.A., looking for work. John offered me the number of his friend, Bruce, who was a director of television commercials. Bruce invited me to an audition that same day for Ritz Crackers. I wrote down the address and on Monday morning, after Koko went to work, I walked out the front door and toward the freeway where I stuck my thumb out. In a short time, I scored a ride that took me the whole thirty-mile stretch, delivering me at the exact address. I'm stunned as I look back and see both how fearless and foolish I was.

    The audition went well, and though I didn't get the part, Bruce took my number and offered himself as a friendly contact while in town. Then I hitched another ride back to Thousand Oaks. That evening, Koko, Rachel and I were sitting around talking about the day. Koko was shocked when I shared that I'd hitchhiked to town and back and offered to rent me a car for a couple of weeks. Rachel could barely contain her disapproval but knew when to stuff it. Meanwhile, I was beginning to find some sordid pleasure in playing the role she'd cast me in. I remember her saying, "I've got it so good here with Koko. I get to enjoy all the benefits of his job and home—but, at the same time, I don't have to sleep with him."

    I responded, "Funny. I feel the same way, but for the opposite reason. I don't have to be all involved with his work, yet I *do* get to sleep with him." That may be the most catty thing I've ever said—and I must admit I got quite a kick out of it.

One afternoon, the three of us were packed into the Porsche, cruising along Ventura Blvd., when Koko pulled into an Orange Julius. The vibe between Rachel and me, as we sat alone in his car was too much to bear, so I got out. Koko was standing in line as I approached from behind, surprising him by gripping his waist and saying, "Boo!" He spun around, grabbed me by the shoulders, lifted me off the ground, and then slammed me back down. My throat tightened and I wanted to burst into tears, but it seemed more important that I straighten him out immediately. So, with all the gravity I could muster, I said, "**You** have to remember that you are **much** stronger than me."

His response was quick and clear. "No. **You** have to remember that."

That afternoon, I gathered up my few belongings, and set about making my exit while he was taking a shower. But then, at the last minute, my base desires got the best of me, and I removed my clothing and stepped into the shower for one last tryst. I was going to miss this guy, and I wanted to make sure he missed me too. I needed to feel that power. And so, I did.

I must say, that even though he didn't turn out to be a total prince, I have always felt gratitude toward the Kokopelli Man for escorting me across America—with *America*.

EATING CAKE

I bought "Malerie", a 1965 Chevy Malibu, for three hundred dollars from Bert, a mechanic that became a key figure in helping me stay mobile over the next few years. A good mechanic in Los Angeles is as essential as a good doctor, which, fortunately, was not something I needed at the time. Meanwhile, the toilet paper commercial started paying off, and soon I was able to manage my own ticket back to New York to gather up the rest of my belongings.

Comparatively, life in Hollywood was like eating cake. The things that seemed to put most people off didn't bother me in the least, like being isolated and always moving from place to place in your own little bubble. My God, what a welcome change! I treasured the protection and the anonymity of the automobile. Another thing that alienated the typical New Yorker was that most of the socializing took place in people's homes. Though L.A. did have some happening night spots like The Whiskey and The Rainbow, the best parties took place in people's homes. I knew which style was for me—I just needed to get invited.

Not long after my arrival, Crystal rented a house in Laurel Canyon big enough to support three of her children (her most recent ex-husband had custody of their youngest daughter), me, and another female friend. I was thrilled to be in on the deal and happily contributed a few hundred dollars a month for my share. Interesting guys, actors and musicians, came by the house regularly to see Crystal. I recall one afternoon arriving home to find Ed Begley, Jr., sitting on the front porch with a boom box, listening to Tom Waits. Clearly, Crystal had stellar social skills but her parenting left something to be desired. One time in particular, when her six years old son dared to walk into the living room while we were hanging out, she snapped at him. "Yes?" He changed his mind and retreated.

She was always scraping money together but I was straight-up furious when I learned that she had called my father and asked him for a monthly contribution toward my upkeep. She told him that she was providing a home and meals for me but failed to mention that I was contributing my fair share. Since I came from the prestigious suburb of Birmingham, I guess she figured my parents were loaded. What she didn't know was that my parents had divorced and my dad had been forced to sell the house and was currently experiencing a financial crisis. I was beginning to see that there were few things deemed too audacious for Crystal, who, like myself, was a woman on a mission.

Crystal became friends with a psychiatrist who lived in a beautiful house at the top of the canyon and soon secured an open invitation for us to use his pool. I loved lying on my back in a sun-soaked, cushy lounge chair, gazing up at the pines, as they reached for the sky and swayed in the breeze. I was so grateful to be looking up and seeing tall trees instead of tall buildings. Those were some sweet California days—days that helped me come out of the state of paranoia that I had been living in for so long—that had seeped into my very bones. I was beginning to relax.

One afternoon, while lying by the pool, Crystal confided in me that she suffered from an aggressive form of rheumatoid arthritis. She knew her window of opportunity was short, so if she had to be a ball-buster to achieve her dream, she was okay with that. Though only thirty-six, she would be hospitalized on more than one occasion, during the coming year.

Driving slowly along Melrose Avenue, I called out to a young woman, "Excuse me! Do you know where the Melrose Theater is?"

"Yes, it's right up here. That's where I'm going, too! Follow me." Jeanine Anderson, an adorable girl with big blue eyes and long blonde hair, introduced herself and welcomed me to the workshop. She sat behind me that day and we got to talking. "So, where are you from?" she asked.

"I just moved here from New York," I said, and then added, "But I'm originally from Detroit."

"Oh, I'm from Detroit too!" she exclaimed.

"Wow! What a coincidence. Actually, I'm from Birmingham." She screeches, "Me too!"

"Stop!" I cried.

"Where did you go to high school?" she asked.

"Marian—for the first two…" but before I could finish, she jumped in.

"That's where I went!" And it didn't stop there. Soon we discovered that our younger brothers (two each) were very close friends. Our bond was established, and we'd only get closer over the years.

Also fresh from New York and attending class for the first time was a fellow by the name of Stanton Coffin. Paul Kent, the teacher and theater owner, assigned us to each other as scene partners. Stan and I selected Echoes, a challenging piece by Richard Nash set in a psychiatric ward.

Our rehearsals would begin with a silence that would eventually morph into an exchange of sounds that became our characters' special language. Sometimes our sounds were shrieks or growls, other times melodic chants. In a mental institution nothing is too far out.

We'd go on long hikes, chanting in character, until we'd eventually get around to the lines. We went to the ocean, and with waves lapping around us, would dive into the dialogue. After several weeks, we put the scene up in class. Our work paid off, and we were the hit of the day.

Stan and I, reluctant to let go, chose to work on another section from the play. When our success was repeated a month later, Paul offered us a full six-week production. He assigned Rod Loomis as our director, who would also play the small role of the psychiatrist. We were the envy of the class as such a speedy road to production was rarely seen. *Hallelujah! I love my life!*

As we got close to opening night and were tending to details, I became frustrated about my failure to achieve crazy-looking hair. I approached Rod and Paul with my concern. "Don't waste your energy worrying about your hair!" Paul blasted. "It's not important! Just focus on your character!" So, I did just that.

The show opened successfully and generated a buzz of excitement. Over the next several weekends, a couple casting directors and agents contacted me for appointments. It was a thrilling time. *My stars are aligned—my time has finally come—and it's all about the work. Yes!* When the first couple of reviews came out as raves, Paul said he'd like to extend the run from six to eight weeks, providing that the Times review concurred. Finally, that reviewer came and we all eagerly awaited the results.

Unable to sleep, I drove to a nearby convenience store before dawn and purchased the Sunday paper. There it was: *Echoes* by N. Richard Nash, reviewed by Lawrence Christenson. My eyes scanned it until I came to my name. "Ms. McCaffrey's Farrah Fawcett hairdo doesn't exactly personify a woman isolated in her own mind." The most complimentary thing he had to say was, "the performances were competent." He spent the rest of the review tearing down the author, whose career was in no way on the line. I was inconsolable—in large part because I knew he was right about the hair. *Why didn't I listen to myself on that one? That one mistake is going to cost me my ticket in!?* I couldn't accept it. There had to be something I could do to turn it around. So, I sat down and wrote him a letter, promising that if he would just come back again, that he would see a true reflection of Tilda's unkempt mind.

I drove downtown to the *Times* building where I was able to walk right up to Mr. Christenson's desk. I stood there with my letter in hand, wanting him to look at me and see my pain—but his downward gaze never faltered. Finally, I set the letter on his desk and went home to grieve. There would be no two-week extension.

Echoes with Stanton Coffin

HIT & MISS

In 1977 *Rocky* took the Oscar for Best Picture, and John Avildsen won for Best Director. I sat with Crystal and friends and watched as he kissed the woman sitting next to him before walking up to collect his statue. *Damn. I wonder if that could've been me.*

Crystal became very angry with me one day when I refused to lend her my car. Perhaps, had she not abandoned it with a dead battery the last time she'd borrowed it, I would have. Displeased with my answer, she stormed into my room, threw open the window and started throwing my clothes out. I rushed over and grabbed what I could from her. She spun around and clamped her powerful hands around my throat, dragging me onto the bed. I got scared and went limp. When she backed off, I quickly pulled my stuff together and got the hell out of there.

Okay. Who can you call for a place to stay tonight? I asked myself. And I thought of Crystal's friend, Karen. She'd been to Dan Tana's with us several times over the past year, and I got along with her pretty well. I had nothing to lose. To my utter delight, she asked, "How would you like to rent a room from me on an ongoing basis?"

That same day I moved into her lovely, Spanish-style house in Beachwood Canyon. Karen, a commercial producer, went out of town frequently and needed a reliable person to look after her cat and home. I fell in love with the neighborhood and made some new friends there, including Hazel, an elderly woman who worked at the Beachwood Café.

I scored another national commercial through Mr. Chairman, who often came to Los Angeles. It was to be the launching of a new instant-playback video camera by Polaroid. It was called Polavision. Ed McMahon, Johnny Carson's straight man on *The*

Tonight Show, was the spokesman for the spot. I was cast as a family member having fun at a backyard party, while being filmed by the new instant video-playback camera.

I followed Mr. Chairman's instructions and met with the casting director at her office. Her name was Jane and her attitude made it evident that she didn't approve of me. Maybe she thought I got everything handed to me on a silver platter. Maybe she thought I was sleeping with the boss. *Whatever!* I was so tired of that crap.

It wasn't always easy keeping Mr. Chairman at arm's length, as his drinking usually landed him in a state of inebriation when he would inevitably hit on me. Somehow, I consistently managed to ward him off without offending him too badly. Still, he was a "good old Joe", and was actually coming through for me, which was awesome.

It was non-stop laughter on the set with the Byers brothers from Youngstown, Ohio, the home-town of both my parents; and the town where I was born. All of us actors were excited about the launching of Polavision because it was likely that we'd make good money in residuals, especially with Ed McMahon being the spokesperson. The product's debut would occur during *The Tonight Show*. When we were given the air date, I alerted my parents and waited in anticipation for the night to arrive. When it did, my dad called afterward to ask what happened.

"What do you mean?" I replied.

"It wasn't on," he said. Stumped, I watched for myself, hoping that, somehow, he was wrong, but sadly that was not the case. The next day, I found out that all plans to launch the product had been terminated because they learned that superior playback technology was coming down the pike. So, there ya go! Another one bites the dust.

with Ed McMahon

GOIN' SOUTH

One afternoon, I was invited to join a friend from New York at the Chateau Marmont Hotel. Lenny was in town with the rocker, Meatloaf, who was riding high on his recently released *Bat out of Hell* album. After hanging out for a while with Meatloaf and his Playboy twin girlfriends, Lenny and I went down to the pool to catch some rays.

A young woman was lounging there, reading a manuscript. After an hour or so, she put it down and looked around. When she looked my way, I said, "Hello".

She offered a warm smile and said, "Hi."

"Is it a good script?" I dared to ask.

"Yes, it's a *great* script." She sat up to stretch her back. She reminded me of myself—she was no Playboy Bunny. "It's starring Jack Nicholson," she added.

"You're kidding," is all I could come back with.

"No, I'm not," she said beaming, as her beauty came to life. "I've been cast as his wife in his next film."

"Oh my God!" I exclaimed. "How did that happen?" She pulled her chair a little closer.

"I was a waitress in New York up until two weeks ago. Al Pacino was a regular where I worked and knew that Jack wanted an unknown for the female lead in his next film. Al set up the audition for me. I was so nervous. I didn't think it went very well, and I never dreamed I'd get the part but somehow he chose me."

"Wow," I said, filled with envy.

"So, what's the name of the movie?" Lenny asked.

"*Goin' South*," she said. We were talking to Mary Steenburgen.

Jack Nicholson was the one actor above all others that I wanted most to work with. And sadly, I surmised that, because this amazing bit of good fortune had happened to Mary, the chances of it happening to me were greatly reduced. I congratulated her and wished her success before Lenny and I took our leave. Later that day, I told the story to Karen and her boyfriend, Hal, allowing my envy to show. Hal grinned and said, "Well, I wasn't going to say anything until I signed the contract, but I just got hired to be a gaffer on *Goin' South*."

"Hal, that might be one set I'd like to come visit you on," Karen retorted. And now my envy-barometer was off the charts. Everyone was *goin' south* but me.

Some months later, I secured a small bungalow in Beachwood Canyon for a mere $160 per month. The house, nestled among rich foliage on the down-slope of a hill, was undetectable from the street. At the bottom of the driveway, I'd take the walkway to the right, go past the kitchen door, continue around the bend to the left, down twelve steps, and finally around to the left again to see a wooden deck and my own charming entryway. It was completely private, peaceful, and beautiful. I was ecstatic to have my own little sanctuary in the hills, directly beneath the Hollywood sign.

The tiny L-shaped unit, which had been unexpectedly vacated by the actress that had inhabited it, came fully furnished—at least until she returned to claim her stuff. Among her abandoned belongings were a couple drawers full of clothes, which was a nice perk since my wardrobe was sorely lacking. There was a tiny kitchen nook, a sleeping area, and a little sitting room. The big bonus was a second deck off the bedroom area which sported a wooden rocking chair and a small table.

On moving day, while I was packing up, Hal, who had just returned home from the *Goin' South* gig, got into a big argument with Karen. It was escalating quickly, as I rushed around trying to gather up the last of my things. Hal made his exit just seconds after my own and without an invitation, followed me to my new place. "How about a cup of tea?" he asked.

I figured he was probably distraught from the break-up, so I said, "Okay, sure." Somehow, I put together a cup of tea for my first guest.

Hal proceeded to tell me about how cool it was to work for and with Jack. I soaked up every morsel of what he had to say. He mentioned that Jack and his girlfriend, Anjelica Huston, were on the outs, and then added that there were a few pick-up shots scheduled for the upcoming week, here in town. Hal was scheduled to work the very next day at Paramount Studios.

"Would you like to be my guest on the set?" he asked.

I'm sure that the widening of my eyes gave him the answer but, nonetheless, I said, "Yes!"

He went on to share with me the rules of being a guest on one of Jack's sets: "You can only come one time. Be quiet and don't stay for more than an hour. After that the only way back is if Jack himself invites you." I was grateful to hear the rules, as the last thing I wanted was to make myself unwelcome.

When I arrived at the Paramount gate the following day, my name was on the list. I parked and made my way to Stage C. At first, I didn't see Hal, so I struck up a conversation with a friendly cameraman who helped put me at ease. Then, I saw Mary Steenburgen in the distance talking to a woman. I went over and said hello, reminding her of our meeting at the Chateau Marmont. She remembered me and was gracious, introducing me to her agent. Then, I wandered around a bit, wishing Hal would show up. I made my way to the craft table and stood near it, without much focus. I certainly wasn't hungry.

Suddenly, out of the shadows, Jack came walking right toward me. He stopped a few feet away, turned his head in the opposite direction and said ,"Sorry it's such a boring set." And with that, he put his hands in his pockets and started to shuffle away.

I had to do something to mark the moment, so thanks to my Detroit training in the "shock and delight" approach, out of my mouth came flying the words, "Ah, shit—yeah, Jack. I'm *real* disappointed." He turned around and looked directly at me. When he did, I let him see my delight. He grinned, and for a moment, our eyes sparkled together. Then he moved on.

Shortly afterwards, Hal made his appearance and came over to greet me. He explained that they were shooting a sequence that took place inside a gold mine. The set was quite dark and I had no visual access to the action, so my hour flew by without seeing Jack again. I hated to take my leave but I was hoping that, after what had transpired, he would take the next step. Meanwhile, I had a dinner date scheduled that night with Mr. Chairman at 7 p.m., so the next chance I had, I thanked Hal and said good-bye. Just then, Jack's voice carried over from the other side of the wall. "Who's leaving?" he called out.

"It's my friend, Frances," Hal replied.

"Tell Frances she doesn't have to leave," said the man himself.

Adrenalin swept through me, as I anguished over why I had to have a damned date with the Chairman. I couldn't think of any way to get in touch with him and I knew he would be at Dan Tana's promptly at 7 p.m. The thought of standing him up was unconscionable, and yet if ever there was a time for that—this was it. I reflected on my core belief that if you want to be treated first-class, then you have to treat yourself accordingly. *What would Katherine Hepburn do?* I knew the answer, so I told Hal that I had plans that couldn't be changed.

The next day, there was a message on my service from Hal. "Your presence is requested at Stage C. Please come by this afternoon at 2 p.m." Thrilled that my gamble had paid off, I readied myself to go back to the studio. Upon arrival, I walked down a long, dark, passageway between the wall of the building and the back of the set when, suddenly, I saw Jack walking toward me. I was ready to say hi to him but when he got close enough, he looked right through me with no response or recognition. My confused heart sank. Through sheer will, my legs kept moving forward while my mind fumbled over what had just happened—or not happened. When I moved into the open, well-lit area, I heard Mary Steenburgen's voice call out, "Is that you *again*, Frances?"

A kick in the chest by a mule would've been preferable. Mortified, I wanted to disappear. How this happened, I couldn't imagine. Only Hal could fill in the blanks, and my anger was building toward him for having set me up for such humiliation. It seemed like forever till he made his appearance, and when he did, he put his hands on my shoulders and started massaging them. Now that really irked me, as it was completely inauthentic within our relationship. He was marking his territory, showing me off like a piece of jewelry that he owned—but was maybe willing to share. I wanted to smack him.

"Who requested me to come back here?" I asked, disengaging from his touch.

"I did," he said innocently.

"You told me that visitors only get to come once, stay for no more than an hour and then return only if invited by Jack. So, why would you ask me back without his permission?"

"Because I thought he liked you," he said. "I thought he'd be glad to see you again."

Close to tears, I said, "You shouldn't have done that," and split.

Hal called later that night and shared with me that, at one point during the day, Jack approached him and said, "What happened to your friend Frances? I saw her, and then she disappeared."

Hal responded, "She'd slit her wrists if she knew you were asking about her. Believe it or not, she felt like she was imposing." Again, I wanted to strangle him for representing me so poorly.

Then he added, "Jack stood there for a moment, looking down at the ground. Finally, he said, 'Funny…little girls,' shrugged his shoulders, and walked away."

So, he did see me, I mused. *Go figure.* It would take months to get beyond the disappointment. All I could do was stuff it.

FRANCINE AT THE WHEEL

It was February, 1979. I had been receiving residuals from two commercials for a couple of years but they were phasing out now, and I had to confront the question—where will the next check come from? Seated by a window at the Beachwood Café, I pondered my harsh reality over a cup of coffee. Hazel, a matronly woman around eighty years old, served both as a hostess and a godmother to many of us orphan artists who frequented the place. Perhaps she was picking up on my worrisome state when she sat down at my table and asked if everything was alright.

"Not really," I said. "I've got to get a job. I'm running out of money and don't know what to do." Just then an actor I knew from the American Film Institute, where I volunteered once a week, walked in.

"Hi, Frances," Michael said cheerfully.

Hazel stood up to allow Michael space, but before leaving, she whispered in my ear. "Don't worry. Something will turn up." I thanked her and turned my attention to my friend.

"Mind if I join you?" he asked. "How're you doing?"

"Fine…yourself?"

"Good—hungry. I've been driving my cab non-stop for five hours." He picked up a menu and considered his options.

"Do you like driving a cab?" I asked.

"Yeah"

Once he had ordered his cheeseburger and fries, I probed further. "Do you choose the hours you work?"

"Yes, for the most part, mainly because I own my own car. It's plenty lucrative too…lots of cash tips."

I couldn't hack driving a taxi for a living—way too exposed for me. I didn't have office skills, other than answering phones and I was desperate to avoid waitressing. Feeling even more depressed, I started jonesing for some pot, and was bold enough to ask Michael if he had any.

"No, I don't smoke," he said. "Wait! Yeah, I do. I have a joint that this crazy guy gave me as part of my tip." Michael reached into his breast pocket and retrieved a tightly-rolled joint, and then slipped it to me under the table. "This guy was bizarre!" he continued. "He got into my cab with a Great Dane and directed me to a sleazy hotel on Ventura Boulevard. Strange dude—but before splitting, he asked me if I wanted to drive a limousine instead of a taxi. He said it would be a decked-out Cadillac Stretch for a studio called The Record Plant. That's when he handed me his business card, a joint, and twenty bucks. But I make too much bread with my cab to be interested."

"Well, I'm interested," I said. And there it was. I could make money driving a limousine. I had never seen a female at the wheel of one—*but why not? You wouldn't be exposed like in a taxi where just anybody can jump in. No, the clients would be wealthy and you'd know who they were in advance.* "It couldn't be all that difficult to drive a stretched-out car, do you think?" I asked. "A little practice is all I'd need." Michael nodded in support of what was obviously a moment for me.

"If no-one in this business will give me a role, I'll just have to create one for myself," I said with sass. The screen in my mind came to life, showing me a vision of myself stepping out of a long silver limousine, dressed in a classy black pantsuit with a chauffeur's cap tipped slightly off to one side. I gracefully stepped around to open the back door for a famous rock-star. Laughing with delight, I said to Michael, "A limousine would be one hell of a prop, wouldn't it?" Yes, the spirit of creativity had been ignited by this idea and I was excited. I motioned to Hazel to come over, and hear my happy news. "Hazel, I'm going to be a limousine driver."

"What a great idea!" she exclaimed joyfully. And so it was decided.

Well, okay then. I need to head on out of here, smoke that doob, and get to work on manifesting this. Michael paid the bill, hugged me, and wished me luck.

Rocking on my deck chair with a bleary-eyed smile, I visualized some of the facets of my future job. I decided I'd go by "Francine." *Perhaps I'll become known as "Francine, the Limo Queen."* And I giggled with delight. The idea was more than a solution to a problem. It was a vehicle, if you'll excuse the pun, to my future. *I'm sick and tired of stagnating my precious time away, waiting for these assholes to wake up.* Thoughts like that helped me overcome the trepidation that somehow did creep in around the challenge of handling such a big automobile. So, that night I threw out a few feelers to see if anybody in my circle of friends knew someone who might be able to direct me toward the next step.

Sure enough, a friend of Crystal's had a connection with an outfit called Music Express, a messenger and limousine service. She called the office and asked the owner what the story was on female chauffeurs. He told her that he had never hired a woman and had no plans to do so in the future. When she gave me the sorry news, I asked for his number anyway, figuring that he might be able to recommend a company that would.

His name was Gerald and he took my call. Maybe it was my story of how I used to drive my dad's luxury sedans around the greater Detroit area, or my proclamation that he should get in step with the times, but somewhere along the way he, ever so slightly, opened up to the idea and suggested I come by his office to discuss the matter further.

As I sat in his rather large presence, he discouraged me with predictions of the many ways that I would surely fail. Then, he smiled slightly and I took that as my cue. "I'll be one of your best drivers, Gerald. Really, you won't regret it."

I worked for Music Express for six months, and once I got going, I worked my butt off. There was a lot to learn, not the least of which was how to use the Thomas Guide, a map book that served as the bible to every professional driver in Los Angeles. Fortunately, I was given plenty of time to learn the lay of the land, as I apprenticed for several runs before being sent out on my own.

For my uniform, I went around to a few friends' homes and, thanks to their generosity, was able to come up with a vintage black jacket with padded shoulders and a slightly thread-bare, braided trim. The threadbare aspect was forgivable because it was otherwise such a classy number. I scored another gem in the form of a white, form-fitted, French-cuffed tuxedo shirt. Then came what was for me a humbling experience, the purchasing of a pair of polyester slacks. Having grown up in the fashion world and developed an appreciation for fabric, I tried to avoid pure synthetics. I knew they would only be to tide me over until I could afford something more chic. But alas, there I was, suited up and ready to go. Gerald approved.

I'd been on the job only two weeks when a major gas crisis hit the country and Gerald required his cars to be at a certain carwash in Burbank at 7 a.m. Even at that hour, the weather was hot and humid, and aside from the constant kick I got out of people giving me double-takes, it was a most unpleasant way to greet the day. Nonetheless, I hung in there and became very much at home in my Caddy, while trying to prove my reliability to my not-so-sure-about-his-lady-driver-boss.

One advantage of this outfit was that you got to take your limo home. Obviously, it was only practical that they be used for some personal business. The unspoken rule was "be discreet." I had great fun taking my friends out for joy rides, while becoming a familiar sight in Beachwood, and other favorite haunts. It also helped to compensate for the disappointing amount of money I was making, for it turned out that Gerald's clients rarely tipped beyond the mandatory fifteen percent. That, on top of the three-dollar minimum wage, totaled an unimpressive six dollars per hour, which I found frustrating, knowing that I was carting around all these rich dudes. That's right; there was rarely a woman among them. Not in the music business, anyway, which we catered to exclusively. So, it was low pay but the job held the promise of excitement, and it did allow me to pay my bills.

FLEETWOOD MAC

A few weeks into it, I found myself standing at a gate at the Burbank Airport, holding up a name card for Stevie Nicks. Even though I was excited about my new role, I believed in my heart that my true calling, fulfilled, would land me in the back of the limo on equal ground with my clients. Standing there at the gate, holding up a sign, felt like a public announcement of my status of servitude and I was surprised by how uncomfortable it made me feel.

As people started filing out of the plane, I tried to be discreet and flash my sign only to who I figured was the right party. Sure enough, Stevie, along with a bearded guy and a brunette woman, saw my sign and gave me a subtle wave of recognition. The guy handed me a couple of light bags as I heard her say, "How bizarre, a female." We proceeded directly across the street to where the limo was parked. I popped the trunk, opened the doors, and once everyone was squared away, took my place at the wheel.

"We're going to Doheny Drive, north of Sunset," the brunette said, and we were on our way. As we wove through Laurel Canyon, they began to tell a story about Rod Stewart. I couldn't help but overhear them and wondered why they were allowing that, and then, just before they got to the punchline, someone closed the divider. *Ouch.*

When we arrived at a magnificent house, I hopped out and opened the door for my rock-star client and her small entourage. Stevie was adorable, wearing a mid-calf length cotton dress with white ankle socks and tennis shoes. This time I had eye contact with her and she offered me a slight smile before heading into the mansion. The gentleman asked if I could wait for them, as they were going to need a car to take them to the studio sometime in the afternoon. I told him I'd be happy to. Then, as an afterthought, the dark-haired woman turned back and invited me to come wait inside. I had been trained to stay with the car in most circumstances, so I graciously declined her offer. When she persisted, saying that it might be hours, I acquiesced.

I stood awkwardly in the grand foyer while people walked by on the mezzanine above, giving me second-glances. Soon, the same lady who seemed to be in a managerial role, came back, introduced herself as, "Gail", and instructed me to follow her into the kitchen. On the way, we walked through a small room with ballet-bars, mirrors, several pairs of pink satin ballet slippers lined up against the wall, and a reflective disco-globe hanging from the ceiling. A small window provided enough light to set off an array of dancing rainbow prisms throughout the space. I felt as if I was being doused with pixie dust.

In the kitchen, a few cool-looking guys sat around the table. "Francine, this is…" and following the introductions, I took a seat among them. Gail poured me a glass of iced tea and then busied herself with food preparation. One of the guys reached into his pocket, brought forth a bag of grass and deftly rolled a joint. He took a big hit and handed it to me. Wisely, I passed it along without partaking, but it did make me think that I was among peers. So, feeling more at ease, I followed an impulse to get up and go into the ballet room and stretch. I went right up to the barre, lifted one leg up, and leaned into a long, smooth stretch. I was extremely flexible and my polyester slacks had plenty of give in them. It felt good to bend and lengthen. But then, as I switched legs, I noticed Gail looking at me in the mirror. I smiled at her and kept on stretching. Moments later, the guy who had ridden with us earlier, approached me and said, "Would you please go out and cool off the car? We'll be leaving soon." Surprised at the suddenness of the transition, I did what he asked, not even sensing that anything was wrong.

While cooling the car, I marveled at the notion that I'd be hanging out with this legendary band at a studio all afternoon.

I imagined that by the time I laid my head to rest that night, I'd be reflecting on a great experience with Fleetwood Mac. Just then, the same chap came out and said sheepishly, "There's been a change of plans. We're not going to need the car after all." He handed me a ten-dollar bill and made a beeline back into the house.

"Okay, thank you. I hope you'll remember me for the future!" I said, wincing instantly. Driving away, it occurred to me that maybe my move to the barre didn't go over too well. *Oh, boy...did I stretch it too far?*

CARRYING MY WEIGHT

I always tried to allow plenty of lead time before a run so I could study my route and avoid getting lost. Being late for a pick-up was not acceptable and Gerald was watching me. He still wasn't comfortable with me as a driver. Ideally, I wanted to work evenings so as to be free to go to auditions and pursue my acting career but it was becoming obvious that most of Gerald's business was in the daytime. I began to view Music Express as the taxi-cab service of the limousine world: a great place to get trained but that was about it.

The fleet of cars included several stretch sedans and a few super-stretched Cadillacs, which Gerald was never going to let me drive. There were easily five airport runs per day and that meant repeatedly trying to assure clients that I, all one hundred-and-ten pounds of me, had no problem carrying or hoisting their heavy bags in and out of the trunk. Most men would insist on handling their own bag but, not wanting my gender to affect my level of service, I always did my best. There were, however, a few situations where it was downright silly and when those moments arose, I understood why Gerald preferred a man for the job.

On one airport run the client buzzed me in to get his bags. When he saw me, he nearly cried. Shaking his head, he pointed at two huge suitcases. "I just had heart surgery. I can't lift these bags. And they're too heavy for you!" I assured him it was no problem and, though it nearly killed me, I managed. I wanted a job where the trips would be more about pleasure than business. I sensed my days working for Music Express were numbered but I used the opportunity to hone my driving skills, familiarize myself with the cars, and learn the lay of the land.

One day, my landlord invited me to come by and meet the woman that would be renting the main portion of the house and living above me. "Pam, meet Frances. She lives in the apartment below," he said.

Pam responded, "Franny? Franny McCaffrey?" Seeing that I was not recognizing her, she added, "The A + Agency? I'm Pam Dawber." And with that, it finally clicked.

"Oh my God! Hi, Pam!" I exclaimed, feeling like a total dunce.

"So, here we are, two hopefuls from Detroit, landing at the same house in the Hollywood Hills. Don't you love it?" she asked, as we laughed and hugged. Soon I learned that she had been cast in the television pilot, "Mork and Mindy", opposite Robin Williams. I was happy for her but a little jealous, too. I was beginning to be troubled by the "*why not me?*" syndrome, something that I knew could only work against me—never for me.

ROYAL ROLLS
1978/79

While mingling with a hundred other drivers in a parking lot at a huge CBS event, I met a dark-haired Irishman named Roger who spoke glowingly about the company he worked for, bragging about his frequent hundred-dollar tips. Before I got around to asking for the name of the company, he was beeped and rushed off to pick up his clients. *Damn*, I thought, *that sounds like an outfit I'd like to work for.* Regardless, it served to get me onto the process of looking.

The first few companies I checked out seemed too regimented: very strict on uniforms and keeping their drivers on call all the time. Then I went to one based in the underground garage of the exclusive L'Ermitage Hotel in Beverly Hills and, to my delight, there sat Roger. Following a warm greeting, he introduced me to Eric, the manager of Royal Rolls Limousine Service, who wasted no time in offering me an application. Once I'd completed the form, he interviewed me.

He liked the idea of having a couple of female drivers on his team, and Carla, their only female driver, was getting more requests than she could handle. Once approved by their insurance company, I was in.

The wage was, once again, a meager three dollars per hour plus fifteen percent, but since Roger seemed so happy with his cash tips, I decided to give it a try. I gave Gerald my two-week notice.

"Thank you so much for giving me this opportunity, Gerald. I am forever grateful. But I think it's time for me to…" and he jumped in, enthusiastically.

"Did you get yourself another job?"

"Yes," I replied.

"Wonderful! Where?"

"Royal Rolls Limousine Service, based in the L'Ermitage Hotel."

"Excellent," he responded. "I'm sure you'll do very well there. Just turn in your beeper."

"But I wanted to give you some notice…"

"That's not necessary," he said, barely trying to hide his relief. It was all fine with me. Gerald was a nice man who had stepped out of his comfort zone to give me a chance at something. I felt nothing but gratitude.

This new company had a couple of Rolls Royce Limousines, four Cadillac stretches, one Lincoln stretch and a few Cadillac standards (only slightly stretched). "There will be a two-week trial period before you're allowed to drive any of the stretches, and under no circumstances will you ever drive either of the Rolls Royces," said Eric. One of the hotel's primo amenities was that guests had free limousine service anywhere within a three-mile radius. Consequently, there always had to be a *duty driver* ready to jump into action.

On my first day of work, when I arrived in my fume-spewing Chevy, Eric winced and directed me two levels underground. That would be my procedure from then on. With great anticipation, I began my first day as duty driver. Within the first hour, a request came in for the Rolls Royce stretch with a female driver. Carla, who had driven this same client for ten hours the day before was not available. Suddenly Eric needed me to step up to the plate. Eager to prove myself, I said "Sure. I'd be happy to."

He escorted me over to the royal chariot, informing me that it was worth over two hundred thousand dollars, and had once been owned by the Prince of Wales. It was the crown jewel of the company, having inspired the name Royal Rolls. In a fifteen-minute training session, I was shown that the driver's seat was on the right side of the car, and that I'd need to use the "Neutral" gear (there was no gear at all for "Park"), along with the handbrake, to bring the massive vehicle to a complete stop. On top of all that, I would be held financially responsible for the five-hundred-dollar deductible if any damage occurred to the vehicle as a result of my error. *Holy shit! I can't believe that I'm being sent off in this regal number on day one, with a fifteen- minute driving lesson!* Then, Eric handed me my trip ticket and pointed out that the pick-up address was a good twenty miles out into the San Fernando Valley.

The body of the car was extra-wide and rode higher than I had ever experienced. I slipped my cap on, took my place at the helm, and hit the road. Driving from the opposite side of the car was unnerving to say the least, and it didn't help any that everyone who passed me honked, waved, hollered, and gave me a thumbs-up. But this was no time for silliness. I gripped the wheel and looked straight ahead in steadfast seriousness.

Arriving ten minutes late with soaked underarms, I found my client waiting in the parking lot of a large apartment complex. Casually dressed, Bobby Martin, a black man sporting a beard, was in his early thirties. The scoop I had been given was that he was a music producer for A&M Records and was on vacation with a three-thousand-dollar limousine allowance. As I held the back door open for him, he offered me a friendly greeting and climbed in.

Per his instructions, I got back on the freeway and headed toward downtown L.A. where his friend, Roscoe, awaited us. When I confided to Mr. Martin that it was my first time driving that particular car, he assured me that I needn't worry; that he was used to it, so I could relax—I was in good hands.

In a sketchy neighborhood in the inner city, Bobby instructed me to enter an alley that wasn't much wider than the car itself. Slowly, I did so, and when I came to a stop, Roscoe approached from a narrow walkway along with a few wide-eyed children. More dapper than his friend, Roscoe was dressed in a cream-colored suit with a wide-brimmed hat. When I stepped out to open the back door for him, the children fell silent, watching closely as I went through the paces of greeting my distinguished client.

Bobby and Roscoe kept the glass divider closed, communicating with me via the intercom phone. They directed me to drive through the neighborhood streets at a slow speed. With their windows down, they waved at people, occasionally hollering, "Hello, there!" Once they'd had enough of that, they gave me my next destination point: a disco in San Clemente, some seventy-five miles south. Really—a disco in *San Clemente? Okay... who am I to question?*

The long drive gave me the opportunity to really get comfortable with the vehicle. I refused Bobby's invitation to join them inside the club, knowing I should stay with the car. After fifteen minutes or so, I told the bouncer that I needed to use the facilities but was concerned about the security of the limousine. He called the manager who came out and assured me that he'd have security keep a close eye on it. He encouraged me to come inside, have a bite to eat, and relax. With that assurance, I grabbed my purse, locked up the Rolls, and went inside.

It was a crowded club with a huge dance floor. I went directly to the dining area and sat at an empty table. Soon, Bobby and Roscoe brought a couple of young women over to meet me. One of the girls was delirious with intrigue and questioned me about my job: "Who's the most famous person you've ever driven? What's the craziest job you've ever had? Is it hard driving that car? Do you make a lot of tips?" I enjoyed sharing information with them, bearing witness to the beginning of their own wheels starting to turn.

When Roscoe asked me to dance to some great song of the day, I forgot about my commitment to be more conservative on the job. Ever since I'd moved west and realized that the paranoia I lived with in New York had affected my ability to move freely,

I decided I would always try to dance as if no one was watching. I was a damn good dancer—for a white girl. And I was the only white girl in the joint, so I pulled quite a bit of focus when I cut loose with Roscoe. Immediately afterward, I took my leave and headed out to the car where I stretched out in the back seat and rested my eyes. The next thing I knew there was a harsh knocking on the window.

I jumped to attention, got out, and offered a ready smile to my clients, but Bobby's expression was sour and I didn't know why. "Back to Los Angeles," he barked. The next destination was The Subway, a popular after-hours club in Hollywood. Adjacent to it was a small parking lot, but to get into it one had to navigate a long and very narrow driveway. When I stopped the car and walked around to open their doors for them, Bobby, friendly once again, told me that they'd likely be an hour or two.

Once I got the car into the small, unlit parking lot, I realized that there was barely enough room to turn the ship around. Then, through my right-hand mirror I saw a tall, thin man approaching me. Quickly, I secured the locks and went to roll up the windows but fumbled as I searched for the right button. Suddenly, this man's face was getting quite close to mine. I gasped as I finally hit the right button. The window nearly clipped him.

"Hey!" he said, as if he were offended.

I brought it back down just a crack and said, "I'm sorry, sir. I just have to turn this car around."

"So, who is this guy you're driving?"

"Look, I'm busy, okay?"

"What's your name?"

"Hey! I don't know who you are and I don't feel like rapping, so please leave me alone." I was now well into my three-point turn when he said loudly, "I'm Ernest Helms.'"

And it clicked: Ernest Helms is the owner of Royal Rolls Limousine Service. With sheer dread, I asked, "Are you…my new boss?"

"Yes," he replied. "I own this car. So, you're the new lady driver?"

I now opened the window all the way and said, "Yes, I'm Francine," awkwardly reaching out to shake his hand. "I'm sorry for giving you a hard time, but at least now you know I've got some street smarts." Stoically, he studied me and stepped back while I maneuvered his pride-and-joy into position. He then told me to take care of the car and walked into the club. Getting off to a bad start with the boss was not what I needed.

When my guys returned a couple hours later, Bobby had a young lady with him. "Fat Jack's, Francine," he said buoyantly. At the nearby hamburger joint, they chowed down on burgers and fries. The stop after that was back downtown to the same alleyway where we'd picked Roscoe up. There Roscoe thanked me for a great ride and vanished into the night. Then Bobby directed me to his lady-friend's apartment, which was also in a sketchy part of the city, and much to my dismay, instructed me to wait in the driveway while he went inside. *Holy shit! It's already after 3 a.m.* And this time, he did not give me a time-frame. So, feeling like a sitting duck, I put my hat on in the hopes that it might make my silhouette look more like a man's. A few minutes later, two shadowy figures walked in my direction. I froze, looking straight ahead, proclaiming invisibility, while reciting the 23rd Psalm under my breath. "Yea, though I walk through the valley of the shadow of death, I will fear no evil, for Thou art with me." They walked on by.

Bobby returned a while later in a sour mood. With the receiver tucked onto my shoulder, we chatted for the entire forty-mile drive back to his apartment. He vented his frustrations to me (apparently he didn't get laid), and I offered what wisdom I had about what women want…to be courted. When he mellowed out and seemed to be feeling better about himself, I took a risk and asked him about his career. He said that he was both a producer and a drummer, one who had played with Stevie

Wonder. I didn't believe a word of it. Then, he brought up the subject of proper chauffeur etiquette, and in no uncertain terms told me that I should not have been sleeping in the back of *his* limousine earlier. Taken aback, I realized that he was teaching me something and thanked him for bringing it to my attention. Finally, back at his complex, he signed the trip ticket, upping the 15% tip to 20%. Bobby thanked me and said he'd be calling for the limousine again soon. I watched through my side mirror as he walked off into the pre-dawn shadows.

Back at Base, I turned in my ticket and headed home in my funky Chevy, wondering who the hell Bobby really was. The next day, when I confided to Eric that I doubted the guy's legitimacy, he called A&M Records and they did in fact confirm that Mr. Martin had a limousine allowance of up to three thousand dollars. When Eric calculated the hours used so far, he realized that we were already over the three-thousand-dollar mark. Suddenly, there was great interest in finding out more about Bobby Martin.

A deeper probe exposed the scam. There was, indeed, a producer at A&M Records by that name, but it was not the same person. Later that afternoon, when Bobby called to order a limousine, again with a lady driver, Eric played along. How bummed he must have been when his next limo sported the LAPD emblem on its side, and his chauffeur was a policeman. I felt bad for "Baby Face Martin", as I came to refer to him, especially when I heard that he was going to jail. *Maybe it was worth it to him,* I thought. At any rate, I had been righteously initiated into my new team of drivers and would not be denied access to any vehicle from then on. Mine was a royal welcome to Royal Rolls.

THE SAUDI CONNECTION

I was headed down to my car when someone called out, "Hey, Francine! Come join us." Inside the white Rolls Royce were three of my fellow drivers: Roger, Jeffrey and Richard.

Jeffrey was an aspiring musician with soft, curly hair. Richard was an aspiring screenwriter with piercing blue eyes and a cynicism that colored most of what he had to say. Roger, a wannabe actor like myself, had dark, sparkling eyes and a gentle masculine presence that made him very attractive. Sadly, he was spoken for. Friendship would be the order of the day with these fellows.

I joined them in the backseat and partook of the joint they were sharing. We got to talking about my experience with Stevie Nicks.

"Was it my move to the ballet barre?" I asked them.

Roger: "Ah, just laugh it off! What the hell. You'll make yourself crazy trying to second guess people."

Jeffrey: "Yeah. Just keep smiling that smile of yours and everything'll be alright."

Richard: "Clearly, someone felt threatened. You should never have left the limo."

Roger: "I don't agree! Why would she stay in the car if she was invited in?"

Me: "I did resist at first. I only agreed when she seconded the invitation."

Jeffrey: "Hey, man! It was an adventure. Only a wimp would sit it out."

But Richard was adamant: "No, listen to me! Stars and the people around them do not want to think of you as a person. They want you to remain distant and impersonal. You'll never get ahead by meeting someone as a limo driver—period."

Roger: "Bah, humbug!"

Richard: "You may get *head*—or even give *head*—but you will not get *ahead*."

Me: "Well, thank you for sharing your infinite wisdom, Richard. But don't let it go to your head." Moans and groans erupted.

Roger: "And on that note, I'm gonna head on outta here."

"Me, too," I said. "Thanks, guys. I'll see y'all later!"

While walking me to my car, Roger asked if there was anything happening on the acting front. I told him that I had a meeting with an agent the following afternoon that might be interesting, as it had been arranged through Darren, an old friend from grade school, who now lived in Saudi Arabia. I left it at that and promised to fill him in after the meeting.

I first met Darren when I was ten years old and new to Our Lady Queen of Martyrs elementary school. A good looking, blonde, blue-eyed boy, he was the school's crossing-guard. During our high-school years he worked as an assistant chef at the Birmingham Country Club where my family belonged and where we often went for Sunday brunch. Sometimes he'd come out from the kitchen to say hello. My dad was impressed by his ambitiousness.

One frosty December night, when I was around thirteen, a bunch of kids from the neighborhood went tobogganing at the club's golf course. Sitting on your butt, on a snow-slicked slab of wood, with your legs wrapped around the person in front of you, while leaning into the person behind you, who in turn has their legs wrapped around you—is a pretty exciting thing for a young, pubescent girl. Add to that, the thrill of riding down a frozen slope, screaming at the top of your lungs—well, it has to be about the most fun a kid can have.

Following a couple hours of such fun, everyone came over to

the McCaffrey house for hot chocolate. Darren and I remained outdoors, chasing each other around, throwing snowballs. Then, there came a moment when we simultaneously fell backwards into a big, soft snow drift. Laughing heartily, and without thinking about it, we kissed—a kiss that would remain frozen in time. Yet when we were old enough to truly explore something deeper, our interests had branched out in opposing directions. Darren went into the military, while I admired those who refused to. After four years of service, he decided to make a life for himself in Saudi Arabia.

Thanks to his staying in touch by phone, I was aware that he was working closely with a royal family, enjoying considerable success. Most often in a drunken state, he would ramble on about the many, mega business deals that he and "the prince" were working on. One night he called to tell me that he had secured a multi-million-dollar railroad contract and that Prince Assad had asked him to suggest something that he could do to express his gratitude, something beyond financial payment. Darren responded, "Please do something to help my friend, Franny, in Hollywood. She's trying to make it as an actress."

Laughing, I said, "But how can a prince from Saudi Arabia help me here in Hollywood, Darren?"

"Because this prince created a company called Cine Mobile in Hollywood several years ago and it was a huge success. It provides trailers for location shoots. He sold the company but still has some good connections there in town. He's already called a producer on your behalf."

Blown away, I could only say, "Damn, Darren. That's unbelievable!"

"Yeah! And the producer told him to have you call a friend of his who is an agent. And that person is expecting your call. You need a break, Franny."

In full agreement, I reached for a pen and jotted down the information.

With warm green eyes and stylish red hair, Sam rose from her desk to greet me. The first thing I realized was that rather than being the agent, she was working *for* the agent…but whatever. Conversation flowed easily between us, as she thoughtfully flipped through my portfolio, studying my photos and reading the reviews. The meeting was going well, until she began tapping her nails on the desk and twisting her lips. I grew anxious with anticipation, sensing that there was some pearl she was about to bestow upon me, but then she said, "Ah…never mind." My heart leapt and sank in the same breath.

Unable to refrain from doing so, I said, "Please tell me what you were going to say."

"Well, it's too bad you're not an Ava Gardner type. Otherwise, I think you'd be a good possibility for Cora."

"Who's Cora?" I asked.

"Cora is the love interest in *The Postman Always Rings Twice*. My friend, Bob Rafelson, is doing a remake of the 1940s classic. Jack Nicholson is going to play the John Garfield role and they're looking for an unknown to play the Lana Turner part. Only this time they want to go in the direction of a young Ava Gardner. Unfortunately, you don't look a thing like her. Otherwise I'd have you meet Bob—but don't worry, there'll be other opportunities."

When she said, "Jack Nicholson", my not-so-deeply buried dream revived. Then I inquired nonchalantly, "So, Bob Rafelson and Jack Nicholson are like personal friends of yours?"

"Yeah, they were over at my place for a dinner party last week. I've known Bob for years through my ex-husband."

Whirling around in my mind was an experience I'd had just a few nights earlier. I decided to take a chance and share it with her. "Sam, I have to tell you something really strange. A few nights ago, when I came home late from driving, I turned the TV on and happened upon an old Ava Gardner film. I'm not even sure of the name of it but, as I watched her, I actually had the thought, 'I have a quality similar to hers.' I saw myself in her."

"Really?" she said. "That's interesting, but I think I know what they meant when they said an 'Ava Gardner type' and I don't think you fit that concept." Then, with a cheerful adjustment, she added, "But Bob has all kinds of projects and I'll definitely introduce you to him at some point. But right now, he's totally wrapped up in this one." I practically had to bite my lip to keep from pressing the issue. I nodded and said I understood.

She wanted twenty-five headshots, offering to submit me for things as they came up. Feigning enthusiasm, I told her I'd get them to her soon and stood to take my leave. "Thanks for coming in, Frances," she said, as she extended her hand. "Prince Assad doesn't send actresses our way every day."

"Did I do the Prince proud?" I asked,

"Yes, you did the Prince proud," she responded with a laugh, and off I went.

As I made my way across town in my dilapidated, fume-spewing car, I raged over the cruelty of the universe when it came to my career. It had taken me a good six months to get over my encounter with Jack. Now, for some reason, I had inspired this woman to think of me for the romantic lead in his next movie, only to snatch it back. I was frustrated because time was slipping away and opportunities were few and far between. I didn't want to fail at this dream. Then, like a bolt of lightning, it struck me. I could demonstrate my Ava quality in a photograph, which I could then show to Sam. And if she was impressed then she'd want to show it to Bob Rafelson. *Yes, I must create the "me as Ava" photograph.*

I promptly called Norman, a hairstylist and make-up artist that Jeanine had recommended. Luckily, he was available and offered his services for a reasonable price. Then I hired a photographer that was referred through one of my theater contacts. Charged with new purpose, I scheduled the photo session for the following week.

Jeanine joined me for a trip to the UCLA bookstore where I purchased a copy of *The Postman Always Rings Twice*. From there, we ventured on to a few resale shops in search of classy 1940's outfits. Suits were very popular back then and were a perfect choice for both Ava, and chauffeur roles. Skirt-suits were acceptable at Royal Rolls as long as they were knee-length or longer.

I found two that day: one black with a collarless jacket, open to the waist, and then cinched by two cloth-covered buttons. Its flounced sleeves had fitted cuffs, which gave it an attractive line. The skirt was made of a substantial, yet slinky fabric, which hugged my hips but flared out easily from there, sexy and ladylike. The second suit was brown-and-black checked with a golden thread running throughout, and black velvet trim on both its collar and cuffs. The pencil skirt had a slit up the back, which was essential for getting in and out of cars. It was a stunner. In addition, I found a pink satin blouse that looked great with the black suit, a pair of black pumps, and a velvet purse to tie it all together. I now had my wardrobe for the photo shoot, as well as for my job. I was jazzed.

When I arrived home that night, a box containing four newly-born kittens was empty and turned on its side. Their mother, Reefer, a tabby that I had agreed to adopt from a fellow chauffer a few months earlier, was nowhere to be seen. I had no prior experience with cats and had no idea that this one was pregnant till the morning I arrived home and there they were. Now, a few weeks later, I was in love with all of them. A terrible sense of dread came over me as I started searching. Three out of four of the kittens were found hiding under the bed. Reefer then appeared at the sliding door, which I kept ajar for her convenience. Finally, I closed and locked it, left only with a prayer for the fourth kitten.

Early the following morning, I ventured down the hillside through thick brush toward the underside of the house next door. "Here, kitty kitty!" I cried, as I climbed over a fallen fence. I saw what appeared to be a ball of fur lying on a slab of cement. Adrenalin pumping, I moved in a little closer and to my abhorrence realized that it was indeed the missing kitty. When I lifted my gaze from its body, I found myself engaged in direct eye-contact with a large, orange cat perched on a ledge about ten feet deeper inside the space. The hair on my arms rose up as a chill traveled down my spine. I turned around and hurriedly walked away, not wanting it to see my fear.

I realized that I was living in a different kind of jungle than New York. There were coyotes and wild cats, and possums and skunks and snakes—as well as demented humans. *No, you can't let your guard down here either, Frances, even when it appears to be Paradise.* I knew I still had much to learn about survival and I was determined to learn it. With a somber heart, I began to read my new book.

MICKEY MANTLE & BILLY MARTIN

The following afternoon I was working as "duty driver" when Eric received a call for an airport drop-off for Mickey Mantle and Billy Martin. With a big smile, he handed me the ticket. "Here ya go, Francine. You're to pick them up in front of the hotel in twenty minutes. They're going to LAX."

"Far out…Mickey Mantle!" I exclaimed. My dad and brothers would flip over this one. As an afterthought, I asked, "Who's Billy Martin?"

Amused, Eric informed me that Billy had been the manager for the Yankees for quite a long time and was a rather high-profile guy. I knew that statement was loaded but I'd have to get educated later.

"Rumor has it that they're tipping everyone with fifties and hundreds," he said with a wink, and handed me the keys to the black stretch.

I glided into position in front of the hotel just as a Volkswagen Bug was pulling away. I rolled down my window to catch the attention of Emil, the bellman, and told him I was there for Mickey Mantle. With a sly grin, he said, "They asked the woman driving that VW to take them to The Saloon on Dayton Way." My jaw dropped in disbelief as he added, "She had just pulled over to ask me directions and before I knew it, they were in her car." He laughed heartily, "But they left their bags." *Oh good—all is not lost.*

"They'll call when they're ready. They're pretty good tippers," he added, as he loaded their bags into the trunk, flashing me a fifty.

When the call finally came, Eric sent me back out but this

time with a warning. "They may decide they'd rather have you drive them to Vegas, my dear. Just let me know. Meanwhile, they've been hitting the juice pretty hard, so do be careful—and have fun!"

When I pulled up in front of The Saloon, a fair-haired, bearded man approached my car. I had no idea what Mickey Mantle looked like, so even though this guy was short and scruffy and walking with a limp, I figured it must be him. I got out of the car and walked around the hood to greet my esteemed client when suddenly it dawned on me that he could be the wrong guy.

"Good evening, sir," I said, apprehensively.

His response was inaudible and his clothes were filthy. I realized my error and offered an apology for having mistaken him for someone else. Then, in words I could clearly understand, he asked my name.

"Francine," I said. "What's yours?"

Unbelievably, he said, "Mickey."

I laughed out loud and told him that I was there to pick up another Mickey. He went back to his mumbling rant and this time I was able to discern a reference made to Vietnam. Just as the sadness of this guy was penetrating my psyche, the real Mickey Mantle walked out of The Saloon. A full foot taller and twice the width of the street man, he was wonderfully awkward as he tried to figure out what was going on.

"Street Mickey" ramped up his rap into a nearly vicious tone. Not wanting to see the situation escalate in a bad way, I said to him, "Mickey, this is Mickey Mantle." He got quiet, his face softened, and he looked closely at the face of the baseball legend. Mr. Mantle offered his hand to the broken veteran.

Then, turning his attention to me, Mickey Mantle asked, "And what's your name?"

"Francine," I responded, as we shook hands.

"Where in the hell have you been all week?" he asked, shining his beautiful baby-blues at me. With a laugh, I moved around to open his door. Just then, Billy Martin walked out. Both of them were sporting ten-gallon hats and cowboy boots, along with a major booze-buzz.

When I moved around to open the door for them, they were having none of it. Amidst a heap of man-giggles, I could feel them checking me out as I walked around the hood of the car to take my place at the wheel. I barely had the engine started when Mickey piped, "Hell, Billy, we can catch a flight to Vegas any hour. Let's spend some time with Maxine here."

"It's *Francine,* isn't it?" Billy asked.

"That's correct, Mr. Martin."

"No, no! It's Billy—Billy and Mickey."

So then, Mickey asked, "Will you come have a drink with us, Francine?"

"Ah, well, I could have a coke with you, if you'd like."

"Great! Take us to the Brown Derby," and they continued to joke around.

When I pulled up to the front of the restaurant, I got out and tried in vain to open their doors for them, but it only sent them into a tizzy. The maître d' showed us to a crescent booth in the nearly-empty restaurant and I sat between them.

Over cocktails and a Coke, we chatted it up. At one point, Billy slipped a hundred-dollar bill to me under the table. "Please put this in your purse," he whispered, as if it was important that Mickey didn't know. That felt weird, so I tried to slip it back to him, but he persisted. Finally, I stuffed it into my purse.

I asked them what the story was on the VW. They told me that the woman driving it was eight months pregnant, so they figured she could probably use a hundred bucks. That's why they asked her to drop them off. Story after wonderful story, I soaked it all up. At one point, three businessmen got up to leave the bar, but before doing so they came over to our table. Faces lit with admiration, one by one, they offered praise and gratitude to the two legends as they shook their hands. I enjoyed being the mystery woman. The drinks kept coming and their flirtatiousness got a little bolder as time slipped by.

"Which one of us do you like best?" asked Billy.

This could get really awkward, I thought. So, in an attempt to bring them back to reality, I said, "Shall I have the hotel reserve a flight for you?" When they agreed that was a good idea, I excused myself and went to the pay phone in the Ladies Room. I called Eric and asked him to secure reservations for these guys on the next available flight to Vegas, which turned out to be the last one of the night. When I returned to the table, they proposed that instead of going to Vegas, they might come to my place where we could have a ménage à trois. Now, the visual of these two hellions in my tiny bungalow, yelping with glee as they tossed their hats and kicked off their boots, was amusing to say the least, and as much as I was a sucker for a good story, I thought, *Nah, I'll save it for the book*. But now that I'm here…well, sorry to disappoint, but it didn't happen.

The ride to the airport was lively, to say the least. Mickey sat up front, while Billy leaned halfway through the divider, talking and jiving. Mickey tried to convince me to go along with them to Vegas, trying to tantalize me with the fact that I'd be staying at Frank Sinatra's suite. When I pulled up to the drop-off area, I popped the trunk and handed Mickey the trip ticket for signature. He reached into his wallet and retrieved a hundred-dollar bill and offered it to me. I said, "Oh, thank you but no. I couldn't. Billy already gave me a hundred." Mickey opened his wallet again, took out an additional fifty, and handed them both to me, saying under his breath, "Please, take it. I can't let him out-tip me." So, I did. Unsteadily, the two legends made their way to the door, as Mickey called out one last time, "Come to Vegas, Francine!"

Several days later, he requested me to pick him up at LAX. Alone this time, he handed me an autographed picture of himself, after taking his seat up front. He truly was a very nice guy.

TO BE OR NOT TO BE—*REAL*

On the designated day, I met Norman at the photographer's studio and we set about our first order of business: my makeup. With a photograph of Ava Gardner taped to the mirror, Norman swiveled me away from it and tended to my face. He was meticulous with every facet of the process, placing particular emphasis on my eyebrows. When done, he turned his attention to my long brown hair, playing around with different ideas until finally committing to a "do" that I can only liken to Princess Leia's in *Star Wars*. And though I was less than thrilled with the result, I was impressed with how it transformed me. Trusting that he knew what he was doing, I embraced it. Hair and makeup done, I was ready to change into one of my new suits when I noticed Jeanine's grim expression while handling a string of pearls. "What's the story on those?" I asked.

"They were my mother's," she said with tears welling up in her eyes. "I overspent last month and now I'm coming up short. I'm going to see what the pawnbroker will give me for them." I reached into my purse and retrieved one of the hundred-dollar bills that Mickey and Billy had given me.

"This is a finder's fee for turning me on to Norman, and for all the help you've given me with everything: my wardrobe, the photos, and even *Echoes* for God's sake (she manned the lights). Truth be told, I should probably be tithing ten percent of everything to you."

"I like that idea," she said, cracking a smile, and reluctantly accepting my offer. After a hug, we shifted our focus to my reflection in the mirror. "You look incredible!" she exclaimed. We were studying my image from different angles when Norman pulled focus to himself by camping it up, showing off his own best angles. Jeanine said, "You *do* look good, Norman. What have you done diff…oh, my God—you've had surgery!"

"Why, thank you for noticing! I spared no expense," he said, as he showed off his profile. "You think you over-spent last month? Huh! I had a chin-tuck and an eye-lift. But I'll tell you, it was worth every penny." Just then I fidgeted with the scarf wrapped around my chest, which caused Norman to stare at that part of me. Finally, I said, "I know what you're thinking, Norman but No, thank you!"

"Why not, darling?" he implored. "You're a perfect candidate for implants, if you don't mind my saying. I mean, we're all girls here, right? So, let's be real."

"Exactly," I said. "'Let's be real'…that's what I want to be—real."

"But, darling, you could be set for life with perfect boobs. God, I'd do it in a minute if I were an actress!"

My mother and I had once argued about breast implants. She felt that, as an actress, I had a real problem with my less-than-endowed chest. Implants were an obvious solution, simple as that. The same thing had been her lot to deal with in life, and though it didn't hamper her popularity any, she was unhappy with them. So, once we kids were grown, she opted for the surgery. Sadly, she let the doctor choose the size and ended up with a more-than-ample bosom that caused her to be self-conscious from then forward.

The idea that she, or anyone for that matter, considered my small breasts to be such a lousy lot in life that I should have to elect surgery to make my body acceptable, infuriated me. Especially considering that I had been blessed with plenty of beauty otherwise. I imagined how sheepish I'd feel if I were in the hospital getting implants for the sake of vanity, while sharing a room with some poor woman who was doing the same but because she'd had a mastectomy.

"I'm not going to surgically alter my body in order to conform to the standards of an industry that's much too focused on tits-and-ass anyway," I replied. "Don't get me wrong, Norman. It's not that I don't wish I had a little cleavage. I do. But surgery is a big deal, you know. Man, I really thought that Twiggy had led us out of big-breast-mania, but I guess it's alive and well in *"Hollowood."* Seriousness diminished as my little pun got a rise out of them. Defeated, Norman made a final adjustment to my hair and announced, "I think you're ready for your close-up, Miss Gardner!" In a dimly lit studio with soft jazz playing, the photographer skillfully guided me into the sultry look I was going for.

As I'd hoped, Sam was duly impressed with the photograph, and sent it right over to Bob. Casting had begun and the word was that they would screen-test the seven final contenders with Jack himself. Getting the part was one thing, but the screen-test alone could start a career. *Oh, my God! Maybe my story will be like Mary Steenburgen's, after all.*

Considering that Darren, from way the hell over in Saudi Arabia, was the source of this opportunity, I couldn't help but feel like fate was at work here. So, with a great sense of purpose, I began to gear up for my Olympic-level competition, finding comfort in the fact that I had a good ice-breaker for when I met Jack; the story of our prior meeting. Meanwhile, I had to suit-up and show-up at the L'Ermitage.

WOLFMAN JACK

Eric gave me a thumbs-up when I appeared at base the next day in one of my new vintage suits. With his usual happy face, he handed me my evening ticket.

"I thought you'd appreciate this run," he said.

"Oh, yeah?"

"Yeah—do you remember Wolfman Jack?"

"Of course," I replied. "The disc jockey. Everybody knows 'The Wolfman!'" Without a doubt, Wolfman Jack was the most famous DJ of the sixties and seventies, known for his raspy voice with a touch of growl to it—as well as for his frequent, full-on howls.

"Good! You're going to pick him up in the blue Rolls at Hollywood Studios at 3 p.m. It's something to do with a television pilot."

"Excellent!" I replied.

Jeffrey pulled into the garage as Billy, the valet, hurried over to open the back door for his passenger. Out stepped Gene Hackman. He smiled at us all and said, "Good Evening," as he made his way to the elevator. He had a nice twinkle in his eyes, and I was jazzed. Then, Eric turned to Roger who was standing nearby and offered him a trip-ticket.

"And you, sir, shall drive the Sheik." Roger bowed his head and humbly accepted his lot. As we walked away from Eric, Roger asked, "So, how did that meeting with the agent go?"

Jeffrey joined us as we went into the small coffee room where Richard was relaxing. They gave me their utmost attention while I shared the gist of what had transpired since my meeting with Sam.

Then, before departing, I asked Jeffrey, "So, is Gene Hackman a nice guy?"

"Totally a class act," he replied.

"Cool," I said, and sailed out to meet my next adventure.

It was mid-afternoon when I pulled into the parking lot. Wolfman, two men, and a woman came out of the building and headed toward me in good spirits. Wolfman looked just like I remembered from pictures of yester-year: a substantial guy physically, with big brown eyes, a full head of dark hair, and a goatee. I introduced myself to him, Tom, Nick, and Casey, and then helped them get situated inside the wide vehicle.

Casey was wearing a Playboy bunny suit, minus the tail and ears. Her voluptuous bosom was enhanced by a black satin corset, while her long, shapely legs were accentuated by her stiletto heels. Once everyone was situated, I was directed to an address on Mulholland Drive. As we rode along, Nick, the director, explained that they were filming a pilot for a new television show featuring "the Wolfman."

When we arrived at the destination, they told me to pull over to the side of the road near the base of the long, steep driveway. Several other vehicles were already parked there, including a movie trailer (I wondered if it was a Cine-Mobile). Everyone got out of the car except Casey who was told to wait with me. Soon, a hair-stylist appeared and tended to her hair, finishing it off with a classic chauffeurs' cap. *Okay, now you're treading on thin ice.* Then, over a walkie-talkie, the stylist announced that Casey was camera-ready.

Tom came over and explained to me that they were filming the opening sequence of the pilot that would be shown at the beginning of each show. The plan was for Casey, who was playing Wolfman's chauffeur, to drive to the top of the driveway—stop—get out and open his door for him. He continued, "But there's a problem we didn't anticipate, you're the only one insured to operate this vehicle. Plus, now that I see how narrow and steep the driveway is, I realize that I can't allow Casey to attempt it. So, Francine, I have to ask a favor of you. Do you have a chauffeurs' cap?"

"Yes, I certainly do." I popped the trunk to retrieve it. I could already sense the good fortune that was surely coming my way.

"Would you please put it on?" he asked.

I slung it seductively over one eye and flashed him a little attitude. "Stay right here," he said.

Really—what were the chances of me landing this particular gig, featuring a female chauffeur for a television show? And now it looked like I was going to end up replacing the girl because I was the only one insured to drive the car. I mean, I was sorry for her loss, but it couldn't be helped. I looked up to the heavens and offered a silent prayer of gratitude. *My life is pure magic.*

Nick, the director of photography, came over and asked Casey to stand next to me. He studied the two of us standing side by side with our caps on, and then nodded affirmatively to Tom. "Okay, here's what we're going to do," said Tom. "You and Casey will both sit in the front seat with your caps on. Francine, you will drive the car up the driveway. When you reach the top you will duck down, making sure you're completely out of sight. At the same time, you, Casey, will step out of the car and move around to open Wolfman's door. Got it?" he asked.

Nervy little thing that I was, I contested, "But, won't you be able to see both of us? Plus, she'll be getting out of the wrong side of the car."

"Not a problem," Nick said. "The tinted windows will allow for your silhouettes to appear as one. The camera can cheat so that the audience will never know that she's not actually in the driver's seat. It'll work. Now, let's get on it while the light is good!" And he ran up the driveway to his tripod.

Wolfman took his designated place in the backseat while everyone else cleared the way. Tom said, "When you see me clap, Francine, start driving. Don't forget to duck as low as you can once you've stopped the car. He gave Casey a wink, took a moment on the walkie-talkie, and then gave me the signal.

As I proceeded up the steep, cliff-side pavement, Wolfman said, "Damn, this car is wider than the driveway." And he wasn't exaggerating. Relieved to reach the top safely, I did the ducking thing, while Casey got out and did her bit.

"Print!" shouted Nick. One take and they had it. Next, they needed some close-ups.

With Casey in the driver's seat, the camera zoomed in on her as she pretended to drive. A couple of crew members rocked the car up and down, creating a nice jiggle for her illustrious bosom. "Casey, reach for the radio knob as if you're changing the station." She followed his direction and then he added, "Now, slowly bring your hand up your thigh." She complied, seductively gliding her hand up her leg."Good girl—very nice! Okay—got it!" And it was a wrap.

"Alright, Francine! It looks like we got everything we need here," said Tom. "We can let you go now." I handed him the trip-ticket and a pen, while he produced a twenty-dollar bill from his pocket. "Thank you, Francine. You were great!"

Reluctant to accept that there was nothing more to it, I inquired, "So, when can I see the pilot?"

"Good question," he said. "Tell you what…I'll make sure that you're invited to a screening. I'll call your limo company when it's time."

Satisfied, I thanked him and got back in the car to leave. However, it soon became apparent that I was unable to turn the vehicle around at the top of the driveway. The only alternative was to go down in reverse. I kicked into my "motor-city-mama" mode and was about to get on with it when Wolfman approached. "Can you give me a ride down?" he asked.

Tom, overhearing him, said, "Hey! Hold on there, Wolfman! I'm letting her go now. We got the scene."

"The Wolfman knows. I'm just hitching a ride back to the

trailer."

Tom persisted. "I wish you wouldn't. She's going to have to back this boat all the way down. I don't want to jeopardize both of you."

Wolfman considered his words and then replied, "Nah—I think Francine is a good bet. The Wolfman is gonna take the risk." With a wink, he climbed in.

My reverse driving was smooth, and once we were back on the main road, I reached inside my purse and retrieved my new tape recorder saying, "Hey, Wolfman. I've got this tape recorder here. I was wondering if you'd be so kind as to say a little something into it?"

"Sure, turn it on," he said.

I did, and in his gravelly voice, he said, "Francine! I hear you got your recorder on. Is that *all* you got on, Francine—is your recorder?" And then he added his classic Wolfman snicker.

I sailed off into the balmy night on a wave of laughter. I still have the recording.

WHEN SHAME PAYS
1979

I was ecstatic upon hearing that Bob Rafelson liked my photo and gave Sam the go-ahead to arrange an audition. Mildred, the casting director's assistant, scheduled the appointment for the following Tuesday. *This is real now. I must use every spare hour from this moment forward to develop "my Cora." Nothing is more important than being as prepared as possible, and I have the ideal job to support me in this endeavor; one with hours and hours of waiting time—perfect for studying.*

That night at home, following a long day's work, I was organizing my new collection of Cora items. I opened a package of black silk stockings and glided my arm through one of its legs. As I stroked it, my mind wandered into the landscape where Cora and Frank resided. I reclined on my bed beside a large book about Jack and drifted into a dream where I was shooting the scene where Cora and Frank kiss for the first time.

Suddenly, a piercing cry penetrated the air and jolted me back to reality. Reefer was standing at the closed sliding door, crying out threateningly. The huge orange cat with its oversized jaw stood on its hind legs on the other side of the glass, glaring at the kittens in their box beneath me. Horrified, I turned out the lamp and adjusted my eyes to the dark, focusing on the unwelcome visitor, whose eyes now glowed red. Reefer emitted unearthly cries and time stood still. Finally, needing to do something, I lunged forward with my arms raised and yelled, "Boo!" He bolted.

"Is everything alright, Franny?" Pam Dawber called down from her balcony.

"Yes, everything's fine!" I yelled back, opening the door just enough to stick my head out. "I had to scare off a cat that was freaking Reefer out and had killed one of her kittens the other day." Pam moaned in sympathy and then said, "I wanted to ask if you would be interested in being my driver for the Emmys."

"Sure!" I replied. "Are you up for an Emmy?"

"Yeah, it turns out that the show's been nominated for Best

Comedy Series and Robin's up for Best Actor. I thought it would be cool to have you as our driver."

"Absolutely, I'd love to!"

"Great! I'd like the white Rolls Royce, if possible. I'll get back to you with more details soon, but it's coming up in a few weeks." With that, we said goodnight.

A few days later, I picked up three fun-loving guys from Philadelphia: Don, Alvi, and Joey. Loaded with mysterious bags full of goodies, they were already whooping it up when I arrived at the Beverly Garland Hotel. Don greeted me with sheer delight. "Hi beautiful!" he said, and then retrieved a wad of bills from his pocket. "This should cover us for the night," he said, as he counted off three C-notes. "But if we start to run overtime, just let me know." Meanwhile, the other two guys were busy setting up house in the inner sanctum of the stretch. Cocktails were poured and we were off to Dan Tana's. I was looking forward to my study-time but was delighted when Don invited me to join them for dinner. A Dan Tana's meal clearly warranted an exception to the "stay-with-your-car" rule.

I was so familiar with the menu that I confidently offered recommendations, and soon we were feasting on Fettuccini Alfredo, Shrimp Scampi, and Caesar Salads. *Heaven!* I learned that they were in town for a hairdresser's workshop and this was their night to party. Don flirted with me, while Joey and Alvi seemed quite taken with each other.

Once back in the car, Don directed me to a popular disco club. I dropped my clients off and drove to a far corner of the lot. I turned the dome light on, picked up my book and started reading. Deep into it, I came to a passage that I read aloud. "And the cat came back! It stepped on the fuse box and got killed, but here it is back! Ha, ha, ha, ha, ha, ha, ha!" I played with that laugh, trying to achieve just the right dose of maniacal. Suddenly, in the midst of my rendering, someone tried to open the back door. I shrieked.

"Sorry," Don said, realizing that he'd frightened me. "But what's so funny?" Extremely embarrassed, I told him that I was working on a scene for class.

"Do you like to dance?" he asked.

Being that my study mode had been ruined, I admitted, "Yes, I love to dance." Leaving my blazer in the car, we went into the club to have some fun.

We'd been movin' and groovin' for a few tunes when "Bad Girls" by Donna Summers came on, elevating the already highly energized crowd even further. Swept into it, I closed my eyes and started shaking my head, to and fro. Then, in a flash, I slammed my face into Don's shoulder. Stunned, my hands went immediately to my throbbing nose.

Don grasped my shoulders, stabilizing me. With one look, he knew that I was hurt and guided me across the room to a staircase where I momentarily released my hands, causing a stream of blood to flow down and saturate my shirt and slacks. Quickly, he led me to the Ladies Room.

Under harsh lighting, we stood in front of the sink, where he dampened several paper towels and held them to my nose. "There's no bone damage," he said with certainty. "You'll just be a little swollen for a few days. Poor thing, we were having so much fun."

I was beyond miserable, thinking about the upcoming audition and having a busted nose. It was bad enough, fighting the battle of small breasts, but to have an extra-large nose to overcome—no way!

"I can clean your shirt for you if you'd like but you'll have to give it to me right away," Don said.

I loved that perfect little shirt with its classic tuxedo collar. If

Don could save it then that's what needed to be done. While I held the towel to my nose, he removed my vest. Then, I went into one of the stalls, all of which were devoid of doors, and removed my shirt. *Of all nights to be bra-less,* I pined, while quickly slipping the vest back on. I secured the three pearl snaps at the waist, which offered next to no security, and took a seat on the toilet.

After several minutes of diligent rinsing, Don proudly held up a spotless white shirt for me to see. "Wow! That's amazing!" I cried, greatly relieved. Then he asked if he could complete the job, indicating the stains on my gray corduroy pants. Fortunately, he said it wasn't necessary to remove them, so I stood there while Don knelt down and gently blotted away the blood from my thighs. The repetitive gesture kind of turned me on, making me yearn to be carried off and made love to… but for God's sake, I had to get a grip. The audition was coming up soon. I had to stay focused. The evening wrapped up with an exchange of numbers that would never be dialed—with memories that would never fade.

My new black dress-suit looked stunning with the pink satin blouse. My hair came together perfectly in a version reminiscent of Veronica Lake, combed to one side with a sexy wave. I put a Band-Aid over my swollen nose, figuring it was best that it look like an injury. *Maybe it'll be a good conversation piece and work in my favor.* I always looked for the gift in any situation.

While quietly studying the sides with a few other actresses, my name was called. Poking her head through the door, a matronly-looking woman smiled as I stood up. After Mildred introduced herself, I followed her down a hallway into a room furnished with only a couple of chairs and a video camera. When she asked about my nose, I told her my tale of the night before, eliciting just the kind of response I had hoped for. Then I asked her where the casting director was. "Terry had to go to a meeting, so she asked me to read with you instead. Then, if I feel that she should see you, another meeting will be set up."

Son of a bitch! I was appalled. Didn't they realize that I came directly through Bob Rafelson? Still, I had to deal with the card I'd been dealt, and that meant winning Mildred's approval. No one was there to operate the video camera, so it wouldn't even be taped. It was solely Mildred's opinion that would count. I gave it my all, doing my damnedest to imagine Mildred as Jack.

"Very good," she said with sincerity. "I am definitely going to recommend you to Terry. You know, they're going to screen-test the seven final contenders—with Jack himself." When I looked into her eyes, I knew she wasn't messing with me. She said those words because she saw me as one of these contenders.

Uplifted, I smiled and said, "I know."

She kicked it up another notch, assuring me that Terry would receive a "stellar report", and that she'd be getting back to Sam soon with my next appointment time. "You can expect it to be within the next week," she said. "Things are moving quickly now."

"I look forward to seeing you again soon, Mildred," I said, wanting to kiss her. And off I went, confident and unwavering in my commitment to render the best possible audition.

Sam's call came two days later. "I'm afraid I have bad news for you." I slumped down on the bed, bracing myself for what was to come. "In spite of Mildred's recommendation, Terry has decided not to audition you. Apparently, she looked your picture up in the Players' Guide and doesn't think you're physically right for the part." Sam went on to say that she had also spoken to Bob, and though he did like my picture, he said that if Terry felt so strongly that I was wrong for it he'd have to support her decision.

Still stuck on the ludicrousness of the "Players' Guide" being the decisive factor, all I could say was, "You're fucking kidding me?" Sam shrank under my ire. I knew she had tried her best but dammit! How could it all come to this stupid end after I'd jumped through every hoop?

I thanked Sam for her efforts and hung up the phone. Then I grabbed a pillow and went outside to my rocking chair. I let that poor pillow have it, but unlike most fits, this one did not lead to a bottomless pool of grief. No, this one led to a fire pit of rage. *Why is this woman standing between me and my success?* I couldn't accept that it was over. There had to be something I could do. *Maybe if I go back there and get her to see me—maybe she'll change her mind.*

I put on the same black suit and went back to the casting office. When I told the receptionist that I would like to see Terry she responded pointedly, "No one sees Terry without an appointment." Then, just at that moment, Mildred popped her head into the waiting room, saw me and smiled. I rushed over to her and whispered, "I thought maybe if Terry met me in person, she'd change her mind." Mildred agreed and told me to wait. Then, a minute later she returned with a victorious smile, motioning for me to follow.

"She's been under a lot of stress lately," she said. "She's really very nice. You'll see." She opened Terry's door for me.

I took a seat across from the dark-haired woman who was busy, talking on the phone. "Yes, she's wonderful. I loved her in that pilot! Definitely, I'll have Mildred get back to you with a time for her to meet Bob. Okay, talk soon." She hung up with a smile and then turned her focus to me.

"Mildred spoke well of your reading," she said. And for a second, I thought we were off to a good start, but then she added, "But if I know someone isn't what they're looking for, I can't go wasting their time." That stung. *How can she sit there, looking right at me when I'm looking so smoking hot—and think that I'd be a "waste of their time?"*

"The best I could do for you would be to set up a reading between the two of us, and then, if I feel…" She paused. "But there really isn't much point. We don't know exactly what we're looking for, but we'll know it when we see it." You'd have thought I was the plainest Jane of all time. Speechless, and reeling from her statement, I then received her knock-out punch. "We're looking for someone a little out of the ordinary, someone who could conceivably turn heads in a diner."

Flashback! Diner—Hell's Kitchen—and the men all turn their heads to check me out as I enter. Having to come up with something, I copped an attitude and said, "Well, that's what I find so amazing…"

"What's that?" she asked, curiously.

"She's in front of you," I said.

And with that, she put her fingers in her mouth and turned to the side as if to puke. I could not believe my eyes. This meeting had now deteriorated to vomit-level. Still, hating to accept that she held the power to block my progress, I managed to find a single strand of hope in the bleak situation. I said, "A moment ago, you said that you could possibly grant me a reading with yourself?" Tongue in cheek, she nodded affirmatively. Ludicrous as it was, I continued, "With you playing Jack's part?" With a look of pure amusement, she nodded once again. Holding her gaze, I stood up, leaned in and said, "I'd like to take you up on that."

"Fine," she said. "Mildred will set it up."

"Fine," I responded, as though I were triumphant, and took my leave.

As I walked past Mildred's office, she smiled and said, "Wasn't she nice?"

"Oh, Mildred—you're a lot nicer!" I told her, mustering up a half-smile. "You're supposed to schedule a reading for the two of us together." Puzzled, Mildred said she'd take care of it.

A few days later, Sam called to tell me that Terry was reneging on the deal, saying that I was completely wrong for the part. There was no counter-move. The wind was simply gone from my sails, and I moved into the day in slow motion.

While gassing up Malerie at a station in Hollywood, someone called out my name. I looked around and saw Michael W., the Programming Director at the American Film Institute, waving to me from his car at the traffic light. We had become buddies during the many hours I'd spent volunteering there. I waved as he pulled into the station. A lovely British gentleman, Michael showed a special interest in my career, and soon I was telling him all about the *Postman* saga. It pained him to hear my disappointing story and made him want to fix it somehow, but sadly he didn't know any of the players involved. Then, he brightened up with an idea for something completely unrelated. "Hey, I do know a director who is in pre-production for a movie and looking for an actress to play a small part. The only thing is she's French. Can you do a French accent?"

"Ah oui, Monsieur," I responded with a chuckle. Satisfied, Michael retrieved his black book from his car and made haste over to the pay phone. I felt enormous gratitude toward him for actually caring about me and my dream. When he returned, he told me to go to Paramount Studios right away—that my name would be at the gate where I would be directed to the office of James Toback.

I hugged Michael and thanked him for being such an angel. With a fresh full tank, literally and metaphorically, I set out toward Paramount Studios. With a giggle bursting forth, I imagined the phone call I'd soon have with my mother bringing her up to date on the latest happenings. Recently, it was she who had the big news. She had married a man she'd dated in high-school and they were now living together in Indiana. Though miles apart, our relationship was close.

The radio was playing too loud for my taste when I entered the bungalow of Mr. Toback. He sat behind a desk, chewing gum and talking on the phone at break-neck speed. With brown eyes, curly dark hair, and an unkempt beard, he motioned for me to come in and sit down. A few minutes later he hung up, and without pausing to say hello, dialed another number.

"Hello there! Are you still serving breakfast? Good. Give me two orders of scrambled eggs with sour cream and onions, two orders of rye toast, two large orange juices, and a bottle of Champagne. Bungalow 12." When he hung up the phone, he asked, "Are you hungry?"

"Actually, yes," I said, which seemed to please him.

Over Mimosas and scrambled eggs, I related my *Postman* story to him, starting with Darren and the Saudi Prince, and ending with the wicked casting director. I will never forget his reaction. "Those garbage-picking, ass-hole, mother-fucking casting directors don't know their ass from a hole in the ground!" He took another swig of his champagne before adding, "Jack's a friend of mine. I'll get you a reading." My eyes widened. "No problem," he continued. "I'll call him today. Absolutely, you should be seen for the part." With more joy bubbling up inside me than I could contain, I let out a howl of laughter. *My life is magic.*

"Thank you so much!" I cried out in all earnestness.

He stood up and walked out from behind his desk. I figured it was the end of our meeting, so I started to gather up my things when he took a stance behind me and began massaging my shoulders. I froze for a second and then broke the energy by standing up. "Well, I'd better be going," I said. When I turned to leave, he looked at me lustfully and slowly approached. I smiled nervously, as he gently pushed me up against the wall. He leaned in and whispered in my ear, "Just let me touch your breasts."

I didn't have the will to stop him as he buried his face in my hair and his warm hand made its way inside my blouse. A few seconds later, following a muffled grunt, he turned and walked out of the room.

In a state of shock, I walked out of his office and drifted back to my car, wanting to undo what had just happened. Then, I was utterly mortified when I discovered semen on my skirt. I didn't realize that he had actually climaxed. *Why did you allow him to do that?* I asked myself accusatorily, never thinking to assign blame to him.

Back home, I stepped into the shower holding my skirt. "Out, dammed spot!" I cried, while rubbing soap onto the area. "Out, I say!" But try as I did to make light of it, I succumbed to shame and guilt, and turned to a prayer of contrition; one emblazoned on my psyche since childhood: "Bless me, Father, for I have sinned…" God may have forgiven me, but it would take much longer for me to forgive myself. And though I would've preferred to call it a day and stay home with my cats, I had to suit-up and show-up for work that evening.

Upon arrival at base, Eric handed me a message. "You had a call a while ago from a 'Jack.'" Eric had no clue as to who Jack was, and I made sure I didn't give him one. Then he asked, "Would you please cover the phones while I go to dinner?"

"Of course," I said, and took a seat at his desk, my heart racing. After the way things had gone, I never dreamed that Mr. Toback would actually make the call on my behalf. *Am I in bed with the devil now?* Fear gripped me.

I took a deep breath and dialed the number. A woman answered. "Hello."

"Hello" I said. "I'd like to speak with Jack, please."

"Who may I say is calling?"

"Frances McCaffrey"

A moment later that unmistakable voice was addressing me. "How're ya doing, Frances?"

"Fine thanks, Jack. How're you doing?"

"Good—real good. So, I hear you want to audition for *The Postman Always Rings Twice*."

"Yes, I do."

"Well, okay then. I'll leave your name with the casting

director, so there shouldn't be any problem setting up an audition."

Dumbfounded, I feigned enthusiasm. "Oh…uh, that's great."

Switching the subject, he said, "So, what are you doing?"

Now it seemed to me that he meant, "what are you doing *right now?*" So, I told him that I was working, that I was a limousine driver based out of the L'Ermitage Hotel.

"Oh yeah—James said something about that." Shuddering, I wondered what else James had said. Jack continued, "Well, was there anything else you wanted?" Pause. "I mean, did you want to meet me?"

Oh my God! I couldn't believe he was asking me that. I took a breath, centered myself, and said, "It would be more than a pleasure to meet you, Jack. But I don't want to impose on your time and I'm more than happy to go about this through the normal channels."

It was common knowledge that Jack loved the girls, so I assumed he'd make a move on me if I went up to his house. He might not take it well if I rejected him, and if I responded to his advances then I feared he wouldn't recognize my value. It was a lose/lose situation. It was imperative that he see me work. Romance could come later.

Jack responded, "Well then, like I said, I left your name with Terry, the casting director."

I had to come clean. "Actually, Jack, I've already met with her."

"Oh?"

"Yeah…she doesn't think I'm 'physically right' for the part," I said, wincing at the sound of the words. There was an awkward silence.

"Well, then…I can get you an appointment directly with Bob, but if he feels the same—then there's nothing more I can do."

"I understand," I said.

"Alright, I'll set it up for you to meet with Bob."

"Thank you. Oh, and hey, Jack…I look forward to meeting

you," I said, as if meeting him was inevitable.

I had just bet everything on my ability to be so frigging irresistibly brilliant that Bob would simply have to see me work opposite Jack. Would I be good enough to make the final seven? I assured myself that I was. *Oh my God, am I back in the race even though I was disgraced?*

I saw Mr. Toback on television the other night. It was in relation to the Harvey Weinstein sexual abuse scandal that recently rocked the country. I had been using an alias for Mr. Toback for decades, never dreaming of revealing his true identity, which I actually forgot over time—until I saw him on the news. Now, I'd feel cowardly if I *didn't* state his real name, for dozens of women have bravely stepped forward to share their Toback stories, and thanks to them, I now realize that I, too…yes—ME TOO—was left with a terrible sense of shame for a man's crime.

TONY BENNETT

Parked in front of a theater in Westwood, fifteen minutes before pickup time, I was distracted from my book by a jostling of the backdoor handle. Snapped to attention, I rushed around the front of the stretch to see a small child, maybe six years old, trying to open the door. Somewhat annoyed, she looked at me and asked, "Is this Tony's limo?"

I said that it was and opened the door for the adorable and oh-so fashionably dressed little girl. I offered my assistance as she settled in but she dismissed me. Clearly, limousines were commonplace to her. Charmed, I reclaimed my post at the wheel and we sat in silence for a few minutes till she sighed and said, "Oh, it's *good* to be alone."

Though her remark slayed me, I caught her eye in the rearview mirror and responded sincerely. "I know what you mean." I could tell she was sizing me up.

"You look familiar to me," she said, tickling me once again with her air of worldliness.

Playing along, I said, "Really? What's your name?"

"Courtney," she replied. "What's yours?" But before I could respond, a chubby boy carrying a bunch of balloons arrived with three other children. Jumping into action, I sped around the vehicle and helped the lively bunch get situated. Once they were all buckled in, I stood up and found myself standing so close to Mr. Bennett that I shrieked. Terribly embarrassed, I fumbled awkwardly and apologized. "Oh, I'm so sorry, Mr. Bennett."

"No, I'm sorry I startled you," he said, probably embarrassed as well.

"I startle easily. Anyway…Hi, I'm Francine," I said, and extended my hand.

"It's nice to meet you, Francine. Please call me Tony." And

he took his seat among the children as he directed me to Bel-Air Estates.

It started to rain as I approached the 405. Sirens blared from behind, so I craned my neck and spotted major congestion on the highway. I quickly maneuvered out of the entrance lane, avoiding the mess. "Nice driving, Francine," Tony remarked. Meanwhile, Courtney told a story that ended with someone jumping into a pool with no clothes on. Uproarious laughter filled the air. *I have precious cargo.*

At our destination house, the lively children stumbled out of the vehicle, one by one, with their balloons in hand. Tony and I were standing next to each other when he said, "Wow—what a handful! Kids are great, aren't they?"

I nodded and asked if he had children. "Yes. I have two sons and two daughters. You?"

"No, no kids here."

Courtney was staring up at us, our profiles silhouetted against an amber sky. Suddenly, she cried out with satisfaction, "It's the nose!" I wasn't sure what she meant but I thought it was hysterically funny and couldn't help but sweep the child up into a big hug.

On the drive back Tony sat up front and I shared with him Courtney's remark about how good it was to be alone. We laughed heartily over that, and then he told me that she was Natalie Wood's daughter. "Oh, wow," I said. "So, she truly is Hollywood royalty."

"Yes, she is," he agreed. I felt embarrassed again for, of course, so was he. I asked what the event was that they had attended and he explained that it was a fund-raiser for a children's charity that he sponsored. "That's wonderful," I said. Little did we know that in a matter of months that child would know all too well what it truly meant to be alone in this world.

Then Tony noticed my *Postman* book lying on the console between us and said, "I remember that movie. It starred Lana

Turner and John Garfield. How is it that you're reading this book?"

"They're doing a remake of it with Jack Nicholson and they're looking for an unknown to play Lana Turner's part. I'm going to be auditioning for it soon."

"That's great! You do have a certain forties kind of look."

"Thank you. I'd love to ask you a question that pertains to my character, if I may?"

"Of course," he replied.

"Well, I was wondering what music my character might enjoy listening to. Like what would she dance around the house to?"

After some thought, he offered, "Fats Waller was very popular back then. Are you familiar with him?"

"The name's familiar but…I can't really…"

"I'll tell you what—drive up to Tower Records and I'll get you a Fats Waller tape. I need to pick up a few things for myself anyway. That'll be my contribution to your pursuit."

"Oh my gosh. Thank you!" And to Tower Records we went. When we eventually arrived back at the hotel, he said, "If you want to hear some great live jazz, I'd be happy to have you as my guest tonight at a studio in Hollywood. Ella Fitzgerald will be recording a few songs. You should come. Also, one of the best saxophonists in the world will be playing—Zoot Simms. They're both good friends of mine."

"Oh, wow! I'd love to. Sure!" I replied, as he got out of the vehicle.

Then he leaned back into the car within earshot of Eric, "I'll phone the address down when I get to my room. You should arrive there at 9:30."

Eric had a twinkle in his eye when I came up from parking the stretch. With no hassle he gave me my freedom as of 9 p.m. By chance, I had a black silk Mandarin-collar dress fresh from the cleaners hanging in my car. Fortunately, I happened to be wearing my black pumps, so I was set. By 9:15 I was dressed in elegant evening attire and ready to step out with Tony Bennett and Ella Fitzgerald. *Oh God, I do so love my life. .*

Entering the dimly lit studio, I saw a woman that I presumed to be Ella. What I knew for sure was that a statuesque black woman was looking at me with skepticism. Tony rushed over to greet and introduce me, first to Ella, which caused her cool expression to morph into a slight smile, then to his friends, the couple that he had come with. There was a small eruption of laughter when the woman and I realized that we were wearing identical dresses.

When the session got going, Tony began to sketch a picture of his friend, Zoot Simms. I treasured every minute as time flew by. After an hour or so it was a wrap, and I was about to depart when Tony invited me to join him and his friends for dinner. "I'd love to," I said, but inwardly cringed when he then asked if he could ride with me. "Ah, sure—but my car is old and pretty funky." Undeterred, he jovially got into Malerie and off we chugged, leaving a toxic cloud in our wake.

Upon arrival at Le Dome, an elegant yet trendy restaurant on the Sunset strip, the valet opened Tony's door, only to see him emerge from the car with seat-stuffing all over his dark suit. Tony cracked up when he saw it, brushing it off as best he could. I helped clear off his backside, laughing uncontrollably all the while. Then, as we approached the entrance, one of the paparazzi cried out, "Mr. Bennett!" Tony stopped and turned around, warmly addressing the gentleman by name, while putting his arm around me to pose for a picture. "Who's the lady?" the guy called out. And I don't know why, but I whispered to Tony, "Don't tell him!" So he didn't.

A week or so later, while shopping at the Beachwood market, I ran into Tom, a character I knew through Crystal, who gave me a knowing grin and said, "You and Tony make a good-looking couple." Baffled, I asked him what he was talking about. Finally, after taunting me for a few minutes, he told me that he saw our picture in The National Enquirer.

I picked up the paper at the check-out counter and nervously turned the first couple pages and there it was—me and Tony. Somehow, someone got my name and then fabricated a little story about me and Tony. I was grateful that it was a decent picture, but still—the nerve of them going through my car to find out my identity! At least, that's what I assume happened.

Tony Bennett, estranged from wife Sandi, is crooning love tunes to actress Frances McCaffrey. The woosome twosome have been dating for several weeks and were spotted gazing at each other over cozy late-night dinners around TinselTown ... Peter Sellers' widow Lynne Frederick wants a future in the movies — behind the camera. She was exec producer of Sellers' last guffaw, "The Fiendish Plot of Dr. Fu Manchu," and now she plans to keep producing.

Beautiful Bo Derek and hubby John bought a 31-acre ranch near Santa Barbara where they will raise Arabian horses. They plunked down an incredible $5½

TONY BENNETT
... crooning love songs.

PLATO'S RETREAT

It was a beautiful, balmy night and I had parked the stretch as close to the water as possible, so as to hear the sound of the waves. Mr. Niles and his lovely young girlfriend, Rebecca, were having dinner at the Paradise Cove Cafe. Figuring that I had at least an hour-and-a-half of waiting time, I over-rode my rule to never sit in the backseat and did just that.

With the moon-roof open, I sipped from a can of Coca Cola and studied a scene from the book. While imagining Jack as Frank, sitting beside me, I began to speak Cora's lines aloud. Meanwhile, my clients were approaching the limo but stopped in their tracks upon hearing my highly charged voice. Then, joined by a valet attendant, the small group listened as I passionately carried on about how I (Cora) was revolted by my husband and "his disgusting Bay Rum that he rubs on his hair every night." The scene ends with Cora saying something about not wanting to ever see Frank (Jack) wind up with a lousy parking-lot job, that that would kill her. End of scene—and I was feeling quite pleased when I suddenly heard clapping. *Huh?*

I stood up through the moon roof to see what was going on, but quickly shrank back in, much like a jack-in-the box, deeply chagrinned upon realizing that the applause was for me and that my clients were part of the audience. Desperate to disappear, I jumped into action instead, quickly stashing my open Coke can in the front seat, along with my book, and then scurrying around to open the door for them, I could feel my face flushing with blood and I strained to contain the hysteria that was pent up inside. Oh, how I wanted to collapse into it. Fortunately, my clients were amused as well, and were in very high spirits as they partook of a little appetizer of the powder variety. All is well.

Later that evening, as I neared the hotel, Mr. Niles said that he and Rebecca weren't ready to call it a night yet. I had been hoping to drop them off and go home, but that's not the way to think when you're a professional driver. "There really aren't any after-hours clubs in this town," I said.

Mr. Niles replied, "But they were talking about a new place on the Johnny Carson show the other night—Plato's Retreat. Could you take us there?"

"Oh wow, that's the new sex-club!" And soon I found myself parked in a dark lot next to an unmarked building. Mr. Niles and Rebecca ventured into the mysterious place. I began writing in my *Cora journal,* but was distracted by a prostitute negotiating a deal in my rearview mirror. She hopped into the man's car and went off with him. Clearly, I was in a sketchy part of town. I kept my engine running, resolved to stay alert, for the car was my only protection—bad-ass as it was. "With You I'm Born Again" by Billy Preston and Syreeta Wright came on the radio. By the end of it, tears filled my eyes, as I longed for a love of my own.

Suddenly, Mr. Niles and Rebecca appeared back at the car. He said they couldn't enjoy themselves while thinking of me outside, all alone. They wanted me to come inside where it was safe. "It's a very relaxed environment," he said. "Just some couples lounging around, taking Jacuzzis and stuff—nothing too bizarre." He was right that I didn't feel safe where I was—but a sex club? That was definitely off-limits.

He continued to cajole me. "Francine, I have enormous respect for you, both as my chauffeur and as a lady, and I wouldn't want you to do anything that you'd be uncomfortable with. But I promise you, if you're concerned about anybody finding out, that's completely unnecessary. In fact, if you'd feel better about it, we can all make a promise right now that our presence here will remain our secret. And, really, Francine, even if you just sit in the lounge and sip orange juice, I'd feel much better knowing that you are safe indoors than out here in this desolate lot." Well, he had me with that, so declining his offer of a line of cocaine, I locked up the car and went inside the club with my clients.

While I was writing a phony name on the registry, some man walked in and tried to convince the manager to allow him entry even though he didn't have the required female companion. Then, when he realized that I was an unaccompanied female, which was allowed, he said to me, "Excuse me, Miss. Would you be so kind as to let me go in as your escort? I just got off work. I'm an airplane pilot. I come here regularly to unwind. Please?" With a smile as intense as his pitch, he offered me his hand and said, "My name is Peter." I looked to Mr. Niles, who in turn looked to the manager, who gave a nod of confirmation. Reluctantly, I shook Peter's hand in agreement.

A handsome guy who looked like a professional athlete ushered the four of us into a unisex locker-room upstairs. "This is where you secure your belongings and 'towel up,'" he said. I looked around and saw a few couples wrapped in towels, making their way toward the stairs. These yellow towels were the uniform of Plato's, and lame as it sounds now, my thinking was that I didn't want to stand out like Mother Mary Seaton in my black pantsuit. Plus, I was kind of keen on the idea of a Jacuzzi. Was I nuts? Probably, but I took the two yellow towels offered. Then, Peter made the gross assumption that I'd be willing to share my locker with him. Abruptly, I set him straight and moved to the other side of the locker room.

With a towel around my waist and another hanging from my neck, covering my precious ones, I took my book and headed for the stairs. *What the hell am I doing?* I must have asked myself. I say "must have" because I really don't remember. But ask or not, I was doing what I was doing with a good deal of nervousness, a sense of adventure, and an absolute certainty that I was not going to have sex with anyone. I just wanted to see what the place was like. So, with images of breasts and thighs, flashing on the wall behind me, I descended the spiral staircase.

A lavish spread of fruit beckoned me at the landing. After

considering the abundance of options, I picked up a gorgeous, fat strawberry and bit into it. As I observed my surroundings, I noticed silhouettes in a purple haze emanating from two hot tubs around forty-feet in front of me. With a fabricated air of nonchalance, I walked in the opposite direction toward the juice bar where I poured myself a drink. I was relieved when I spotted an empty pinball room off to the side. There I nabbed a small table and settled in to study—but that was not to be, as the studly guy who had led us to the locker room soon strolled in and asked if he could join me.

Sitting there, clad only in a couple of towels, having an exchange with a fully dressed attractive man, was bizarrely erotic. A med-student, working his way through school, he seemed like a solid person. I was enjoying his company but he must've been beeped or something for he suddenly had to leave. However, he did hand me his card and invited me to contact him. "Unfortunately, my only free night is Monday," he said, as I slipped his card into my book. Enlivened by the encounter, I felt emboldened enough to go explore the Jacuzzi situation.

"Francine!" Mr. Niles called out in a piercing voice. I offered a small wave in response, already regretting my decision to leave the pinball room. "Francine, how are you doing?" he persisted, motioning for me to come closer.

"I'm alright, Mr. Niles," I said. "How are you doing?"

"Great! Call me Woody."

"Okay," I said, not letting myself go to the giggly place.

"Come on in. The water's beautiful," he implored.

So, there I was, facing the moment of truth. I flashed back to Woodstock when Randy and I came across the scene of naked people, slipping and sliding together in the mud. I was so uptight back then about my body and about nudity, and though I still wasn't casual about it, I kind of wanted to be. So, I said, "In honor of Woodstock, I surrender," and stepped into the hot gurgling water.

"Were you at Woodstock?" Rebecca asked.

"Yes, I was."

"Really—what was it like?" she asked.

"You must have been seven years old!" interjected Woody.

"More like seventeen," I replied, enjoying the compliment.

"Did you swim in the nude there?" she asked.

"No. I didn't have the nerve at the time."

"Well, see…now, you do!" Woody exclaimed.

There were a few people in the whirlpool a step above us, most notably a man sitting on the edge of the pool with some woman's head in his lap. *Oh dear—that is too much. I can't hack this place.* I averted my gaze to a wall of curtains just as Peter emerged from them. When he saw me, he approached and stepped into our hot tub and sat down next to me. I ignored him and moved closer to Rebecca, but in an instant his hand landed smack on my thigh. When I pushed it off, he angrily climbed out and headed back through the curtains. I hoped that the threat of Peter was over, and that I might actually get to enjoy the Jacuzzi, but that was not to be.

Peter re-emerged a couple minutes later, only this time flaunting what I could only assume was a very large erection beneath his towel. I felt like I was in an X-rated comedy spoof, but this was no time for laughter, as I was the intended brunt of the joke. When his greedy little eyes darted my way, I knew I had to get the hell out of there. I excused myself and went to the locker room.

It was strangely quiet on the ride back to the hotel. At base, I was relieved when Woody smiled and handed me a hundred-dollar bill. The three of us had a weird bond now. I knew I could trust them. What happens at Plato's—stays at Plato's.

MAKING WAVES

A couple nights later, I dozed off while watching my kittens wrestle their way toward independence. I was jarred from my sleep by Reefer's unearthly cries only to see the devilish orange cat standing on its haunches, trying to open the door. My roaring lurch proved successful once again but there would be no peace as long as he was about.

Nearly two weeks had gone by since I'd spoken with Jack, and still there was no audition scheduled. It was time to call Sam to find out why. When I did, she reluctantly told me that Bob didn't want to "make waves" with the casting director, so he was going to abide by her judgment. *This is unbelievable! Am I going to have to go in from above the director?*

The rain was pouring down when I arrived at Base for a noon pick-up. Eric, in an exceptionally happy mood, helped me prep one of the stretches. We cleaned the glasses, stocked the bar, filled the ice-bucket, vacuumed, etc. He let me know something was up that pertained to me but he was going to have his fun teasing me before coming out with it. Finally, he said, "I have a message for you, Francine." I cringed. "It's from a hotel guest," he added, rolling his mischievous eyes. *Oh, Lord—don't tell me that Mr. Niles said something?*

"He called to reserve a stretch limousine with you, my dear, tonight. However, you are to be his *guest*, not his driver. He even offered to pay double, if necessary, just to make sure that *you* are available."

I felt embarrassed and confused. I couldn't imagine that Woody and Rebecca would request such a thing. The only other possibility was Tony Bennett. Yeah, it had to be Tony. "Listen, Eric. Don't jump to conclusions. I thought he kind of liked me, but I didn't think he'd go to this extreme."

"Who?" he asked

"You say it first," I said.

"Nope, you've got to say it—or I may not be able to let you off."

Meekly, I answered, "Tony?"

He howled with laughter. "I knew you and Tony…mmm hmmm." Finally, when he'd had enough of my suffering, he said, "Darren."

"Darren?!!" I screeched. "Darren's here?"

"Yeah. Darren must be some kind of big shot, huh?"

"He's a friend since fifth-grade, Eric. He's the one who started this whole audition process for me." Taking real pleasure in my joy, he added that Roger would be our driver for the evening. "Far out!" I cried. I had a great night ahead of me and a very important day before that. This was the day I would call Jack again.

My jaw dropped when the elevator opened and revealed a character that looked like he was ready for Halloween. He was a heavyset African American man, sporting sunglasses, a wig with long bouncy curls, white Levi's that looked like they'd been sprayed on, and a Hawaiian shirt. Eric introduced me to Sydney, my client for the day. "What the hell?" was written all over my face but Eric just shrugged his shoulders. Hotel management had cleared this guy for limousine usage with the caveat that three hundred dollars cash had to be collected before returning him to the hotel by 6 p. m. With disco music blaring, and a bad feeling in my gut, I set sail into a heavy rainstorm. First destination: a stamp and coin shop in Hollywood.

As soon as he'd gone inside the store, I ran through the rain to a nearby phone booth. With a quick prayer, I put my quarter in and dialed Jack's number. I gave the woman my name and soon Jack was on the line. "Yes?!"

Oh, crap. He's annoyed with me.

"How're ya doin', Jack?" I asked, hoping to warm him up.

"Doin' alright. How're you doin'?" he asked in a more pleasant tone.

"Good, thanks, but I'm having trouble getting an audition with Bob," I said.

"Jeezes!" he exclaimed. "Okay, listen. Call this number, 213-999-9999. Talk to Jolene. Tell her that you just spoke with me, that you've come highly recommended, and that you are to be seen for this part—and that I don't want to hear another thing about it! Got it?"

"Got it. Thank you," I replied, while scribbling the number on the back of a business card.

"And good luck," he said.

"Thank you, Jack," I said, and then added, "Oh, and Jack—I look forward to meeting you."

Immediately, I called Jolene and repeated Jack's message verbatim. She laughed heartily and said, "Hold on one moment, Frances. I've got Terry Liebling on the other line telling me that we are definitely not to audition you. Ha!—I can't wait to meet you!"

When she returned, she asked for my number so that she could call me within the next two days with an appointment time. "I have to be sure that Terry's out of the building when you come, so you might not get more than a couple hours' notice. Okay?"

"Okay" I replied.

"So just be ready," she said, and that was that.

Loving the rain on my face, I ran back to the car just in time to greet Sydney who directed me to the Hyatt in Pasadena. "And haul ass, please," he commanded. "I have to be there in fifteen minutes,"

Feeling my own power in that moment, I quipped back, "Well, that's impossible. I suggest you relax for a good half-hour ride—if we're lucky." And I hit the road.

Along the way he held up a piece of paper and said, "Do you know how much this check is worth?"

"Sure do not."

"Well, guess."

"Ten-thousand dollars."

"Nope. Twenty-four thousand."

"Oh, a mere spit in the ocean," I sassed back.

He then assured me that he worked very hard for a living, adding that he was Donna Summers' producer. *That's funny,* I thought. *I drove someone else who claimed to be her producer. How many could she have?*

"Mmm…cool," I said, hoping to end the conversation.

At the Hyatt, I couldn't believe it when he waited for me to get out and walk around in the deluge to open his door for him. Then, without giving me any indication of how long he would be, he gave his curls a toss, and swished toward the front entrance. Only because he left his briefcase did I have any faith that he would return.

Three hours later, still waiting, I called Base. "This guy is a fraud, Eric," I said.

"You may be right, but hang in there a while longer, and make sure that you collect the cash when he returns. Get him back here by 6 p.m., Francine. And please do be careful."

Sydney returned soon afterwards and directed me to a jewelry store in Korea Town. I was still well ahead of the 6 p.m. deadline, so I acquiesced. The driving was treacherous, with flooding in most intersections. After twenty more minutes of waiting, I went up and knocked on the door. A woman opened a miniature window at eye level and said in a soft voice, "Ten minutes."

When he finally got back to the car, I said, "I need to collect three hundred dollars from you, sir." His response was that we had to make a stop in Westwood first. Well, there was no way that was going to happen, so I told him, matter-of-factly, that I'd take him back to the hotel where he could sort out the finances and begin anew with a fresh driver. I took my place at the wheel and started back to Base.

"I wasn't able to get hold of any cash today because the credit offices in New York closed early." At that point, I knew for sure that this guy was going to stiff us. When I didn't respond, he closed the divider, shutting me out. I drove as fast as safely possible and was nearing base when he called on the intercom, commanding me to pull over to the phone-booths up ahead. I figured he would run away if I did, so without answering him, I sped right past them. My heart was pounding as loud as the rain at this point, and when I came to a stop at a red light, I deftly leaned down, picked up the receiver, and called Base. "10-1," (our code for emergency) I whispered. "ETA five."

When I finally pulled into the underground garage, Billy opened the back door as if everything was cool. Sydney exited the car with his briefcase in hand and sauntered over to the elevator. I looked to Eric whose face assured me that the situation was under control. Later I learned that Security was supposed to intercept him when he got off the elevator at the lobby level. But for whatever lame reason, that didn't happen. Instead, Sydney walked directly out the front door, unchallenged. I could not believe it. *What the hell?*

Eric was more relieved that I was okay than he was concerned about the money and assured me that I would not be held responsible, that I would be paid in full. "Go home and get ready for your night on the town," he said kindly.

Roger and Darren arrived just as the rain ceased. After a joyful greeting and a quick look at my pad, Darren and I walked up the driveway to the waiting white stretch. I noticed a star shining from between the parting clouds and felt a sense of shared triumph. Darren opened a bottle of Dom Perignon Champagne and we toasted to life and friendship, as Roger made his way to Bob's Big Boy, a drive-in restaurant in the valley where Jeanine worked. There, Roger joined us in the backseat and we all chowed down on burgers and fries, while Jeanine stepped in now and then, sipping on a cherry Coke. I brought them up to date on the amazing saga that had resulted from Darren's call, and how I was now assured an audition with the director. Of course, I did omit my moment of shame with Toback—that would remain my dark secret.

As much as I wished I had the stamina for a night on the town, I was exhausted and asked to be taken home following dinner. After Darren said goodnight, he directed Roger to the Sunset Strip.

Early the next morning, Eric called and said, "Good morning, Francine. Sorry to bother you so early but Sergeant McLean from the police department is here and would like to speak with you."

"Oh, great," I said, sarcastically. The officer then asked me questions about my day with Sydney and kindly requested that I come to the hotel as soon as possible to look at mug shots. Sydney, it turned out, was an ex-con who had actually been robbing the shops I'd been taking him to. *Oh, lovely. Now, because of everyone else's ineptness, I have to drag my tired ass out of bed and haul it across town to look at pictures of the guy that I tried to tell everyone was a crook!* "I'm on my way," I said politely.

Many of the pictures fit his basic profile, but since Sydney never removed his shades, and because of his wig, I couldn't be sure. I didn't want to be guessing at something that held such grave consequences. Plus, it maddened me that no one heeded my warning cries. So, as far as I know, Sydney got away with it, and I'm forever grateful to have survived the ordeal.

After the questioning, Darren took me out to brunch and shared the rest of the events of the night before. He was at the Rainbow Club at closing time and was ushered out the side door. While making his way down the steps, he noticed a crowd gathered in the parking lot. Curious, he moved in closer, and quite unbelievably saw that Jack Nicholson was standing in the center, outside of his car. I could hardly believe what I was hearing, but Darren continued and shared with me the exchange they had.

"Jack! Jack! You've got to help my friend, Franny!" Darren yelled. "You've got to put her in your movie, man!"

Oh, God! I could clearly imagine Darren, in a drunken stupor, pushing his way toward Jack. Then, he continued. "Then Jack opened his car door to get in, but before he did, he turned around and I swear to God he said, '**Franny**?' Do you mean **Frances McCaffrey**?' And I said, 'Yes! Do you know her?' And he answered, 'No, but I talked to her on the phone today.' And then I said, 'Hey, man! She's a great actress. You've got to put her in your movie!' He nodded at me and got into the car."

Oh, my God! I was dying—though it was kind of wonderful to think that Jack had my name on his mind. *Something's happening here…*

BOB RAFELSON

A few days later, Jolene called at 11:30 a.m. to set my appointment for 2 p.m. that same afternoon. After a heartfelt prayer for good fortune, I set about the process of becoming Cora. I put my Fats Waller tape on and stepped into the shower. Then, wrapped in a towel, I applied my make-up and arranged my hair so that it fell gracefully onto my shoulders. Next, I put on a pair of white full-bottomed underpants, a garter belt, and a padded bra. Then I carefully slipped each leg into a black silk stocking, securing the straps at the thigh. The unfamiliar underwear (I usually wore the bikini style with pantyhose), had a powerful effect on my character, but it was when I stepped into the checkered suit that it really came together.

Even the contents of my purse were authentic forties items: the red lipstick, the compact mirror, and a white glove that had been left in my limousine by Irene Dunne, a great film actress of Cora's day. When I had called Ms. Dunne to tell her that I had her glove, she told me to keep it for good luck.

Once satisfied with my physical preparation, I poured myself a shot of banana liquor, snatched a manila envelope from my dresser top, and took a seat outside on the deck. From the envelope, I retrieved three scenes that I had typed out on Pam Dawber's typewriter. Since I'd had no access to the actual script for the past six weeks, I was hoping that I'd be able to audition from the book. With Fats Waller still playing, I reviewed each scene, slowly sipping the sweet, sticky liquor. Soon, it was time to go.

I started the car and turned off the radio, wanting to keep Fats fresh in my mind. Ten minutes later, I arrived at the building where my failed meeting with Ms. Liebling had taken place. My heart accelerated and my hands turned to ice. Moving slowly, giving calmness every chance to show up, I walked into the building. Over an intercom, I announced myself. When I got off the elevator and started down the hall, a woman with a welcoming smile approached me.

"Frances?" she asked.

"Yes," I replied and she reached her hand out to shake mine.

"I'm Jolene. It's great to finally meet you. Bob's in a meeting right now but he won't be long." Together, we walked to the office suite where she invited me to take a seat on a couch just outside Bob's office. She then opened his door a tad and told him I was there. As she started into her own office, she turned back around and said, "By the way—you're beautiful!"

Good as it was to have her on my side, I was still a nervous wreck. Soon Bob's door opened and out came a gentleman who blatantly checked me out as he made his exit. Bob then closed the door, but not completely. I could hear him tinkering with something mechanical. Then, suddenly, the music of Fats Waller filtered out into the hallway. My stress vaporized with each familiar chord, as a sense of peaceful confidence took its place. I was exactly where I was supposed to be. Then Bob opened his door. "Frances, please, come in."

Somewhere in his forties, he was tall and, though not classically handsome, very appealing. Naturally, I made a reference to the fact that I, too, was a Fats Waller fan, which got the conversation off to a great start—*thank you, Tony*. Soon thereafter, he got down to the business at hand. "So, I understand you want to read for the part of Cora."

"Yes"

"Well, Jolene will give you a couple of sides from the screenplay when you leave. We'll schedule another time for you to come back and read."

I couldn't believe my ears and risked coming across as impudent by responding, "I've been working with the book for the past six weeks. I'm ready to read any scene from it, but there are three in particular that I've been focusing on."

He then told me that he had read a few people from the book early on and had decided not to do it anymore—that David Mamet had his own style and that he thought it was wise to stay true to his version. "Besides, the print is so damn small that I can't read the lines, anyway."

With that, I picked up the manila envelope, retrieved the three scenes from it, handed them to him and said, "I anticipated that possibility, so I typed the scenes out, double-spaced them, high-lighted your lines…and I know mine."

Taken aback, he put his glasses on and scanned through the pages. "You remind me of Jon Voight," he said. "He is always incredibly prepared." He considered my request further and then responded decisively. "But I'm sticking with my policy." And he handed the papers back to me. Shifting gears, he said, "So, tell me something about yourself. I hear you're a limousine driver."

Doing my best to make the necessary adjustment, I said, "Yes…based out of the L'Ermitage Hotel."

"What's the most bizarre experience you've had so far?" he asked.

I poured myself a glass of water, while I considered my options. I could tell him the Stevie Nicks story, that was kind of fun. Or there was the story of Sydney—that was a winner. But there was also "Baby Face Martin", and who wouldn't love that one? For God's sake, any one of them would've been a good choice, but this was Bob Rafelson I was talking to—a great film director—one who had given us *Five Easy Pieces*. This guy had the bar set very high on story-telling and I needed to make the best possible choice. As much as I preferred to keep it to myself, it was going to have to be Plato's Retreat. I took a long drink of water, summoned my cojones, and starting spinning my tale.

"It started out as a typical run, taking a couple of hotel guests to dinner…" and on I went, holding him captive every step of the way.

"When I finished, he said that it was a great story and added, "I'll bet you have lots of them."

"Yes, I do," I said.

"Have you written them down yet?" he asked.

"No, but I did buy a little tape recorder for that purpose."

"Great! You should definitely keep track of your stories."

"Yeah, I know. I think it'd be great material for a movie…" I said, fishing.

He pondered the notion for a moment but then brought our meeting to a close. "Thank you for sharing your story, Frances." He stood up and added, "And Terry was wrong for not allowing you to audition."

Happy for the vindication, I thanked him as we walked to the door together. "Jolene will give you some sides to take home and we'll call you back within a few days. You'll read with me. Until then, have a great time and start writing your adventures down."

"Okay, I will. Bye for now," I said, feeling confident that his word was good.

Late afternoon, a few days later, I was sitting on my deck with Jenkins and Boots, two of my kittens. I had a tall glass of vinegar water and was combing fleas out of Jenkin's fur. Reefer and the third kitten, Melrose, were asleep in the box. When I had captured most of the fleas in the vinegar water, I tossed it out and began gathering up my things. I stepped inside ever-so-briefly to answer the phone when I heard a kitty shriek. I dropped the receiver and tore out to the deck just one big step away, and to my utter horror, I saw Hell Cat running away with Boots in his mouth.

"Oh my God—**NO**!" I screamed, while snatching up Jenkins and placing him safely in the box. Then I closed the sliding door, grabbed a broom and went running out into the overgrown hillside. "Drop her, you son-of-a-bitch!" I yelled at the top of my lungs, while thrashing the broom about like a wild woman. "God dammit, you fucker!" I wailed, as I shook the fence that now separated me from them. If it weren't for the barbed-wire on top, I would've climbed the damned thing. I looked around and cried for help. "Pam! Bobby! Anybody! Help! Someone, please… anyone!" But no one was within hearing range. I howled in agony. I couldn't bear it, and yet it was what was happening. The psycho killer cat had gotten another one of my precious babies! My only hope for Boots now was that her suffering was brief. I was sick with grief.

A short time later, when it was nearly dark out, I got clarity on what I had to do—go to the store and buy rat poison. So, while walking up the driveway and rummaging through my purse in search of car keys, a man's voice commanded me to, "Stop right there! Put your hands in the air!" With a scream, I dropped my purse and put my hands in the air. Walking down the driveway toward me were four police officers with their guns drawn.

"Who are you?" one of them demanded.

"Frances McCaffrey. I live here."

"We got a call from a neighbor who said a woman was screaming as though she were being stabbed to death. Do you know anything about that?"

"Oh…yes, Officer. That was me. I was chasing a cat that ran off with one of my kittens. It's the second one he's gotten!" I started bawling.

They rolled their eyes at each other and then he said, "You can put your hands down." They all relaxed and put their guns away, while a female officer put her arm around me and offered me her condolences before leaving. I got into my car and kept on my mission. It was going to be a long dark night.

Later, I laid in bed waiting, wanting the murderous devil to devour his last meal. I didn't want to torture him—I just wanted him gone. It was heavy, but I held my ground with Jeanine who put forth an opposing argument. The next morning the bowl was empty. The deed was done.

Sam called to let me know that Bob would see me at 4 p.m. the following day. She said that Jolene suggested that I bring an outfit change. A summer dress, perhaps, so they could see me in a different look. I didn't have a summer dress that would work for Cora, and besides I thought the request was a little strange. *Maybe they're trying to get a look at my cleavage—or lack thereof.* Anyway, I let it go in one ear and out the other.

After serving as duty driver that afternoon, Eric requested that I go home in a Cadillac stretch so that I could drive it to my audition and then head directly to LAX for a pickup. As I was about to get into it a rear window of the Rolls Royce glided down, allowing a waft of marijuana smoke to escape.

"Come on in," Richard said. "We've got a killer bowl going." So, I joined the guys in the backseat. Just as I told them that Eric had freed me up for the night, Richard's beeper went off. "Crap! Eric's looking for me. I bet I'm working the night shift to cover for you!" he barked, as he took one last hit.

"I'm sorry!" I said.

He grumbled and said, "Yeah, well…when you're a big star maybe you'll remember how I helped you out when you really needed it. Maybe you can get one of my movies made."

"I promise I will do all I can to help bring your scripts to the silver screen, Richard…providing that they're good."

"Good? What the hell does 'good' have to do with it?" He climbed out of the car, "Sex and violence, Honey—that's what sells. That's where the money is." He was almost out of sight when he looked back and shouted, "Embrace it, Francine! Don't try to change it!"

"I'm not going there," I replied.

"I know you'll dazzle them," Roger said, as the rest of us piled out of the car.

For the second meeting with Bob, I wore the pink satin blouse with the black skirt-suit. Bob sat on the couch next to me, sides in hand. There was a pint of milk on the table. Together, we read a scene that takes place after the murder of Cora's husband, when their trust in each other had deteriorated. When we wrapped it up, he said, "I want you to do it again, but this time I want you to give me more annoyance at the top." He lit a cigarette while I took a sip of water and then added, "Keep the energy taut throughout. I want to put it on its feet this time."

I removed my jacket, stood up and placed myself near the door. Bob went to the window, leaned against the wall and said, "Whenever you're ready." I took a deep breath, turned around and began the scene. Soon it was over, and he motioned for me to take a seat. "You're the only actress who I've auditioned that I'm going to tell the results to. The reason is because I respect you and the tenacity it took for you to get here." *This isn't sounding good.* "You just read better than seventy-five percent of all the actresses I've auditioned…and I'm talking about actresses the likes of Faye Dunaway. You incorporated my direction beautifully, and I'd recommend you to anyone. Unfortunately, you're not Cora."

Stung, I quipped back, "You mean, I'm not your Cora." For at that point, no one could tell me that I was not Cora.

He released a sigh of exasperation…or perhaps I had even angered him. "Do you have any idea what this is like for me? I wish I could put your face in my movie! Someday I will. But it's just impossible this time. There's only one other female part and that's been cast from the start." I knew he was referring to Angelica Huston. My disappointment was palpable and it took great effort to remain composed. Then, he added, "Hell, I don't know who's going to make the best Cora. I have to please not only myself but the studio executives and now they're pressuring me to go with a name."

"Are you still looking for an Ava Gardner-type?" I asked.

"Ava Gardner? Where'd that come from?" I couldn't believe

my ears.

"From Sam—she said you were looking for an unknown—an Ava Gardner-type." But Bob didn't recall having ever said such a thing. Poof! So much for Ava.

"What about screen-testing the seven final contenders with Jack?" I asked.

"Oh yeah, that was a nice idea, while it lasted. No time, and no point now. I'm going to be choosing soon, and I'm going to be choosing someone who won't need to be screen-tested."

I grappled with the finality of it, refusing to accept that nothing was going to come of it all. "You said you would be willing to recommend me to anyone?"

"Yes, I'd be glad to," he affirmed.

"Thank you. I may take you up on that."

Kindly, he smiled and said, "Please do."

As I put my jacket on to leave, he added, "And I'd like to encourage you to start writing your limousine adventures. I think there's real potential there."

"Yeah, I know," I said with lackluster. "I've got great stories. But I'm not a writer."

I opened the door to take my leave when he reached over my head and closed it again. "I think you need a kick in the ass, Frances. And I'd like to provide it for you. I'd like to advance you a thousand dollars to write your limousine memoirs."

Speechless, I stood and watched as he went over to his desk and retrieved his checkbook. A moment later he handed me a check. "Write at least a hundred and fifty pages of your stories within the next six months. In exchange, I want first option on the material. Once it's completed, you can try to sell it to anyone you want. If you get an offer, let me know and I'll decide if I want to exercise my option. If I choose not to, then you'll pay me back a thousand dollars when you get paid. If you write it and never sell it, you don't owe me anything. If you never write it, you owe me a thousand dollars."

I listened to his every word, as he continued. "It's not about me making the movie, but someone in this town will want to make it, and I'd like to be part of making that happen." He put his arm around me and walked with me out into the hallway. "Keep in mind, Frances, that it's not the extraordinary tales that will make it interesting, but rather the ordinary things, as seen through extraordinary eyes." I was floored.

"I suggest you pick up a copy of *Basketball Diaries* by Jim Carroll. He is a first-time writer who speaks in his own unique voice, and that's what you want to do. Check it out. I think it could be helpful." Just then, his phone rang. He kissed me on the cheek and broke away to get back to the business of making a movie.

Jolene, who had heard the tail end of our meeting, walked me to the elevator. With a warm hug, she said, "We'll see you again, Frances." Clearly, I had won some sort of victory here, but had lost something as well. My emotions were confused.

I stood in the parking garage, reluctant to get into my limousine. *Maybe Jack will happen to cruise in.* After a slow count of ten, I took my seat behind the wheel. I allowed another ten-count before starting the engine. Finally, I backed slowly out of my spot and circled the area once, giving fate a little wiggle room. But Jack wasn't keeping his appointment with destiny. He wasn't anywhere in sight. I drove out onto the street.

Tears welled up in my eyes on the way to the airport. I needed time to grieve over a movie that I wouldn't be in, and a movie star that I wouldn't meet, one who was alive and well, who knew my name and took my calls! I knew all too well how few and far between such opportunities were, and I feared that this was likely the end of my dream to become a great film actress. It was hard to accept that with all the challenges I overcame, and the magic I manifested, that the ultimate answer was a big fat "**no.**" My tears won out and crying commenced.

A few miles later, I realized that my sobs were keeping time with the music. I played with that rhythmically for a bit, until finally cracking myself up. There was no way that I could truly despair. This was simply one of life's disappointments. A big one, granted—but not a devastating one. After all, there was a thousand-dollar check from Bob Rafelson in my wallet.

When I called Eric to let him know that I was at LAX, standing by, it so happened that Roger and Jeffrey were both on the intercom. They were all eager to hear how it went, so when Eric asked me—they were all ears.

I choked up and couldn't get the words out. Finally, Roger broke the silence. "Roger to Base."

Eric: "Go, Roger."

Roger: "Francine, we know you did great. We love you, Francine."

Jeffrey: "Jeff to Base"

Eric: "Yes, Jeff. Go."

Jeffrey: "Hey, Francine, you made it to the finish line. Congratulations!"

Feeling a little more buoyant, I responded. "I did good, you guys. I'm just not *his* Cora".

Eric: "Well, you may not be his Cora, but you're our ace-number-one, baddest little chauffeur in town!"

Me: "Shoot, Eric, you don't mean it."

Roger: "You've got *winner* written all over you, Francine. It's just a matter of time."

Calmer and more composed now, I said, "Thank you, Roger. I love you guys. Eric, it's a pleasure being on your team."

Eric: "That's what I like to hear. So, are you ready to rock and roll?"

"Ten-four," I said.

Eric: "Good. Do you have your sign?"

The name card was lying on the passenger seat, face down. I

said, "Ten-four, Eric. I'll see you back at Base." I hung up the receiver. When I turned over the card I saw "QUEEN" written in bold black letters.

I wiped away the tears, put my sunglasses on, and cruised up to baggage claim. Just as I pulled up, the exhausted world-traveling rockers straggled out. Grateful to see their limousine, they happily climbed aboard. The road manager introduced himself as Mal "their babysitter", and took a seat up front. He was full of fun and flirtation, but at this point I wasn't easily charmed.

The sky was a glorious blend of coral and lilac hues, as we sailed off toward the 405. One of the guys opened the sun-roof, eager to feel the warm California air. Another one lit up a pipe (filled with tobacco), and in a most charming British accent said, "Home, James!"

And there was music,
And there was laughter,
And there would always be a morning after.

Stretched out on the floor at home that evening, while on the phone with Jeanine, Reefer and her two kittens slept peacefully in their box beside me. Then suddenly, I thought I heard a distant meow. I stopped talking and listened intently—but nothing. I continued to speak but in a much quieter tone now and sure enough, I heard it again. This time I set the phone down and reached up to the knob and opened the door. There, right in front of me, stood my darling Boots!

"Jeanine—it's Boots! Boots is alive!" I cried, as I scooped her up into my arms. "Oh my God! I'll call you back," I said, as I hung up the phone. Then, ever-so-gently, I explored the bloodied fur on my kitty's head where Hell-Cat—never to be seen again—had bitten into her skull. Bittersweet tears streamed down my cheeks as I held my precious Boots.

So, God does love me, I thought. But I so wanted it all. Could I really let go now? After getting so damn close? I had no doubts about being talented enough, or good enough. It seemed to be more a matter of being lucky enough. My father had often referred to himself as being unlucky. I wanted to change that belief. Still, the ten-year time-line was upon me, and I had to face the very real possibility that it might not happen for me.

I carefully analyzed the situation. Opportunities were far too sparse; I was pushing the dreaded thirty, and I didn't have any representation worth beans. On the other hand, I was making ends meet while enjoying a rich adventurous life experience in the beautiful City of the Angels, and remote as it was, my life did hold at least the possibility of success. Additionally, I now had a new mission, to write a manuscript financed by Bob Rafelson. Not bad. *Yeah, I'll give it another five.* And so, it was.

Over the next period of time, I would have many more amazing adventures, ranging from dark tawdry tales to wonderful, funny, and every now and then, romantic encounters. Tony Bennett, Pam Dawber, Gene Hackman, Mary Tyler Moore, Prince, Francis Ford Coppola and others would grace my limousine. Those stories will be available in a separate book titled *My Limousine Memoirs…and More.* Meanwhile, there's a lot of ground to cover here.

Photo by Patrick Cragin

PART TWO

THE MANUSCRIPT

Within a few months, I had compiled a hundred and fifty pages of limousine adventures. Around that time, Steve De Jarnatt, a friend from the neighborhood, and I were having breakfast at the Beachwood. We were tossing around ideas for a title when he came up with *Home, Jane!*

"I love it!" I cried. "You're brilliant! Thank you! But I think I'll add a "y" to the spelling, just to spice it up some—she's no 'plain Jane.'"

When I turned the manuscript in to Bob Rafelson, Jolene warned me that it'd likely be several weeks before he'd get around to reading it. Meanwhile, I was free to go out and try to sell it, keeping in mind that Bob held first option.

The next day, I had an airport pick-up for Antony G., who worked with Hemdale Productions. On the way back to the hotel, I told him about my manuscript and he asked if he could read it. Within the week, I had a script development deal on the table.

The offer was ten-thousand dollars, to be paid in three equal payments: one up front, one midway through, and the last upon completion of the script. Thrilled, I called Jolene with the good news. Bob was very happy for me and chose to release his rights. We agreed that I would pay back his thousand in thirds, coinciding with my payments.

The fact that I was not a screenwriter didn't faze Mr. G. in the slightest. He simply told me to find someone who was. So, without hesitation, I chose my good friend, Miles, who I'd come to know through my theater connections, and who had always taken great interest in my stories. Miles had so impressed me with one of his earlier scripts that I used my connection with John Avildsen to try and help him get a break. Amazingly, that worked out, and John did in fact option Miles's screenplay, which kick-started his career. When Hemdale Pictures issued me the first payment of $3333.33, I wrote a check to Bob Rafelson for $333.33, and paid the other three thousand to Miles.

The red flag came when Miles revealed that he was going to craft the storyline around a romance between me, (the "me" that he alone decided should be fictionalized), and another chauffeur. He would be pulling from women he had met at bars etc. I sadly came to realize that he could not be inspired by a woman whose career took precedence over her desire to have a primary romantic relationship. This meant that for years I had mistaken his interest in me and in my stories as understanding and respect. I thought our friendship was one of mutual admiration and support for one another's dreams. Now, when I really needed him to come through for me, I was instead worried that he didn't get me at all.

My waning hopes plummetted as I read the finished script. It was a formula romantic comedy with a few limo runs woven throughout. It bored me to tears. He even went so far as to replace my cats with a talking parrot. I, Franny/Frances/Francine, was unrecognizable in it.

It came as no surprise to me when Mr. G. expressed his disappointment. His partner, David Hemmings, famous for his role in *Blow Up*, agreed to meet with me over dinner to discuss the matter. At Harry's Bar in Century City, I did my best to salvage the opportunity but to no avail. He did, however, agree to release all rights back to me in lieu of the final payment. In turn, Miles agreed to forego his final payment and released any and all claims on the story and/or script to me. He had been a "pay for hire."

Why hadn't I included myself as a co-writer on the deal—with creative control? *Hello!* For God's sake, I could have hired a coach to guide me through the process. But no, I handed it over to a man that I deemed to be more capable than I to write my own story. And what did I learn? That he didn't respect me. He didn't understand my heart. It was one brutal lesson.

It took a few months to save up the last three hundred and thirty-three dollars owed to Bob, but it felt great when he called and told me that I was the first of many artists who he'd helped over the years to pay him back.

Some months later, I was featured in a Los Angeles Times article on the "Limo Scene." From that, I scored a meeting with a producer at Paramount Studios. Maybe it's not over yet, I thought, as I walked across the lot, trying to suppress the cursed flashback of my encounter with Mr. Toback. This time, thank God, everything was proper, but I could not believe my ears when the producer told me that it was Pam Dawber who he had in mind to play my role. *Wow! The universe is sure having fun with me.* It was just too much to take. But in the end, the project never took off. Meanwhile, I co-founded a theater company with twenty other actors, called The Los Angeles Theater Unit, and worked on original plays from 1980 to 1984.

Sometime mid '82, my first boyfriend, Randy, contacted me, saying he was in town on business and wanted to get together for a drink. Over a couple of beers at a pub downtown, I sat across from my handsome love of yesteryear, trying to rise above my desire to sidle up next to him and start things up all over again. I maintained composure and listened as he shared with me how badly I'd hurt him. He also let me know that his net-worth had hit the million-dollar mark and that he had recently purchased a condo for his sister. If he was trying to make me envious, it was working. At the end of our time (he had a business meeting to attend), he asked if I was free for dinner the following night. Happily, I said, "Yes."

That night, I lay in bed, realizing how lonely and weary I was from the rat race of it all. I longed to find someone to soar with.

Could I soar with Randy? I wondered. The thought of it both excited and terrified me. *What if I tried and then concluded the same thing as before? Is he too conservative for me? Could I be happy being a wife living on the east coast? And if not, then what—break his heart again?* But no worries, just then the phone rang. "I've thought better of things," he said, "and I can't make it tomorrow night." I told him I understood and wished him all the best.

In 1984, I scored a small part in a film called *Fraternity Vacation*. I was cast as the prominent of two hookers. In the beginning it was being talked up as another *Fast Times at Ridgemont High*, introducing several young actors, including Tim Robbins. Unfortunately, it fell way short of expectations, and following the screening, I felt sad when I saw Tim at a popular Russian café downtown, sitting alone with his head bowed over his beer. Little did he know that soon his star would rise and he'd be playing opposite Susan Sarandon in *Bull Durham*.

Meanwhile, my work on the film earned me the exact amount of money I needed to move, for my enchanting bungalow was falling apart and the house was scheduled for repair. Thanks to a Tarot Card reading from Brinke Stevens, an attractive young woman who a friend referred me to, I had received the heads-up on the matter. Brinke told me, in no uncertain terms, that I was soon to be, "out of my home."

When I arrived back at my bungalow following the reading, a six-week eviction notice awaited me in the mailbox. Had it not been for her warning and assurance that I had *the magician* working with me, I would've been traumatized. Much later, when a friendship developed between us, I learned that I was Brinke's first paying customer.

Simultaneous with the move was also a change of employment.

After much resistance, I accepted the unlikely position of West Coast Sales Representative for Technidisc, a laser video disc manufacturer based in Troy, Michigan. The company's owner, Mr. T, remembered me from the Cinema Club days in Detroit, and when he came into town, he stayed at the L'Ermitage—always requesting me as his driver. He often invited me to join him for meals, and over a period of several months, we learned quite a bit about each other. One day he surprised me with a job offer.

"Anybody who can do what you do on a daily basis here in Los Angeles—has all the intestinal fortitude I could ever hope to find in a sales rep." Mr. T then carved out the job to suit me. He accepted that I wasn't willing to call it quits on my acting career, though I was definitely ready for a break from the driving. My lack of knowledge of his highly technical product didn't concern him. I was "trainable."

The package for this part-time position included a good salary plus bonuses, a new car, and a quarterly trip back to my hometown. That part really attracted me, for I missed my family terribly. Once I accepted his offer, he insisted on purchasing a few outfits for me, shoes and all, from Saks Fifth Avenue. *Maybe he's working an angle,* I feared. It was a shame that I didn't feel any chemistry with him because he was a very interesting person and divorced. But that's the way it was, so I pointedly asked him if he had another agenda going on. "Absolutely not," he said assuredly. So, after nearly five years, I quit the limo scene.

The digitally encoded, album sized, reflective discs offered a quality of video far superior to all other formats available at the time. Technidisc was one of three facilities in the United States that manufactured these discs—and both of the other companies specialized in the industrial markets. After millions of dollars and several years of preparation, Technidisc was poised to enter the feature film market for home viewing. My new boss assigned me the task of pioneering that mission.

Denise Beaumont & myself...Fraternity Vacation
personal collection

CHERRY 2000

Steve De Jarnatt hired me for a bit part in his movie, *Cherry 2000*. It was scheduled to shoot in the desert near Las Vegas and would star Melanie Griffith and David Andrews. Fortunately, because my new job was only part-time, there was no conflict. Steve invited me to bring a friend, promising to give them a day's work as an extra. Lisandre, the woman who had introduced me to Brinke Stevens, was available and interested, so I brought her along.

Being into quartz crystals in a serious way, Lisandre often drove to Arkansas with a pick and axe and mined them herself until the trunk of her Chrysler couldn't handle any more. She had recently returned from one of those trips and brought a bag of the sparkling rocks with her on our jaunt. Time sailed by as she educated me about their special qualities. I was fascinated.

The setting of the movie was a futuristic nightclub. I was slated to be featured as a "Glu-Glu Club Patron" entering into the negotiation of a sexual encounter. My potential sex partner would ask the mediator if he could use a cattle prod on me to which I would respond, "Deal breaker!" Yes, it was another classy moment for me on the silver screen. Unlike *Fraternity Vacation* however, *Cherry 2000* has become a cult classic, enjoying some notoriety to this day.

Just in time, I found a house for lease in the Hollywood Hills with a separate guest unit. The asking price was $700 per month for the house and $450 for the cottage. The triple-lot on Woodrow Wilson Drive offered panoramic views to the north and east. The expansive grounds were laden with a variety of fruit trees and outdoor patio spaces. It was beyond anything I had imagined, even with Brinke's directive.

The 1920 craftsman house was built into the hill, reminding

me of a ship riding a wave. Windows dominated what had once been a sun-porch but was now an extension to the living-room, the main feature, aside from the fabulous view, being a fireplace. A vintage, art deco, brass peacock fan stood in front of it. The mantle above ran the length of the wall and was book-ended by two small square windows that opened inward. Stunned by the beauty and charm of the place, I slowly turned around, taking it all in. A majestic pine tree hovered over the garage and hidden within its branches I spotted a two-story treehouse. The Hollywood Sign reigned omnipotent in the hills beyond. I was in love.

On the far side of the kitchen, in a little hallway, there was a steep, wooden stairway that led to a huge loft. Crouching, I climbed up to find a long, wide, carpeted room, where I could stand fully upright at its peaked center. It featured a big window that offered the most stellar view of all—it was magical. *I will put my bed at the far end*, I thought, and in that moment, regardless of the fact that the rent was three times what I was used to, the commitment was made. I had found my new home. Overwhelmed with joy, I envisioned the five-star review that my cats were sure to give it.

Sitting on the airplane, headed for Detroit, I marveled at how my Hollywood life had circled back around, taking me home to Michigan and in the capacity of a sales position, the kind of work I had excelled at in high school. Even though I'd not met with success as an actress, I felt good about the fact that a prestigious company was investing in me, and that I was traveling on their dime, rental car included. These were things that impressed my dad, whose approval remained a core motivator for me.

I was excited to see him, my sister, Lee, and my brother, Russell, the only two of my five siblings still residing in the area. Nancy was a single mother now, living in Berkeley, California. Mark was getting his doctorate in Spanish at UCSD, and Billy was working for MCI in Chicago.

My parents were both were remarried now. Dad and Joan, a lovely woman with two adult daughters and a six-year old boy, resided in a townhouse in Southfield, not far from Technidisc. Mom and Ken had moved into a trailer home on Lake Chemung so as to be close to Lee and Lou and their two young children. On my quarterly visits, I would split my time between the two areas, appreciating the opportunity to be "Aunt Franny" to my niece and nephew.

In my second quarter on the job, I met with success, bringing in a sizeable purchase order from Image Entertainment, consisting of several different titles, including *Fraternity Vacation*. My client showed me the LVD jackets and to my utter shock there was a photograph of me with my sidekick hooker on the back cover. I didn't let on but I could have screeched for there I was all decked out in red spandex hot pants with hair ratted to the high heavens. Back in my car, I laughed my butt off, imagining Mr. T's reaction if he were to see it.

In addition to Image Entertainment, I secured an order from Warner Brothers. This was a client that obviously held huge potential for Technidisc, not to mention mega-bucks for me. My newfound status brought me respect and bonuses, allowing me to breathe a sigh of relief regarding finances. Unfortunately, that lasted for only around six months before I received a call from the head of distribution at Warner Brothers. "Frances, your discs are being returned to stores at an astonishing rate. Apparently there is a problem with the quality of the picture." *Oh, dear.*

Over the next several weeks, I endured multiple embarrassing meetings, which ultimately led to a total recall of the product. It was concluded that oxidation was causing degradation of the digital encoding after the product left the factory. I took it in stride but felt terrible for Mr. T, who desperately tried to restore the client's vote of confidence while he searched for a solution. Meanwhile, my job hung precariously in the balance.

Cherry 2000

KEEPER OF THE FLAME, 1986

One night during this tenuous time, I had a date with Chuck, an entrepreneur/actor. We were enjoying champagne and pizza in my living room, when I suddenly wanted to have a candle burning on the mantle. I went into the kitchen and searched around but came up empty-handed. "No household should be without at least one candle," I said, reprimanding myself. Then, I remembered a box of odds-and-ends that my mother had sent—stuff she'd picked up at garage sales. Among the items were three miss-shaped, colorless candles with embedded seashells and wicks secured by pennies. I thought they were too ugly to have sitting around, so I banished them to storage to be forgotten till now. Chuck followed me out to the laundry room where he pulled a dusty box down from a high shelf. I started digging through it, and *voila!* There they were—the three ugly ducklings.

I placed one of them on the mantle, lit it, and watched as the flame found its calm and reached toward the ceiling. The room became radiant with a romantic, peaceful ambiance, and what I had perceived as ugly before was now showing itself as exquisitely beautiful.

An hour or so later, the glow weakened, and I went over to investigate. I discovered that one of the seashells had floated on to the wick and was about to snuff out the flame. I went to the bathroom and got a pair of tweezers. Once I removed the shell, the flame flourished again. I wiped the hot wax off of the shell and marveled at its intricate design. "I think that if someone came to fully understand the evolution of a seashell, that they would be enlightened," I said, oh-so profoundly.

Chuck, not quite as ethereal as me, was a good listener and encouraged me to continue. "Look at this amazing thing," I said, holding up the tiny spiral wonder. "No human being on Earth could re-create this—ever. Yet, we don't attribute any financial value to it." I looked back into the candle and spotted another shell moving in toward the wick. That flame wasn't going to get snuffed out on my watch! So, I retrieved it and wiped it off. Then, I wondered aloud, "What else could come out of a candle?"

Chuck stood next to me in silence until I answered my own question. "Crystals!"

Chills swept across my scalp and down my arms. Then I elaborated. "Crystals, and Rubies, and Sapphires, or *any* precious gem could come out of a candle." Goose bumps ran down my legs as the questions and ideas exploded into play.

I needed help understanding the basic science of candles so Chuck did his best to explain. "Most wax comes from petroleum. It liquefies when it's heated. That liquid then fuels the fire by way of the wick, which becomes saturated with the liquid fuel." But it wouldn't be until I made them myself that I would fully get what he was saying. What did become clear, however, was that it was a relatively simple and inexpensive craft.

Neither one of us had ever come across the concept of buried surprises in candles. We had seen candles with seashells and flowers embedded in the outer rim for decorative purposes, but none with buried treasures intended to be discovered through the burning process.

"There must have been someone," I said. "Like, maybe in ancient Egypt, who had this same idea. Think about it…a robber could come into your home and steal everything of value but never think twice about the ordinary-looking candle sitting in the middle of the table, containing all your diamonds and rubies. Oh, my God, it's brilliant! Seashells will be honored…and quartz crystals, too," I continued. "Yes, 'treasures of the Earth' will be buried inside each one." The candle wasn't the only thing on fire.

It seemed fitting that Chuck should be my partner in this venture, not only because he was present when I conceived the idea, but also because I thought he could help bring to the table what I was short on—capital and know-how. The problem was that he had recently started his own real estate business, so I wasn't shocked when he passed on my offer. "I would, however, like to contribute a hundred dollars toward your initial printing costs," he said. I thanked him for his generous offer before saying goodnight and returning to my newfound dream—"The Treasure Candle." I spilled over with excitement and laughter as the ideas kept coming.

Though yearning to share my concept with one of my closest friends, I managed to keep it to myself. It was something that needed to be **done**, not talked about. The idea itself was a great treasure, and this time I was not going to make the mistake of giving it away. No—this one was all on me.

Technidiscs' oxidation problem didn't matter in the long run because the entire technology would become extinct before it had a chance to take off. Meanwhile, I was being pulled by a new and powerful vision. Yes, it was time to change tracks, and set about the task of becoming an entrepreneur—time to let go of the pursuit of an acting career.

The fact was that for fifteen years now, no matter how much magic I created, or how many influential moguls I connected with, the universe just wasn't giving me what I wanted. It seemed obvious that I wasn't destined to share my acting talent with the world after all. It was a tough thing to admit, but I took my metaphorical bow and cut my ties with the theater. Then I cried and wailed for three consecutive days before turning the page and becoming an apprentice candle-maker. Fortunately, I'd be able to hang on to my job for another six months, for those steady paychecks took the stress out of start-up costs, modest as they were.

At a candle shop in the valley, I bought a beginner's kit. Then, I went downtown to the jewelry district and purchased charms and pendants to add to my collection of stones, crystals, and seashells.

I poured hot red wax into two pillar molds, filling them up 1/3rd each. Once the wax hardened substantially, I used long tweezers to secure the treasures inside, and then repeated the process for a second layer. With great anticipation, I removed my first prototypes from their molds, disappointed to see that the finish had harsh demarcation lines between the layers. But that didn't deter me, for I knew, as the ugly ducklings had shown me, they'd be beautiful in a dark room, burning.

When I presented my festively wrapped gifts to friends and family that Christmas, I made it clear that I had made the candles, which surprised everyone, as I'd never been a crafty kind of gal. I encouraged them to burn their candles but gave no hint about their hidden surprises.

Several days went by without any feedback. Finally, I asked Brinke if she had burned hers yet. She said sweetly, "Yes, I've been burning it. And it's really lovely, Franny. But I think you could enhance the look of it even more." I stifled my laughter and humbly accepted her criticism, realizing she had no notion of the buried treasures.

Finally, the feedback started coming in, and as I expected, the reaction was fantastic. Next, I ordered twenty heart-shaped molds. My plan was to have a hundred hearts ready for market by Valentine's Day, 1987. That would be my official launching, and I'd sell them for fourteen dollars each.

Lisandre generously presented me with a batch of quartz crystals as a start-up gift. Ceremoniously, she set them out on my living room floor, encircling the small ones around a large point that she called the "mother generator." Then, with a prayer, we infused the "mother" and all her babies with the mission of transmitting positive energy into the lives of all who would receive them. They were to become secret agents of love, a notion that tickled the mischievousness in me.

The unattractive line of demarcation between layers was an issue that would require much trial and error to figure out. The problem was that I didn't have the luxury of waste, so I bought some paisley-printed cellophane to wrap each candle in, camouflaging its imperfections.

I consulted with a trademark/patent attorney in the hopes of being able to secure a patent but was told that no one could own the idea of burying something in a candle—even if it'd never been done before. "Your best bet is to be the first, the fastest and the best," he said. He advised me to create a logo and trademark it along with the name. I consulted with two more patent specialists just to make sure, and they all agreed. So, I doodled around until I came up with my logo: a heart with two smaller hearts within, and a flame rising out of its center.

When Valentine's Day arrived, I had one hundred heart shaped candles, wrapped and ready for market. Each one had a card secured by a pipe-cleaner, explaining the special nature of the gift. I blessed them all with a prayer that went something like: "Mother, Father, God, I infuse these candles with love and ask that you guide them into the lives of people who will be delighted, amused and touched by their magic and beauty. I thank you with all my heart for choosing me to bring this special light forth to the world. And thank you in advance for the abundance, the joy, and the many opportunities that this endeavor will reward me with. I am forever grateful. Amen." I packed them into the car and headed for the Beachwood Market.

Happy to support me, the owner of the grocery store allowed me to hang around outside and try to sell them. I sat on a brick ledge in the parking lot and called out to each passerby, "Do you need a Valentine gift?" It was humbling, for sure, but I was heartened by the receptive response and by day's end I had sold forty of them. Several more were sold through word-of-mouth, and when the final tally was in, I'd earned back my start-up costs plus a few dollars profit. I was off and running.

One morning, as I was taking candles out of their molds, I was shocked to see Mr. T. coming up the steps. He walked into the house amidst candle-mania, and there wasn't a thing I could do but try to convince him that this was only a hobby. He had one thing to say about it, "There's no money in candles, Frances."

In July of '88, while back in Michigan for the quarterly meeting, I was finally cut loose. The reason given was, "low sales figures." Oh well, we all knew that had nothing to do with me. Mr. T. looked at me lopsided when I said, "Okay, that's fine—but keep your eye out for 'The Treasure Candle.'"

I was grateful for having gotten the axe in the morning, as it was a warm sunny day in Michigan and I wanted to make the most of it. I called Jeanine who happened to be in town for a high-school reunion and was thrilled when she invited me to join her for a day of boating with some of her friends. By 2 p.m. I was lounging on a raft in the middle of a sparkling lake, laughing and waving good-bye to my past. *Perfection!*

Photo by Brinke Stevens

ALICE IN BUSINESSLAND

Typically, I'd come down from the loft in the morning, open the blinds, feed the cats, make a pot of coffee, and begin to take apart the molds that I'd poured the night before. One such morning, I was taken aback by the exceptional beauty of each heart-shaped candle. Their sheen was so lustrous and their rainbow colors so gorgeous that I could hardly believe they came into form through my hands. As I opened the third glorious creation, a wave of ecstatic energy moved through my chest and up my throat—but rather than allow it expression through the exhilarating yelp that it sought—I squelched it and continued on with my task. Soon, the part of my brain that was aware that something had just happened was asking, "What was that all about?"

The answer came quickly. "That was **joy** moving through you."

"Why did you stop it?" I probed.

"Because it wasn't coming from acting success," I replied.

Wow. Blocking joy? How foolish is that? Am I really going to be one of those people who walk through life inhibiting joy? "**No**" was the answer to that one. So, with a deep breath, and a vocal release of gratitude, I surrendered that constraint forevermore. *From now on, I will always be open to joy, wherever it comes from.* I cannot overstate the weight that was lifted with that revelation.

Every few days, I drove to the supply store and loaded my trunk with eleven-pound slabs of wax that I would carry up the twenty-four steps to my house. Of course, I was just as often hauling the finished product down the steps and into my car, so it was a constant schlepp. But I was in excellent shape and mostly appreciated the workout. On quite a different note, I pretty much ruined the oven, totally trashed the floors, and came damn close to burning the house down more than once. I can only credit my angels for getting me through those situations unharmed.

One day, there was a flyer in the mailbox from someone looking for housework. I called the number and asked the woman if she'd be interested in learning how to make candles instead. Enthusiastically she replied, "Yes!" Tali, a twenty-year-old army veteran from Israel, had recently arrived in California and was living with her boyfriend. With a high work-ethic and the sensibilities of an artist, she quickly developed a talent for the craft. Less than a year later, she governed her own little factory in a rented garage, filled with supplies that I provided. We were jamming.

Over the next couple of years, I'd set-up and train over a dozen other individuals who also created their own production facilities in their garages or their kitchens. They were independent contractors paid by the piece that I lovingly referred to as my "peace-mealians." Tali, my superstar candle maker, earned more money than she had ever imagined possible, while I grew a booming cottage industry. Meanwhile, I kept looking for a real manufacturer who could take on production and allow me to grow the business to the million-dollar level and beyond.

One rainy day, the pyramids came out of their molds riddled with pock-marks. Who knew that candles were sensitive to humidity? Since waste was not an option, I desperately needed to find a way to turn ugly into beautiful. At a local craft shop I found a fire-friendly paint available in several luscious metallic colors. With several tubes in hand, I hurried home to test them out. Voila! So fantastic was the result that I ended up creating a demand for metallic pyramids—and the more texture to them the better.

In November, 1989, the Berlin Wall came down. Through

television the world bore witness to the celebration as thousands of people clamored for their souvenir: a piece of the wall. *I want a chunk of that wall. Then I'll figure out a way to cut it into pieces small enough to bury in a candle—and it'll be a limited edition. Yeah, and I'll call it The Freedom Candle...and I'll share part of the proceeds with Amnesty International. Yes, yes, yes!*

On the boat the day I got fired from Technidisc, I met a woman from Germany, so I called Jeanine to see if she could put me in touch with her. That proved easy enough, and as fate would have it, the woman had a cousin in Berlin who was delighted to secure a chunk of wall for me in exchange for a hundred dollars. I wired him the money, and a few weeks later I had a piece of wall, graffiti and all.

Lisandre's husband, a professional stone cutter, sliced my chunk into small cubes, which I then wrapped carefully in tinfoil. In addition to that special treasure, I also buried a sterling silver dove pendent and a tiny quartz crystal in each dove-shaped candle. Once I had fifty of them made, I contacted the Los Angeles Times. Within two weeks they published an article on The Freedom Candle. What I hadn't figured on was the article getting picked up by the UPI (United Press International), causing orders to come in from gift shops around the country. *Yikes! Now I need a shipping department.*

Lisandre stepped up to the plate and became my first employee, technically speaking. Her garage became shipping central and her spare bedroom served as the main office. Not only did she become the head of operations but she and her husband were able to guide me to great treasure resources.

I continued to produce candles in my own home, while focusing on sales and training. Wherever I went, I had candles in the car. Be it a store or a person I encountered, there was no stopping me from selling. One day, while soliciting a potential retailer in Venice, I met a bright-faced, engaging salesman by the name of Guy (pronounced Gee), who was representing a few

New-Age lines. He fell completely in love with The Treasure Candle, and after an hour or so of talking, we entered into an agreement. He would represent my line in any store he could open, as he traveled the California coast. Lisandre and I always loved it when Guy showed up with a beaming smile and a pile of new orders. The enthusiasm was building. I had a tiger by the tail.

One afternoon, I read a compelling letter from Tierra Del Sol, a school for mentally disabled adults, seeking financial contributions. At first, I felt bad that I couldn't afford to write them a check but then an idea struck: *What if I designed a candle in their honor and shared with them a set amount from the sale of each one?* The concept was already working with the Freedom Candle, so I decided to give it a try.

The foundation's director responded enthusiastically and invited me to come meet the art teacher. That gentleman then created a contest for his pottery class: to design a sun-face that would represent their school, one that would be painted gold and mounted on a dark green candle. Two stunning designs resulted and I committed to both. Tierra Del Sol and The Treasure Candle were destined to go a long way together over the coming years.

In retrospect, I'm able to see that, even though I was blazing a new trail in life, I was utilizing several of the same skills that I had employed as an actor. The creativity and resourcefulness that I brought to a character was now being used to remove obstacles and create new opportunities, which in turn led to expansion in sales. Knowing how to be a good listener and connect well with people aided me in developing lasting relationships with suppliers, retailers, bankers, and employees. My natural ability to sell served me well and having a product other than myself to promote made it so much easier. On the rare occasion when someone rejected my candle, it didn't faze me—I knew that they just didn't get it.

During the period of time when I worked the craft show scene, I befriended an angelic looking jewelry artisan named Alura. When she and her boyfriend broke up, I offered her a place to stay in exchange for help with my business. I welcomed the creative energy that was in constant play between us, giving way to trust and friendship.

Around 1990, my sister, Nancy, came down from the Bay Area to help me find a warehouse to lease, for we were quickly outgrowing Lisandre's garage. Within the first hour of our search we found a place. Alura accepted the position of warehouse manager, while Lisandre continued to govern finances from her home. Keeping up with the demand remained my biggest challenge.

Eventually, I connected with John, the owner of a small candle factory in Santa Cruz. I arranged for John to come and observe Tali for a day, and though she was reluctant to reveal her secrets, her resistance soon melted, for he had nothing but admiration and respect for her skill. Inspired by my growing business, John and I cut a deal. Finally, I'd have some real strength in manufacturing. He would deliver the product on an as-needed basis.

I remember driving around town in December, 1990, making last minute deliveries to stores that just couldn't keep enough Treasure Candles on their shelves. I felt such joy—such fulfillment—that I cried. I loved my new story. I loved my life.

Photo by Paul Aratow

The Tierra Candle

BREAKING A MILL

It wasn't long before we had outgrown our warehouse space. Alan, the landlord, offered me the front section of an empty, beautifully refurbished, fifteen-thousand square foot building in North Hollywood. He saw that I had a burgeoning business and offered me what I needed to grow it. This was one of many examples of what I saw as grace operating on my behalf.

The building had a dome-shaped ceiling, secured by giant redwood beams that supported beautiful new light fixtures. There were ten offices upstairs with polished oak floors that opened to a long, mezzanine walkway, overlooking ten-thousand square feet of warehouse. It was awesome. It even had the added charm of being located alongside a defunct railroad track, and on warm days we'd open the wide sliding doors to a loading dock where my employees would enjoy their cigarette breaks. On birthdays and other occasions, we'd set a grill out there, and have a company cookout.

Christmas sales represented two-thirds of my annual income. That made it extremely difficult to create a budget because production had to be financed as early as June, when sales were at their lowest. I needed a line of credit but the bank kept turning me down because I didn't have any personal assets. I did the best I could with what I had and required everyone to pay cash-on-delivery. "In COD we trust," I used to say.

Still, in 1990, in order to meet the demands of the upcoming Christmas, I needed to get my hands on more capital, so I applied for a Small Business Loan. Thankfully, I was approved, and a small independent bank in the Valley made $75,000 available to me. When I met with the bank president to sign the documents, he told me that I had to take out a life insurance policy, naming the bank as the beneficiary. "Oh. So, how do

I go about that?" I asked. That's when he introduced me to a gentleman representing New York Life Insurance. His name was Joel and he would become the agent for all my insurance needs for many years to come.

A year later, The Treasure Candle was doing extremely well at hundreds of stores in California and beyond. My biggest customer was Tops Malibu, regularly sending a truck to load up on as many Treasure Candles as I was willing to sell them. During the crazy busy holiday season, I did my best to refill their orders but was irritated by the owner's constant pressing for a deeper discount, (I was already giving her five percent). But I held the line and said "no", for mine was a sold-out show and discounts were not necessary.

Because Nancy had a passion for operations, and my growth had created the need for an operations manager, I accepted her offer to move down to L.A. and fill that position. At the same time, I moved Alura into product-development, while Lisandre, now pregnant, continued to do the bookkeeping from her home.

Nancy moved in with me just as Alura moved into the adjacent cottage. The Woodrow Wilson compound became all about The Treasure Candle. Alura even set up a small production facility out on her patio. It was an awesome time where everything seemed to unfold in perfect order. We were a happy crew, throwing parties to celebrate holidays, employees' birthdays, and big sales. But the best party of all was at Christmas time when I gave generous bonuses to everyone, slipping hundred dollar bills into their Christmas stockings, along with some more personalized gifts. I loved circulating the abundance.

The next two family members to come on board were my dad and my brother, Russell, both in a sales capacity. Russell had quick success with a chain called Wicks'n'Sticks, whereas my dad worked the malls around our home town. After thirty years of dealing with Teamsters, selling his daughter's candles to nice ladies in gift shops was quite appealing to him. In time, when he really needed it, I was able to set him up with a nice salary, something that humbled both of us.

By the end of 1992, The Treasure Candle cracked the million-dollar mark. *Wow! If they could see me now.* And one by one, my family came to do just that. My mother, who I deemed to be the godmother of the business for having sent the inspirational ugly ducklings, was thrilled beyond words over my success. But I cannot overstate how impactful my dad's response was when he came to T C headquarters. As I led him through the building, introducing him to each of my twenty-plus employees, he could barely contain how pleased and proud he felt. And what a kick it was when I showed him my new forklift. You know you're a friggin' serious business woman when you own a forklift.

Meanwhile, Nancy, Lisandre, Tali, Guy, Alura, John, Brinke, Jeanine, and many more gathered in celebration as we moved into 1993. This was the year when I would finally let go of the burden of having to prove my worth to the world. Instead, I would focus purely on the task before me: taking this baby as far as possible. I set my sights on eight million in five years. Yes!

At the Chicago trade show, I met a distributer who suggested that the candle should come with a fable. That idea struck a chord with me, so when I next got together with Jeanine for dinner, I put forth the challenge of coming up with an idea for a fable. Cynthia, from the Melrose Theater, joined us and rendered the following suggestion: "There was a beautiful princess who fell in love with a brave young knight, but he was imprisoned by an evil king…" That served as the crux. I took it from there.

THE FABLE OF THE TREASURE CANDLE

> *Once upon a time, in a distant land, there lived a fair Princess who was in love with a brave young knight. But alas, the*

Knight was imprisoned by a most evil king.

After longing for her beloved for many a month, the Princess conceived a clever plan. She traveled to a mystical kingdom deep within the Earth where she gathered crystals and stones with magical powers.

Upon returning home, she made a candle in which she concealed the treasures. Then she arranged to have it delivered to her lover in his cold dark dungeon.

The sad and disheartened Knight welcomed the gift of light and immediately burned his candle, unaware of its special powers. When the crystal revealed itself, a rainbow appeared from within. A wave of joy and love swept through him as he realized the special nature of the gift.

At that moment, the crystal in the candle the Princess was burning also shimmered with a rainbow. Then lo and behold, the two tiny rainbows soared out into the heavens and became one. The power of their love was so great that they were drawn into the rainbow's arc where neither prison walls nor evil kings could ever keep them apart.

Within each 'Treasure Candle', you will find a crystal and other gifts of the Earth, each with their own special power. Hold your crystal up to the light; you just might see the beginning of your own magical rainbow.

With Love and Rainbow Wishes,

The Keeper of the Flame

Franny, Brinke, and Jeanine

TC Office with Nancy

Dad and Me

MY BABY'S BEEN KIDNAPPED!

In the first week of January, 1993, Cynthia called from New York to inform me that she had seen and purchased one of my pyramid candles at Henri Bendel's (not an account of mine), but that it bore the name "Tops" on its face. Horror gripped me. She agreed to send it priority mail that same day. Two days later, when I opened the box and saw for myself the Tops logo on my candle, my heart nearly stopped. *My baby has been kidnapped.*

Upon further investigation, I found that even though my card was still attached, my company's address had been cut off. Then, unbelievably, when I unraveled the fable, I discovered that there also the company name and address had been cut off. Can you imagine the outrage, the fury, the pain I felt? Holy shit....what to do?

First, I decided to confront **"Her"** directly. "What the hell are you doing selling my candles to Henri Bendel's—with your name on them?!"

She didn't shrink from my ire, but rather acted like I had blown my opportunity to work with her. "Well, you were so rigid about offering me a better discount that I had to do what I had to do."

"What are you talking about?" I screeched, unable to contain my outrage.

That's when she went on to explain that she would be introducing a similar but uniquely different version of a candle with the same concept, and "yes, they will be pyramid shaped, but with an entirely different look than yours." I probed further to see if there was some way to talk her down from this and that's when she divulged that she had already set up a factory in Oregon. I nearly fell out of my chair. I could not believe that she felt free to do this—but she did, and by the time we hung up, I knew that nothing short of a court injunction was going to stop her. *God dammit! Now I have to find a lawyer and put my fucking energy and money into stopping this bitch!* Yes, I could get ugly sometimes.

"If you're going to draw your gun, Frances, make sure it's loaded," Alan, my landlord said. "You should use my lawyer, Madison. He's solid, he's tough, and he'll take care of business." So, that was that…I had my fire-power. With solid evidence in tow, Madison led me down the path of litigation.

Through a lengthy deposition with the owner of Tops and her husband, we learned they were getting divorced and banking heavily on this candle being a substantial part of her financial future. We also learned that she had searched for related patents and actually did find one! It belonged to a doctor somewhere in the Midwest. He had secured the patent for the idea of burying a capsule containing a message inside a candle. *What?! So, it **was** patentable after all?* But it wasn't that simple.

Being a savvy business woman, and one of means, Tops made a deal with that doctor whereby they leased the patent from him. That is what allowed them to announce at the L.A. Gift Show that they "held the patent on the candle", implying that they were the originators of the idea. And to further her plan along, she used my candles to secure prestigious clients like Henri Bendel's, selling them at a loss. I was being horribly violated. My candle business was my baby. It came through me and from me. I gave my all to it, and now this ruthless woman (an ex-actress no less) was attempting to crush it—to crush me.

Madison's professional opinion was that going to trial would be too costly and not necessarily a victory for me. Sure, I could prove she was guilty of trademark violation and perhaps more, but it wasn't definite that I'd be able to get a Cease and Desist order—and that's what I desperately wanted. Madison urged me to settle.

"Take the money and grow your business with it. Compete with her. You can tell everyone your story. You just won't be able to tell them the dollar amount you settled for. But you'll always be the original."

I listened, and after tormenting myself over the matter for days, finally caved to his reasoning and accepted the six-figure settlement. From then forward, The Treasure Candle and Tops would be fierce competitors. I must admit that the competition gave way to dramatic growth for my company, putting us quickly into department stores, and I certainly did have the better story to tell. However, if I had it to do over again, I would at least have secured a second legal opinion. Who knows, maybe I could've won that Cease and Desist. In any case, it was a terrible injustice to have to deal with, and one that gnawed at my gut for years to come.

Thanks to a buyer with some morality, Henri Bendel's shifted their orders to me, going for the Tierra Candle in a big way. I made a promotional appearance at the Fifth Avenue store during the following holiday season, and I'm pleased to say that Tierra's proceeds surpassed the thirty-thousand-dollar mark by year's end. Thanks to Bendel's, Macy's, Bullock's, and thousands of other retailers across the country, I sold over three million dollars' worth of Treasure Candles in 1994. As a reward to myself, I booked a trip to the mystical ruins of Machu Picchu, Peru with a group from a spiritual center founded by Michael Bernard Beckwith known as Agape, a place I had always heard great things about but hadn't found the time to explore. The community, insights, and inspiration experienced on that sojourn would serve me in ways that I couldn't even imagine for many years to come.

Meanwhile, Tops was going strong, too, and countless other copycats jumped on the bandwagon. I couldn't stop them from making candles with surprises in them, but the minute they used the phrase "Treasure Candle," or responded "Yes" to someone asking, "Are those Treasure Candles?"— I was all over them. My trademark was the only thing I could protect, and I did so diligently. Nancy nicknamed me *Litigia*.

One huge, international merchandiser known as Russ, and famous for having brought Troll Dolls to the marketplace, quite boldly introduced his new line of "Treasure Candles" at the Chicago Gift Show. I was so furious that I made my way past his protective sales people and confronted him. "Sir, you are violating my trademark! I am the originator of this product and did not schlepp forty pounds of wax up and down steps for three years only to wind up coming to a show and finding imposters like you making money off my creativity! I won't have it!"

Russ, who was known to be tough as nails said, "Hey, calm down. Let's find a win/win here." He guided me away from the gawking salesmen and said in a low tone, "Why don't I pay you a royalty?" The next day, we signed an agreement. In the end, his made-in-China version didn't have the quality needed to become a hit and no great fortune was made there, but I did appreciate his willingness to try to right his wrong.

One day, while making my rounds to local retailers, I spotted a sphere-shaped candle with a gold angel mounted on front. It was wrapped like my candles and had a similar card accompanying it. When I read it, my heart sank. Yes, it had a quartz crystal within. I recognized the workmanship of that candle, and so to confirm my worst fear, I asked the store owner who he purchased it from. "Her name is Alura," he said. I felt like I'd been punched in the gut…again.

Alura had moved out of the cottage and left her job at TC in order to return to her jewelry business—or so she said. Upon further investigation, I discovered that she had rented a space downtown where she had set up manufacturing. I didn't have the stomach to accompany Nancy and our head of shipping when they personally delivered her Cease and Desist letter. But to add insult to injury, they saw that she was using stolen TC molds. So, there you have it; Alura was no angel after all—and certainly no friend. Had it not been for some of life's more serious challenges, I likely would've suffered more from these heartbreaks and betrayals, but my dad had a major surgery coming up, and he was someone in my life whose love was real.

It was the final quarter of 1994, and all six of us kids managed to get back to Michigan for my dad's quadruple bypass. I planned to stay on for a couple of weeks, if he should be so blessed as to survive. I wanted to relieve as much of the burden as possible from his wife, Joan, and from my sister, Lee, who was stretched far too thin with her many responsibilities. I'll never forget how, on the day of the surgery, the doctor came out to the waiting room and said to us, "Your father's heart is actually very good, but I've never seen lungs like that on a *living* person." *Whoa!* So, that's what happens after thirty years of smoking.

On a ventilator in ICU for three days, things were looking grim. Seeing him with that horrid hose down his throat was so upsetting that I had to dart into phone booths to release my anguish. In the hospital chapel, I lit a candle and prayed for his full recovery. On day four, due to some improvement, they tried and were successful at taking him off the ventilator. *Thank you, God.*

I was sitting near him while he slept that day, operating the saliva tube (that's what love can do to you), when suddenly he became agitated and started cursing. "Son of a bitch, Frank—help me up. God damnit, Jim! Help me!" Jim and Frank were two of his three brothers who had already passed on.

I nudged him awake, and asked, "What's happening, Dad?"

"I was stuck in the bottom of a well—and Jim and Frank were up at the top, looking down at me—but they wouldn't lift me up. I'm so mad at them."

"It's not your time yet, Dad. You're going to stay here a while longer…with all of us. And I'm so happy for that."

Because there was a steady pressure from buyers to continually introduce new models, I had to invest most of my profits into research and development. Meanwhile, my manufacturers were making a good, reliable profit, while not incurring any of the costs of growth. That imbalance caused me to face a very big fear: bringing manufacturing in-house. But that's why we have fears, isn't it—so we can face them? And so, it came to be, I took on the very intense responsibility of manufacturing. I'm talking about huge vats of wax cooking all day long—extremely hazardous materials and chemicals. But as grace would have it, a couple of key employees stepped up to the plate and proved their reliability. In general, I was humbled by the dedication that most of my employees showed toward me. It was a beautiful thing and I loved them like family.

One day, I got a call from a buyer at Target saying that she was going to carry Top's candles but wanted to see my line before she made her final decision. I was hesitant to sell to a major chain store. I knew the *Ma and Pa* stores wouldn't like it, but when she offered me an extremely large purchase order, I decided to move forward. I convinced myself that if I offered them exclusive models then the smaller stores might be okay with it.

At that point, I needed for Lisandre to either move accounting in-house or move on to something else altogether. Even though we had outgrown her skill level, I would have remained loyal to her since she'd been with me from the beginning. But, because she wanted to be a stay-at-home mom, she gave me two weeks' notice. To make the close of this special working relationship memorable, I told her that I planned to give her a twenty-thousand-dollar severance before she moved on. I set a lunch date for us on that final day.

With her severance check and a chilled bottle of Dom Perignon in my purse, I called her to say that I was on my way. During that call, she sheepishly revealed that she had already written herself the check and deposited it into her account.

"You did what?" I said, stunned. "Why? That was for me to do. I can't believe you robbed me of the opportunity to give you the most generous gift that I have ever given anyone." Hurt beyond words, I said, "Well then, goodbye," and hung up. I'd enjoy that champagne with someone other than Lisandre, someone that I could truly call a friend.

To meet the increased warehousing demand created by the Target account, I leased another fifteen-thousand square foot building. From there, we shipped massive orders for a couple of years and all was well for a time. But then, the boutique shop sales shrank, due to both the Target exposure and the novelty wearing off. The bottom line slowly began to reflect a downward trend.

Mark, Billy, Russell, Franny, Nancy, Lee

TO HEED OR NOT TO HEED—ADVICE

The idea of sliding into bankruptcy was unacceptable and I was hell-bent on doing everything possible to avoid it. Still, I needed to make sure that if the worst-case scenario did happen, I wouldn't be left with nothing to show for it all. Broke is how I began this journey—it was not going to be how I ended it. I needed to do something smart with my modest savings, so I expressed my concerns to Joel, thinking he might have some suggestions.

"How much are you looking to put away?" he asked.

"Well, I've got forty-thousand, so maybe half of it," I replied.

"Your timing couldn't be better," he said. "My friend, Ed, and I, have just started a new business, and we're looking for some investors."

Joel had already proven himself to me a few years earlier on another investment. That one was for a business run by his brother in Texas that refurbished American luxury cars and then sold them to other countries. The arrangement of our deal was: I loaned Joel twenty-thousand dollars in exchange for a twenty-five percent annual return, to be paid quarterly. He would invest the money into his brother's company and when it went public in two years my principal would double or possibly even triple. At that point, I could either cash out or become a stock-holder. It sounded pretty solid, so I decided to go for it.

Three months later to the day, Joel showed up to take me to lunch. The Smokehouse on Barham was his place of choice. From the valet service to the steak and seafood menu, the Smokehouse offered the feeling of a country club. Seated in a red leather crescent shaped booth, he handed me an envelope as crisp and white as the linens on our table. Inside it was my first payment: twelve hundred and fifty dollars. From then on, I looked forward to our quarterly lunches and Joel slowly became a trusted friend.

At the two-year mark, Joel went to Dallas to help his brother take the company public. When he returned a couple weeks later, he was disheartened and sorry to have to disappoint me; the company would not be going public after all, and I wasn't going to be receiving forty or sixty-thousand dollars. He continued, telling me a dramatic tale about how their lawyer suffered a fatal heart attack the day before it was all supposed to go down. Then everything came to an abrupt halt and he and Ed decided to remain a privately-held company. With a sad face, he handed me an envelope containing a check for twenty-thousand dollars, my original loan amount. Sorry to see the arrangement come to a close, I asked, "Is the company still doing well?"

"Oh, yeah, very well," he replied.

"Well, I don't suppose I could…just keep the twenty in, and continue with the quarterly payments…could I?"

"Yeah, I could do that," he said.

"Really…but I could never get my principal back again…right?"

"Well, I'd need thirty days' notice in writing, but yes, you could still cash out your principal."

I sometimes wondered if he might be harboring a secret attraction toward me. But if he was, he never made anything of it. I believed that he just liked me and wanted to let me in on a good deal. I do recall one time, however, at a luncheon with him and my mother when he said to her, "If I weren't a happily married man, Edna, your daughter would be in trouble." But that's as far as anything ever went along those lines. I told him to hang on to my twenty grand, that I'd continue rolling with the twenty-five percent return. That had been working smoothly for years now, so when he told me that my timing was perfect, and that he and Ed had just started a new business and were looking for investors—I felt like it was divine order.

"What kind of business?" I asked him.

"We're installing ATM machines in hotels," he said.

"I've never used an ATM machine but I know they're becoming very popular," I interjected.

"Yeah, well, last year, Ed and I invested in a few of them with a guy who placed them in convenience stores. We were supposed to receive a percentage of the income they generated but the guy was bad news and skipped town with our money. And then, as we did our due-diligence to try and track him down, we learned a lot about the business and decided to take a stab at it ourselves. So, we bought a few machines and put them in some local stores.

"It wasn't long before we concluded that the maintenance of them was more hassle than it was worth, and we decided to bail on the whole idea. Then, while talking to my brother about the situation, he said, 'Wait. Before you throw in the towel, come to Dallas. Let me put you together with a guy I know who manages a chain of Hilton Hotels. He recently mentioned that he was considering installing ATM machines in the lobbies.'

"So, I flew to Dallas, had dinner with the guy, and by the end of the night had agreed to do a test run in a few of his Hilton hotels. That was six months ago." With a pleased grin, he added, "Let me put it this way, Frances. The test was extremely successful. Ed and I now have a contract with the Hilton chain to install eight hundred machines."

"Eight hundred!" I exclaimed. "Wow! But that must be a huge expense for you guys—buying all those machines." He nodded in agreement, as it dawned on me why they wanted investors. "Oh, I see. But why don't you just go to the bank with that contract and let them give you the money?"

"Because Ed and I have both worked very hard to acquire what we have, and neither one of us wants to hawk our homes and everything else to the bank. We'd rather let investors enjoy a percentage of the profits and remain independent of the bank.

I've got plenty of clients from my years with New York Life who are always looking for a good investment, and I believe we're offering a winning formula."

"Which is?" I asked, my interest peaking.

"An investor purchases a machine for $19,800 and leases it back to us at the same time. They are never to be bothered with the machine's maintenance. It's a passive investment. We take full responsibility for the insurance, maintenance, and upgrading when necessary. Those costs are all covered in the initial purchase price. The investor receives fifty-cents per transaction, per machine, paid out monthly along with an itemized statement of activity for that period. And due to the high traffic prime locations, we're able to guarantee a twenty percent return."

"How much is that per month?" I asked, slightly disappointed that it wasn't as high as the twenty-five percent I was making on the other investment.

"Approximately $330," he said. "However, if a machine performs beyond the twenty percent mark, then that months' check will reflect the increase."

Three hundred and thirty dollars per month would not be all that impactful to my life. On the other hand, I knew it was a good rate of return and did appreciate the guarantee. Still, it would be five years before I'd break even, and Lord knows a lot can happen in five years.

"I don't think I can afford to invest in something where I can't access my principal again," I said.

"Oh, you can sell your machine back to us any time after the first two years."

"Not for the full purchase price though…right?" I asked.

"Yes, for the full purchase price. You just have to give us thirty days' notice."

"But why would you offer that on top of such a high return?

"Because we'd be happy to have the location for ourselves. You see the true value of the deal is not in the machine—but rather in the location. It's our contract with Hilton that's golden here. Besides, we're only offering one third of the machines to investors. We'll be keeping the rest for ourselves."

Now it was beginning to make sense to me. "This is going to be big," he said, and I caught his excitement.

"Would I be your first investor?" I asked.

Chuckling, he said, "Well, not the first, but certainly one of them".

"It sounds like something that would be good for me. When can I sign up?"

"I have a contract in the car."

"Why am I not surprised?" I said, as we enjoyed a good chuckle. "So…when will I see my first payment?"

"Calculations will begin on the first of next month, but the check representing that month will be sent out at the end of the following month. It's always one month in arrears. We need that time to do the paper work. You'll be sent a 1099 at the end of each year."

Everything seemed quite reasonable, and by the end of the day I was a proud owner of an ATM machine in a hotel in Kissimmee, Florida. I put the machine in my mother's name, figuring that she and I could split the monthly income. *Excellent!*

That night, I called my dad and spoke to him and my brother, Billy, about it. They both thought it sounded too good to be true. "But I've been getting my check every three months like clockwork on my other deal," I cried, failing to sway them. Disappointed in their response, I decided to seek another professional opinion, so I called Madison. He felt the same way and advised against it.

Desperately needing some support, I reached out to one more professional, my CPA of many years. And though he was somewhat intrigued by it, he did think it sounded risky. He, too, advised against it.

"Oh, poop," I said, completely deflated. And, as much as I

hated to, I felt I had to heed their advice. Sadly, I called Joel and left the dreaded message.

An hour or so later, as I was walking through the warehouse, I was paged for a call over the loudspeaker. I picked up the phone in the shipping station.

"Frances...why?" Joel asked.

Not wanting to hurt his feelings, I hedged, saying, "I, um—I'm sorry, Joel, but that money, along with my other investment with you, is most of my savings, and I really shouldn't put all my eggs in one basket."

"I'm stunned," he said. "I don't know what to say."

How about "That's fine, Frances. Do what's best for you," and let me off the hook. But instead, he said solemnly, "I'm so sorry that you don't trust me." Pause. "Okay, I'll send you your check back." When we hung up, my stomach felt like a pit of pain. Nancy, who was working nearby, saw my face and knew something was up.

We stepped out onto the loading dock and I brought her up to speed. "He seemed like he was truly hurt by my doubting him, Nancy. I mean, I felt like he was going to cry. Oh my God, I feel terrible. Oh crap. Why does everything that sounds really good have to be *too good to be true?*" I bemoaned.

"It doesn't have to," she responded emphatically. "Look, Joel has come through for you in the past, right?" I nodded. "Dad wants what's best for you but he doesn't always have the answers. I know he has always regretted not investing in Frank's business back when he had the chance." Frank is our super successful cousin.

"Oh yeah, I remember hearing about that."

"Yeah, he would be a rich man now if he had. And Billy is smart but he's young, and has not amassed as much wealth as you have, in case you need be reminded. And, as far as your lawyer and accountant go—well, it's their job to be skeptical. They almost have to advise you against it. I say go with your own gut."

"You might be right, Nancy. This could be my *Frank* opportunity. I'd hate to miss out on it because of other people's fears."

"Good!" And with that, I felt a sense of relief and called Joel to give him the news.

As promised, the first check and every one that followed showed up in my mother's mailbox by the 3rd of each month. Humble as the amount was, it was sweet to share it with her. Then, after a few years of observing the steady income, her husband decided to purchase one as well. And that's how it rolled.

It was August, 1997, and my company had slipped deeply into debt. I knew I couldn't hang on much longer. Painful as that was, it paled in comparison to the loss of my precious niece, Leta, only twenty years old, from Leukemia. It was a terrible time, but a time, nonetheless, where I had a perspective that allowed me to rise above that which is transient in this world. My focus became to find someone to buy my business, so as to avoid bankruptcy. Amazingly, at the New York Gift Show, I found such a candidate while waiting in line at the snack counter.

His name was Jerry and he was a partner in a new enterprise called GiftStar. Their plan was to procure three entrepreneurial gift companies that hadn't been able to make it past the three-million-dollar mark and move the manufacturing to China. And though the *China* part didn't appeal to me, the rest of it did. "Well, that's me," I told him, and then led him to my booth. Impressed, he and his partner flew out to see my operation and, literally, one day before UPS was going to cut us off, we finalized a deal.

With a half-million dollars of debt, I certainly wasn't able to get the kind of terms that I would've liked. However, I did manage to get enough so that I could chill out for a couple of years, following a gradual transfer of the business. The specific terms were that GiftStar would make monthly payments to me over a four-year period, while doing the same with the bank that held my loan.

Was this the way I wanted this story to play out? Hell, no! I wanted the Treasure Candle to continue on for the rest of my life. I wanted it to set my financial future on solid ground. And with my newfound wealth I would produce my own movie. I even had an idea that when it was time for the premiere, I would provide limousine service for anyone who could produce a picture of me as their chauffeur. I hung on to my old broken-down Chevy for years so that it could be used in the movie. But life wasn't giving me my fairytale ending, so sadly, I can't give it to you. I was moving on in a different way, and circumstances being what they were, all I could feel at the time was gratitude.

One day soon thereafter, Joel showed up to take me to lunch and give me my quarterly check. Following a celebratory glass of champagne and a toast to my future, he presented me with a pile of business cards. They bore the name Nationwide Automated Systems, Inc., and to my surprise, Frances McCaffrey under the title "Sales Representative" a presumption that missed the mark, for I could not have been less interested.

"I really appreciate your vote of confidence, Joel, but I don't know diddly about ATM machines. I've never even used one. Plus, I am really looking forward to taking a nice long break from everything." But he insisted that I could still take the break, and that all I had to know were the basic terms of the deal.

"And," he added, "There won't be any pressure on you to meet a quota or even attend office meetings. I just want to meet you for lunch once a month. Do you think you could manage that?" I grinned, knowing that he knew I enjoyed our lunches. "You'd be an independent contractor, working for yourself. Why not make some extra money?"

"I don't know many people with twenty thousand dollars

sitting around. Besides, I don't think I'd be any good at it, Joel."

"You'll make a ten-percent commission on every machine you sell, as well as on any future machines that that person buys—and for sales that come through anyone that they refer."

He sure was sweetening the deal. *Damn, at two-grand per pop that could amount to a nice income.* "Okay. If I happen to talk to someone who has that kind of money and happens to be looking for an investment, then I will gladly tell them about my experience with you and the deal you're offering. Then, if they have further interest, I'll direct them to you and you can take it from there. Cool?"

"Cool," he replied, and we raised a toast to success.

MATTERS OF THE HEART

Having fallen in love with Agape during the Peru trip, I eventually made my way to Greece, Morocco, Egypt, Italy, and Maui on further spiritual sojourns led by Reverend Michael Beckwith. I had found my spiritual home.

It was here, and while traveling with "the Rev" and other like-minded people, that I began to release my resentments and heal my wounds while making new friends. I cannot overstate, just to share one highlight, how incredible it was to sit inside the sarcophagus in the King's Chamber of the Great Pyramid, meditating with eighty other sojourners while Cal Bennett poured his heart out on the Saxophone. My spirit soared and continues to soar through the Agape experience and the power places it takes me—within and without.

Meanwhile, two years had already gone by and I hadn't sold a single ATM. Then one day, Nancy called to say that her life-long friend, Shankari, had sold her house and was interested in talking to me about my investment. After that talk, Shankari committed to five machines, around a hundred thousand dollars. Out of the hefty commission I made, I gave Nancy a generous referral fee. It was a win-win all the way around.

I loved my Woodrow Wilson home but had to face the fact that after nearly twenty years my days there were numbered. The landlord was tied up in court with an estranged brother-in-law who claimed rights to the house and wanted me gone. I thought my smartest move would be to become a home-owner, and I figured my chances would be best if I had an insider's advantage. So, I decided to go to real estate school and at the end of 2001, I hung my license with Dilbeck Realtors in Sherman Oaks.

At the end of 2002, having saved enough money for a down payment, I zeroed in on a condominium in a prime location.

When I discovered that it had both a pool and a Jacuzzi, I was sold. *This is my new home*, I said to myself. Now, fifteen years later, I sit writing in my office, while a lovely breeze wafts in from my private garden, gently embracing me and my beautiful cat, Bello. I am incredibly blessed to love my home as I do.

    With real-estate values on the rise between 2002 and 2005, twenty offers per property was commonplace. And though the competition was fierce, I spent countless hours cultivating potential sales and furthering my education. Meanwhile, Shankari bought another five machines and turned a few heavy-hitters onto the deal as well, enabling me to purchase a couple more machines myself. With that, my investments created a decent amount of monthly income, taking some pressure off me, which began to attract the interest of my friends and associates. Soon Lee and Lou, Brinke, Jeanine, and several other friends got in on the deal. By 2005 the ATM income was triple my real estate earnings. And though I liked many things about real estate, I wasn't in love with it, and felt I could be happy retiring from it—so I did.

My dad was diagnosed with lung cancer shortly thereafter and had very little time left. At eighty-five, he was twenty-five years older than he thought he'd ever live to be and surrendered graciously to the end. I wanted to be with him in his final hours but I was needed here in Los Angeles with my mother and brother, Russell, who was in a nearby hospital recovering from a serious prostate condition. So, my dad and I said our goodbyes over the phone. I reminded him of a dream I'd had as a child where I died and he greeted me on the other side with a glass of water. He promised to do just that when my time came.

    Three days later, as my mother and I awaited the imminent call, a flurry of birds gathered around my outdoor fountain. There must have been at least a dozen of them, fluttering about and chirping up a storm. I stepped into the open doorway and watched the spectacle, as chills swept across the crown of my head. "Mother, come quickly" I yelled. The two of us stood together in awe, allowing the grace of the moment to wash over us. He was gone, as was confirmed by the phone call that soon followed. I would miss him terribly.

2006–2009

Thanks to good health, a happy disposition, a loving family, great friends, and a steadily increasing income, my life became such that even I envied me. Not only were all of my needs met, but I was able to pick up the slack for others. If a sibling had an out-of-state event to attend but was strapped for cash, I was there for them. Be it family dinners, gatherings, parties—no problem. It was my pleasure to pick up the tab. I went on trips whenever Spirit moved me, and in 2007 it moved me to attend a retreat in Hawaii, headlining Rev. Michael Beckwith and Ram Dass, the iconic spiritual leader who brought us *Be Here Now* and so much more.

People came from all corners of the globe to sit at the feet of these wise men and listen as they discussed matters of the heart. On registration day, my interest was piqued by an attractive man who was a key supporter of Ram Dass's, and who was managing the audio end of the conference. When the first session got underway, his gaze zeroed in on me and our eyes connected for an abnormally long period of time. Finally, I couldn't sustain it anymore and broke the connection. Later a woman said to me, "I think that guy, Cliff, is really into you." *Oh, boy, here we go.*

Over the next few days, Cliff and I crossed paths several times between the sessions, allowing us to find out a little more about one another each time. And whether the session was poignant or humorous, we were always emotionally moved. The vibe was fun, celebratory and full of love and devotion—and all in the setting of a rainforest at the ocean's edge. It was Paradise, and Cliff was beaming his love light at me. Yeah, it had been awhile, and I was ready.

One day Cliff asked me to join him while he did some errands. I agreed, and on our return, he pulled over to a parking spot on the beach, took a blanket from his trunk, laid it on the sand, and wasted no time getting around to kissing me. One serious first kiss was all there was time for, and then we were back in the car and off again. It was odd but I didn't dwell on that as the kiss was really nice.

"So, what were you thinking when you were looking at me the other day?" I asked on the ride back.

After a considerable pause he said, "I was receiving a download. I was being shown the entirety of you."

"Really? What does that mean?" But before he could answer we were back on the scene and he just ran off, laughing. I'd have to wait to hear his answer.

Most people probably would have run the other way upon hearing such a thing as, "I received a download on you," but we were part of a community where miracles happened regularly, and besides, I'd always been open-minded about such phenomena. So, when he later invited me to accompany him to the "Ram Dass swim day", I happily extended my stay.

I had heard about this swim day—that it was a VIP affair where everyone would go into the ocean with Ram Dass. Once out there, a massive amount of flower blossoms would be released by one of his devotees. The flowers would float freely around the group, way out there in that turquoise ocean water. Afterwards, Ram Dass would take everyone to lunch. It sounded heavenly and I longed to experience it myself.

The group that day included Reverend Michael, his wife Rickie, and a dozen or so other of Ram Dass's inner circle. Most of us were already in the ocean when the most romantic thing happened. Cliff, all 6'3" of him, walked into the water toward me, carrying a beautiful Hawaiian lei. When he reached me, and with all eyes upon us, he placed the lei around my neck, swept me up into his arms, and twirled me around while kissing me. With our spiritual mentors bearing witness to the moment, I felt like we'd just been married.

The next morning, before my return flight, Cliff told me that he knew that he was going to love me for the rest of his life, and that he was not averse to moving to Los Angeles if that's what was required for us to have a life together. "I don't understand," I said, "And you didn't answer my question. What did that download tell you about me?"

"It told me that you are my Beloved, the one that I have been searching for…for lifetimes. It showed me where all the issues would be, and I know there will be some, but you are the One. It's absolutely clear."

Oh my God, is he nuts? Or am I nuts if I don't give it a chance? Though I couldn't match his certainty, our chemistry was scintillating and my heart was aching to open to someone.

It didn't take long for me to slip into the love groove with him, and for the next two years we did the long-distance dance. Happy to be in a deep, meaningful relationship, I also treasured the opportunity to soak up the mana of Maui and the highly spiritual world of Ram Dass. Cliff was a beautiful man that I developed a great affection for. But there was at least one red flag that showed up around six months into the relationship. Cliff came to disdain my mother and wasn't all that fond of my siblings. He felt strongly that I spent too much time with them.

In June of 2009, Billy and his wife threw a graduation party for my nephew, Ryan, in Atlanta. As the date drew closer, the list of attendees increased to where it was looking to become a family reunion. Sadly, I was going to miss the gathering because I had recently seen most everyone and was planning to go to Maui the following week. Additionally, I was experiencing some dizzy spells that followed dental surgery a couple weeks earlier and wasn't completely recovered. My general practitioner suggested that I take it easy and drink plenty of Gator Ade. I did so, and sure enough, the spells ceased.

At the last minute, the sadness expressed by several family members about my mother missing the party got to me. There was no way that she could handle the trip to Atlanta on her own, so I booked a flight for the two of us, figuring on a quick turn-around for myself. Divorced again, after twenty-six years, Edna had moved to California and was living in a retirement community in Apple Valley. I drove the hour-and-a-half to pick her up and then another two hours to the John Wayne Airport, where we caught our stop-over flight to Atlanta. The party was a great success and served as a righteous pat-on-the-back for my nephew. I was happy that I'd made the effort.

The following day, while on my solo drive back to the airport, a dizzy feeling swept over me. It passed quickly, so I kept driving, but a pit of fear took root in my gut. It happened again and I became afraid that I was going to lose consciousness. My heart started beating hard, and there I was on a frigging freeway in Atlanta. I thought about pulling over and calling my family for help but I didn't want to ruin everyone's day, as they were planning to spend it on a lake. I kept driving and somehow finally arrived at the car rental drop-off area. I sat for a few minutes trying to calm myself down but the spells continued. Finally, I summoned an attendant and said, "I think I might be having a heart attack. You better call an ambulance."

By the time the medics took my vitals I had settled down and everything checked out fine. When they gave me the option to go to the hospital or continue on with my trip, I chose the latter. They did authorize an attendant to escort me by wheelchair to and from all gates that day. My anxiety was so bad at that point that I welcomed the assistance.

The next call I made was to Cliff, who was in the midst of conducting a retreat. Just having him to talk to at such a moment was helpful. He took charge and made arrangements for me to get myself and my car home safely. He instructed Skyler, my one nephew who had not attended the party and who was now living in L.A., to meet a limousine driver at my place and ride with him to the John Wayne Airport where my car was parked. Skyler would then drive me home in my car. It was a clever plan.

As I sat on the plane in Dallas, after a relatively calm two-hour lay-over, the spells kicked in again at an even greater intensity. There was no question that I was having a major medical event and was close to passing out. So why didn't I reach out and get help? Well, I did—to Jesus and my angels, but in this dimension…I just wanted to get home. *I'd rather die on the plane than end up in a hospital, alone, in Dallas.* Very stupid I know, but that was my position. Only by the grace of God did I survive that flight.

Thanks to Joel, I had an excellent health insurance policy and when I asked for his help in finding a doctor, he referred me to his own cardiologist team at St Joseph's in the Valley. Two days later, a medical monitor recorded my heart at over 360 beats per minute. "It's called ventricular tachycardia, or sudden death syndrome," the doctor said. "For ninety-five percent of the people who have what you have, the first symptom is death." *Whoa! I knew I had something but I didn't know it was all that!*

Good as that team of cardiologists were, my case turned out to be beyond their experience and a super specialist was sought out. Meanwhile, after ten days in the hospital, they sent me home with a defibrillator vest—a new invention—one that monitors your heart and goes into 911 mode if you start to have an arrhythmia. If it gets serious enough it will start to sound a siren and the person wearing the vest is supposed to push a button to let the machine know that they're still conscious. If you fail to push the button it will assume you have passed out and will prepare to shock you. Few doctors even knew about this vest. Fortunately, mine one was one of them, and he fought ardently with the insurance company to secure it for me. Cliff came out twice over the next period of time, but when the harsh reality of my tenuous condition began to show up for him as an inconvenience, he became agitated, distant and cold. Soon he received a new download. "Maui is my truth. Maui is my truth," he repeated over and over until he left—at my greatest hour of need. *Excuse me…was it 'Your Beloved' that you called me?*

Lee dropped everything to come and be my person for my second catheter ablation. The procedure is one where they run a thin catheter through an artery in the groin up to the heart. They then burn specific cells in the heart, which creates scar tissue that stops the deadly arrhythmia from completing its course. It is possible that an ablation can cure the issue. That's what I was going for and why I refused to allow Dr. Swerdlow to implant a defibrillator in me, as he recommended. I figured I'd rely on the vest until we had success through ablating. However, while I was getting ready in the pre-dawn hours to go to the hospital for the second ablation, I had another dizzy spell. This time it took me out.

Poor Lee was in the bathroom getting ready when she suddenly heard the sound of a siren inside the house. She ran to my bedroom only to see me laid out on the bed. A disembodied voice bellowed out, "Do not touch the patient! A shock is about to be delivered." A moment later—Pow! The shock was administered and I popped right back up off the bed. When I opened my eyes, I saw her standing in the doorway looking terribly affright.

"Lee, I think I had an episode."

"Franny! You were shocked."

"No, I wasn't."

"You were shocked and I'm calling 911," she said, taking control.

"Lee, I'm good now. Let's just get in the car and go. The ambulance will take me to St. Joseph's but I've got to get to Cedars!" Reluctantly, she agreed, and we grabbed what we needed and hit the road. She drove aggressively across Laurel Canyon in the darkness. Calmness was key—but my anxiety was raw. It was imperative that I not talk about it, while going through *it*. Music was helpful, as I employed my best effort to ground myself in a sense of peace.

As we were pulling into the emergency entrance it happened again, but this time I did not lose consciousness. The amazing vest and its startling siren announced my arrival. None of the staff had ever seen such a thing. I was a marvel of modern medicine. *Oh, the glory!* When they undressed me, I learned that my back was covered with blue ink, something that the vest releases in order to conduct the shock. "Lee, you were right. I have been shocked. Wow, so that means I would have died then…or maybe I did die and came back." She couldn't waste time thinking about such a thing, as she was my responsible, on-the-scene person. This was a role she was far too familiar with, but one she shined in. "Damn. I wish I'd had a near-death experience," I said, trying to humor things up. How grateful I was to have her there, giving me the love and support I needed.

Alright then, if I have to have an implant in order to have my life, then so be it. Maybe I'll be lucky and never need it. Maybe the second ablation will do the trick. One could hope. So, I finally acquiesced to Dr. Swerdlow's plea, and following the second ablation became a bionic woman at age fifty-seven.

Life simplified dramatically for me after that. I took solace in my home, my loving family, my friends, and Agape. I used those next couple of years to focus on healing myself, physically and emotionally, while trying to garner the lessons of love. I counted my blessings regularly, putting Joel and his business high on the list. To go through those years without a financial worry was a huge gift.

Anxiety, post-traumatic stress, and occasional wooziness all plagued me for a time but to this day, the defibrillator has never had to kick in again. That second ablation must have done the trick after all. *Thank you, Dr. Swerdlow.*

What I eventually came to see about myself in my relationship with Cliff was that I had knowingly embraced the *illusion* of love. I dove in head first because I deeply desired for it to be true. I was due for a great romance and just couldn't resist. When various red flags arose (and there was more than one), I told myself to hang in there, that love would prevail. And you know what? It did—self-love that is. My heart was not about to let me shut out those whose love was long established in my life. Nor could it allow me to love someone who wanted such a thing.

Oh—and if anyone ever tells you that they've received a "download" on you—run.

Me, Ram Dass, Rev Michael Beckwith

THE SKY IS FALLING

A rare summer shower had invigorated the air on Saturday morning, August , 2014. I sat toward the back of the church in an empty pew. It was a Catholic mass, and though I hadn't attended one in decades, I felt as if it had been yesterday. At the end of the service, as the pall-bearers came forward and stood beside the casket, shafts of colored light beamed through the enormous stained-glass windows, while a bird serenaded the congregation from just outside. I imagined that I wasn't the only one who took that as a sign of Ellen's presence, a woman who I'd spoken with on the phone many times over the past seven years but had never actually met.

I wanted to pay my respects in person and meet some of her family members who I'd spoken with on the phone. I also wanted Joel and Ed to acknowledge the passing of a long time and very significant investor, so I took it upon myself to order an extravagant flower arrangement and sign the card in their names. Joel was on vacation but I was sure he'd be pleased. He was such a softie. The card was placed on the gorgeous, heart-shaped arrangement of white lilies and roses, mounted on an easel alongside her photograph. Somehow, I was surprised to see that Ellen was a brunette.

She had been referred to the ATM investment by a close friend who was happy with his investment and bought into it heavily right from the start. At the time of her death, she owned twenty-some machines, around four hundred-thousand dollars' worth. I think it was in 2011, when she was diagnosed with lung cancer, that she started making gifts of her machines to the people she held dearest in her life: her daughter, siblings, nieces, nephews and close friends. One such friend was an elderly nun who worked in the penal system in Tijuana. Another was an aged priest who lived in an assisted-care facility. She had come to know these *servants of God* during her time running a home for wayward pregnant girls. Ellen was beloved by all who knew her.

The ATM investment, Ellen believed, was the most valuable legacy she could leave to her loved ones, for it offered a reliable, steady income. Sometimes, during our phone conversations, we would express our heartfelt gratitude for the good fortune of being a part of something so special and so bountiful. We gave thanks for Joel and Ed and blessed their company with many happy returns.

I was feeling rather melancholic while driving home from the funeral service when a call came in from Joel. He never called unless it was important, and never when he was on vacation. Uncharacteristically sharp, he jumped right to the matter.

"Frances, I had to come back from Hawaii for an emergency meeting with Ed. He told me that Shankari had called a couple of her hotel locations."

"I know. The reason she made those calls was in an attempt to prove to her friend, Adrielle, that the investment was legitimate."

"I don't care why she did it. She's been a client for fifteen years! How could she doubt me?"

"Well, see Adrielle is the daughter of some very close friends of Shankari and had just sent you a check for a hundred thousand dollars, which represents most of her inheritance. But then she did some online research and found that one nasty blog out there, and after reading that she panicked. Shankari thought she could put her at ease by proving to her that her machines were real, that they were up and operating. She forgot all about the clause in the contract that restricts her from calling the locations. I told her she should have called me first." He was quieter now, so I dared to address the thing that was bugging me. "But, Joel, the owner of the hotel told her that he owned the ATM in his hotel—that he'd never heard of NASI."

"They don't **own** their machine, Frances. I really can't believe that she would do such a thing after fifteen years of making so much money. Tell her that I want her to send me a letter immediately saying that she wants to sell all of her machines back. I don't want to deal with her anymore. I have no time for people like that—people with no gratitude." Ooh, I did not want to see this go to such an ugly place. Nothing like this had ever happened before, but he was the boss. "I mean it," he continued. "Tell her to get me that letter right away. I no longer want her as an investor."

"Okay," I said meekly, realizing that meant he was eager to cut her a check for around two hundred and fifty thousand dollars, just to get rid of her.

And what kind of an answer was, "They don't own it?" I asked myself. Then, in an effort to shift the energy, I told him that I was on my way back from Ellen's funeral. He took pause upon hearing that and expressed some sadness at the news. That was more like the Joel I knew.

"So, can I also tell Shankari that she can assure Adrielle that you'll be sending her check back?" I asked.

"Yes, I'll make sure that's taken care of," he responded.

"So, may I ask what the emergency was that you came back for?"

"It had to do with our main distributor, and let me tell you, Shankari's mistake nearly cost us hundreds of new locations. This guy is very serious about not wanting investors poking their noses around in that end of the business. You have to make it very clear to your people, Frances, that they should call me if they have any concerns or questions. Fortunately, everything worked out this time." Hearing that was a relief.

Joel had told me about this distributor before. He was an elderly man who owned a vast network of ATM machines, mostly placed in gas stations and convenience stores. Joel and Ed had been buying large increments of his portfolio over the course of the last five years, keeping two thirds for themselves and offering the rest to investors. Loving the reliable passive income, and feeling secure with the longevity of the business, investors were eager to go deeper. For some folks it was straight up addictive.

Two days later, I received a call from an investor who I'd known since my theater days. She had not received her August check and was feeling rather anxious. A skeptic at the beginning, she'd slowly come to relax into the deal. A couple years later, she purchased her second ATM. Now, like a mother hen, she was trying to protect her nest-egg.

Joel had always been punctual, getting everybody's checks to them by the 3rd of each month. I thought she was overly concerned and assured her that it would likely arrive the next day. She took comfort in my confidence but when her check did not appear the following day, she panicked. So, I called Joel.

"We decided to switch over to a check distribution company this month and they screwed everything up. I'm on my way over there now to try to straighten things out. Tell your people they'll be receiving their checks very soon. After nearly twenty years of being perfectly on time, you'd think people might cut us some slack."

I was glad to hear they were implementing procedures that would up-level the functionality of the business, for there had been a steady increase of mistakes each month due to their antiquated system of calculating. I agreed that a check distribution agency might be a step in the right direction, and then, wanting to point it out to him, I said, "My clients are pretty chill, Joel, just as long as they know that the company is solid." He assured me that it was and that they'd be bringing check distribution back in house the following month. "Well that's good, I guess. So, on another matter—have you and Shankari spoken?"

"Yes," he said chuckling. "She called and begged for my forgiveness. All is well. She's staying in." Though not at all money-savvy, Joel acknowledged that Shankari was one of the sweetest people one could ever hope to meet, one who operated strictly on trust. Not only did she have her life savings invested with him, but her mother's and sister's as well. When I told her that Joel wanted her to cash out, she was crushed.

"And did you send Adrielle's check back?" I asked.

"Yes. Ed took care of it."

"Great! And are we still on for lunch this Friday?"

"Sure. See you at Monty's at 11:30 (Monty's had replaced the Smokehouse when the business moved to Calabasas)." I breathed a sigh of relief.

On Thursday many of my people received their checks and I felt assured that things were coming back into balance. Shankari arranged for me to bring a couple bottles of fine wine to Monty's for Joel and Ed, as an apology gift. She included a note, expressing her gratitude for being able to continue sharing in the abundance of their brilliant business. Joel smiled when I handed him the bag, saying, "It's just what we need." We laughed and kissed each other on the cheek before I slid into the booth. First off, as always, he handed me my commission check in its standard crisp, white envelope.

Joel ordered a well-done steak with no sauce and plain vegetables, while I went for the blackened salmon with garlic mashed potatoes, and a side of spinach. His hunched shoulders and the dark circles under his big brown eyes told me that he'd been suffering badly under the stress. He said that the investors were hostile and rude toward him, and that if he had it to do over again, he'd never bring investors into the deal at all. I hated hearing that and felt some anger of my own at those mean ungrateful people.

"I don't know if I can take it anymore, Frances," he said. "I'm going to retire, and I'm going to do it soon. I have to for my health." In his early seventies now, Joel was a self-proclaimed hypochondriac who saw his doctor on a regular basis and nipped anything in the bud that threatened his wellbeing. He was always on a diet but never appeared overweight during the twenty years that I'd known him. His soft, fleshy face gave him a boyish look that was somehow endearing.

He told me that he would be holding a meeting over the weekend with his son-in-law to discuss his taking over the business. This was a plan Joel had been speaking about for a long time now. It was scary trying to imagine someone other than Joel at the helm. Supposedly, his partner, Ed, would continue to manage the finances, but Ed was a prickly sort of character and would be terrible in customer relations.

I wondered if that meant I had to retire from my sales position. My creative juices had been dormant since the Treasure Candle days and I'd become a bit complacent, ignoring the faint voice within that had been calling me to something new for quite a while.

"If possible, Joel, I would like to continue working for another year. That would allow me to get all my ducks lined up. Do you think that's possible?" I asked.

"I'll submit your request at the meeting this weekend," he said, sounding weirdly vague.

"Can we still have lunch together next month?" I asked, reluctant to see our ritual come to an end. He assured me that we could.

Things were going to change and that was unnerving, but at least I knew that the company was still stable and that everyone's money was safe. So, with somewhat of a light heart, I went to visit Lee and Lou in their new Arizona home. Their August check arrived the same day I did, which meant that probably everyone else's did as well. *Thank you, God.*

A couple days later, I received an email from Nicole, a loan broker and close friend of Nancy's. Nicole regularly received two separate checks because she had invested both personally and through her IRA account. The news was that both of the checks bounced. Additionally, she had a client whose check had also bounced. A knot formed instantly in my gut and my heart started to pound, while out of my mouth came the words, "Oh, God! The sky is falling."

"What does that mean?" asked Lee, who overheard me as she was walking down the hallway. I knew I couldn't get away with keeping anything from her. She knew me far too well. Meekly, I replied, "It just can't be so." I turned back to the computer to compose an urgent email to Joel. The notion that the whole thing was merely a house of cards had never been a possibility in my mind, although I do recall someone once asking me what I would do if it all turned out to be a Ponzi scheme. My response had been, "I would have to leave the planet."

"What happened?" Lee persisted.

Cringing, I answered, "Three investor checks have bounced." I couldn't look at her, feeling the fear running through her now. I hit the send button.

Moments later Joel called, and sure enough, had an explanation. "A three-million-dollar check from one of the service providers did not clear our account yesterday. That, in turn, caused a bunch of investor's checks to bounce. Ed and I spent the entire morning at the bank. It wouldn't have happened if our regular bank manager had been there. He would've known to take care of it, and he would've made sure that the investors' checks didn't bounce. But he wasn't there and it caused a horrible mix-up. We figure there are probably over two-hundred checks that won't clear because of it. Meanwhile, we have no way of knowing which checks they are because we had to close our accounts and no longer have access to those records. We opened up new accounts at a different bank but it will take us some time to figure it all out."

"Oh, my God," I replied helplessly.

"I promise you, everyone's check will be made good. Make a list of whose checks bounced and for how much and send it to me. I'll take care of it. It's been one hell of a day, Frances."

"But, Joel," I asked incredulously, "why would the account ever be so low that it depended on a single check clearing?" He had always been quite cavalier about their cash wealth, saying that NASI was liquid enough that they could buy out all of the investors if they had to—all two thousand of them.

"We have several different accounts, used for different purposes," he said. "It's complicated but trust me, Frances, there's no cash problem here—just logistics. This has been a nightmare." *Oh, poor Joel.* But my gut was telling me something different. I couldn't bear to face it, so I continued with my head in the sand.

I would've opted to curl up in a fetal position and moan for the rest of the day but Lee dragged me out to join her weekly dance group. I moved my body to the eclectic music while trying to prevent my dark thoughts from overwhelming me.

On our way home that evening, Lee told me that she was going to keep this to herself for a couple of days. She didn't want Louis to worry, not yet anyway. "Maybe we'll be lucky and our check will clear. God, I hope so," she said. Like so many of my investors, they relied on that income for monthly expenses.

Calls from clients whose checks had bounced started pouring in. To each one, I repeated the story of the three-million-dollar check, assuring them that the ship would soon right itself. "How the hell do you know it will?" I asked myself repeatedly, no longer certain. By the time I arrived back in L.A., I had a nagging cough and serious back pain.

Then, wonder of wonders, the replacement checks started showing up as promised—and they were clearing! *Hallelujah, praise the Lord!* But my relief was short-lived once again, for only some people received a replacement check. The dreaded calls kept coming. By month's end there were still dozens of people with either no check or a bounced one. I finally had to face the fact that I was being lied to by Joel, by Ed, and by their staff.

Meanwhile, there were eight people on my list who were

supposed to send in their money for new machines by the end of the month. Even though I knew it might create panic, I contacted each one and told them to hold back, to wait until things got straightened out. One woman named Linda was of particular concern to me. She was a new investor who had gone to see Joel the day that I'd last had lunch with him. He made her feel so comfortable about the security of the investment that she decided to go for six machines instead of five ($118,800). When Joel and I spoke later that afternoon he told me that she was a lovely woman, one who surely, "had been a knock-out in her day." When I called to congratulate her, she shared with me that she was a widow and that that money was what her husband had left her. Now, I was very concerned.

    I called Joel and leveled with him that I couldn't, in good conscience, allow my people to move forward until everything was back in balance. I told him that I was especially concerned about Linda's money. "She cancelled her order," he said emphatically. "You don't have to worry about her. Everybody has cancelled their orders." I believed him, so when I learned months later, after Linda returned from Europe, that he never refunded her money, I was sickened.

    When it was time for September's checks to arrive, the investors received a letter instead. It stated that due to the inordinate amount of work that the office had been burdened with following the mess-up with the bank, and due to all the thousands of phone calls from anxious investors, the September checks wouldn't be going out until the 10th of the month. Calls started coming in to me now in droves. Meanwhile, my cough had rooted deeper into my lungs and the doctor had put me on inhalers, warning me that I was pre-asthmatic. I also had the worst back pain I'd ever experienced. Meanwhile, I tried desperately to hold on to some hope that Joel would right this ship.

THE LAST LUNCH

In September, 2014, I received an email from Joel saying, "Your government is so greedy that they're willing to put a twenty-year-old company out of business over a matter of a disputed securities license." He elaborated further, saying that NASI was under investigation by the Security Exchange Commission and that their lawyers had advised them to stop paying investors until the investigation was complete. My heart flip-flopped. He ended the email saying that our lunch date the following day was still on. Anxious to have a face-to-face, I hoped that he'd tell me that they were going to survive this situation.

We arrived simultaneously at Monty's at 11:30 a.m. sharp. He looked drawn, his smile forced, and there was no white envelope in sight. When I took his hand and leaned in for our customary peck on the cheek, I noticed it was clammy and shaking. Once seated, he shared with me a legal document: a notice from the Security Exchange Commission stating that NASI was under investigation. That, alone, was a lot to absorb, but the date of the document, June 14th, 2014, informed me that he'd been under this cloud for three months already…which had all kinds of ramifications that I didn't have time to ponder in that moment. I read on further and came to a clause that demanded all records relating to sales people be turned over. "Does that mean they'll be contacting me?" I asked naively.

"They might," he said. "And if they do, take my advice and do not speak to them without a lawyer." *Oh shit, this is getting heavy.* But I was still far from grasping its fullness.

"Is this all because you should've gotten a securities license?"

"Yes," he responded emphatically.

"Well then, won't you be able to work out some kind of deal

with them? You don't have to stop the whole business…right?"

It's painful to admit how ridiculous I was being in holding on to the illusion of legitimacy at this point. I wish he would've just told me to wake up and face the fact that I'd been swindled for the last seventeen years. That it was all just a big fat lie, and that we were all screwed. But he didn't, and I continued to believe that the business was real—that there was just a very big problem that needed to be solved.

But Joel appeared to be completely defeated and dropped a bomb when he added that they had already let go of their staff. Upon hearing that, I sank into the leather seat beneath my sorry ass and said, "So…it's all over?" He nodded yes.

"No more checks?"

"No more checks."

"What about the machines? Who's going to manage them?"

"What will happen is that the SEC will appoint a person called a "Receiver." That person will take control of the business and their first priority will be to make the investors whole."

"Well, thank God for that," I said. "At least the machines will keep making money and everyone will be able to get their principal back—right?"

With a slightly menacing grin, he said, "Well, the Receiver's idea of whole and your idea of *whole* may not be one and the same."

"What do you mean?" I asked fearfully.

"They'll focus on the people who came in last, who didn't make back equal to what they invested. They'll take care of them first."

For me and most of my friends, it was because we knew we could sell our machines back that we invested so heavily. Suddenly, I was realizing that we could lose both our principal and our income. At the same time, there were a few dear friends on my mind who had recently invested heavily, people who were going to be truly devastated if they lost so much so quickly. It was an unimaginable nightmare. I still couldn't believe the picture could be so bleak.

"Some of the investors, Frances, have been horrible to me," Joel said, shaking his head in dismay. Then, in a whisper, he added, "One man came storming into my office and actually pointed a gun at me. Can you believe that? He threatened to kill me if I lost his money. My wife is scared to stay at the house and has moved in with one of our daughters. I'm going to check into a hotel tonight. I don't feel safe. How can people be so cruel?"

"People are crazy when their money is involved," I offered, lamely. Then, feeling slightly guilty about bringing the conversation around to myself, I asked, "What am I going to do, Joel?"

With absolute certainty, he said, "You're better off than you were," referring, I suppose, to seventeen years earlier when I'd just sold The Treasure Candle. Could that be true, I wondered? God knows, I had enjoyed a lot of prosperity over the years, but I was now sixty-three years old, and without NASI, had no income. To make matters worse, many people that I loved in this world, maybe even most of them, were going to be hit hard by this…and all because of me. I wasn't feeling so "better off."

As we sat together in that familiar crescent booth, I looked at my old friend and saw that he was suffering terribly. Suddenly I felt worried for his well-being and wondered if he might be suicidal. "Joel, you're not contemplating anything rash, are you?"

"No," he said. "I thought about killing myself but I couldn't do it. I enjoy life too much. I want to play more golf and enjoy my family."

"Joel, I think this might be a time when you could use some spiritual advice and support. I know I've gotten through some rough times due to the support I found at Agape, and particularly from Reverend Michael. I wish you had a Reverend Michael."

He managed a smile and said, "I have my own relationship with God, believe it or not. And, yes, there is a Rabi I could talk to. Maybe that's not a bad idea."

Somewhat relieved, I refocused my thoughts on how to find some way out of this disaster. "Look, Joel. So, okay…you and Ed should have filed for a securities license. Fine! Why not face the music and pay your penalty? Then you can pick up the pieces and continue to carry on." I wondered if he was even listening as he looked blankly at me. With extra enthusiasm, I continued on. "The investors will work with you, Joel. Maybe you only pay them ten-percent, something like that. Because when all is said and done, if there's still a golden goose standing, why not save it?" But he just looked defeated and shook his head no.

We picked at our meal in silence until he said, "They're going to take everything away from me—everything I've worked so hard for all these years." His eyes welled up with tears, and I have to admit, I was touched. I put my arm around him and squeezed him for a good long moment. But then, I just had to ask, "Joel, is there any way this could end up a criminal case?"

"No," he replied.

He then advised me to send him a letter, the sooner the better, stating that I wished to sell all my machines back. "Maybe the Receiver will work on a first-come/first-serve basis." I took the yellow-line pad I'd brought with me, tore off a blank sheet and wrote out the request. He folded it and put it in his pocket. Then I gave him the other two sheets which had a list of clients who had not yet received their August replacement checks. Included in that list, was an investor who had accidently sent two checks, $39,600 each, for two additional machines. Both checks had been cashed. I brought that situation to Joel's attention and he promised that he'd send the gentleman back his money that same afternoon. I believed him.

"You know, Joel, it has been a great journey, and I'm grateful for having been a part of it for all these years."

"Whatever happens with this, Frances…we'll always be friends," he said, as we got up to leave.

My complete awakening to the truth came three days later, by way of a published SEC report, naming NASI a classic Ponzi scheme. I thought, for sure, that my defibrillator was going to go off when I read those words. It was my worst nightmare made manifest. I would have happily died in that moment—but I couldn't stop reading. The report went on to say that, in fact, there were only two hundred and some ATM machines, nothing like the purported **thirty thousand** that had been *sold*, not to mention the two-thirds that they supposedly owned themselves. But, beyond description, was how I felt when I read the part that said that Joel told the FBI agent that he used the Yellow Pages to select locations for machine placement, that he would run his finger down through the lists of hotels or convenient stores and land on one at random. That elderly distributor that he told me about was completely bogus. All of it—had been completely bogus.

But how could it have gone on for so long, I wondered. The two-thirds of the ATM machines that they claimed they kept for themselves didn't exist. All the money they brought in from new investors went to pay other investors and themselves. The pressure on them to keep selling got greater and greater but the appetite of investors grew incrementally as well. Passive income—everyone's dream. We were all suckers who supported the fantasy.

I was lambasted by the enormity of Joel's betrayal, along with the shame and regret I felt for having brought so many people into his trap. On top of that, I was terrified for my own financial, emotional and physical well-being. I had entered Hell.

My friend, who I had trusted with my life, lied to my face for over twenty years. And what was worse—used me and my ability to elicit trust from others, to lure those others into his web of deceit. My integrity had been horribly abused. I had been horribly abused. How could I have been available to such deceit—to such a scam?

BURNING THE SCANDAL AT BOTH ENDS

The phone rang incessantly, and though I had a debilitating cough, I tried to speak with each person that called, feeling a need to suffer through their painful stories with them. I didn't pick up when I read the word "Federal" on the caller ID window. I assumed it was a marketing call of some kind, but when I heard the message my adrenaline surged. "This is Agent Farnsworth from the Federal Bureau of Investigation. I want to speak to Frances McCaffrey about her involvement with Nationwide Automated Systems. Have her call back as soon as she gets this message. We know where you live and will come to your home if you don't call back immediately."

Holy Crap! Oh, dear God. They're coming after me! Just then the doorbell rang. *No, it can't be them already!* I stood frozen, looking at the door. A moment later there was a loud knock. Finally, I called out, "Who is it?"

"It's me—Guy."

I had forgotten my friend of twenty years was coming by to repair a chair. At that moment, though quite an unlikely angel, he was an angel, nonetheless. No sooner had I filled him in on what just happened than the phone rang again. This time I could see clearly that it said Federal Bureau of Investigation. I stood there, unable to answer. Moments later, we listened to the message, this one from a different man, who identified himself as the lead investigator on the NASI case. He said that I was being summoned to appear before a Grand Jury on the following Tuesday. He demanded a prompt return call.

Guy, an eternal child of the sixties who is most in his element when smoking a joint and playing Beatles tunes on his guitar, was stunned upon hearing the latest happenings in my life. Maybe it was even kind of exciting for him, though his concern for my well-being was the predominant factor. We were both members of the "lucky to be alive" club, having gone through life-threatening heart ordeals some years earlier. His very presence provided some calm for me.

I picked up the phone and called my nephew, Holden (Nancy's son), a business lawyer who had offered to serve as my legal counsel should I need it. I needed it.

Surprised at how fast things were moving, Holden offered to make the call to the FBI on my behalf. I embraced the offer. Ten minutes later, he called back to share what had transpired.

"The investigator said, 'This scheme is imploding so quickly and is so massive in scope that it's an all-hands-on-deck situation.' He also said that they're moving quickly toward securing indictments. He's going to be submitting a summons for you through my email within the next few hours. They want you to go before a Grand Jury."

"Oh my God," was about all I could say.

Holden suggested that I call my cousin, Tom, a top-level business lawyer in Texas who might have some advice and possibly a referral. "And you might want to call your other cousin, Jack. He's a prosecuting attorney in Pennsylvania and will understand clearly what lies ahead." Then, before wrapping it up, he had one last thought. "And why not give Madison a call?"

"Oh, wow, I haven't spoken with Madison in fourteen years. I don't know if he'd be so keen on hearing from me. Plus, he advised me against the investment in the first place."

This was one of those times when I wished I had a partner in life, someone who was really there for me—but that was not my story. So, when Guy offered his shoulder to cry on, I took him up on it. Then he hung out, quietly reading the paper, while I had conversations with my cousins who clued me in on what might lie ahead.

Cousin Tom was concerned about possible criminal liability for me through not having a securities license, and referred me to a specialist in matters dealing with the SEC. After sharing my story with that attorney, he adopted Tom's view that I had exposure. His fee was eight hundred dollars per hour and he was available to take my case. Fear gripped me, as I told him I'd get back to him.

My cousin, Jack, thought that I'd be viewed as an innocent victim by almost any judge but warned me that I had a long, difficult, and expensive road ahead. He would remain available for advice and support but had no west-coast referrals.

I took a shot and called Madison, leaving an urgent message. Early that evening, he returned the call. "Hi, Franny," he said, endearing me immediately.

"Hi, Madison. How are you?"

"A little older but still kicking," he said. "I'm visiting my daughter and grandchild in Colorado Springs right now. Life is pretty good. But what's happened to you?"

"Oh, I'm in a hell of a jam, Madison. Remember that ATM investment I got involved with way back when? Well, I've continued to reinvest with them for the last seventeen years, while also representing the investment to others, and the other day it was discovered to be a straight-up Ponzi scheme…" And so on.

"I'm flying back early Sunday evening. I could go straight to the office. Why don't we meet there at 7:30? We can walk over to a quiet restaurant a couple blocks away and have some dinner. Then you can tell me the whole story." *Oh, what a relief! A friendly, familiar person who knew me when.* Yes, Madison would be my warrior and would guide me through the rough waters ahead.

On Sunday night, I cruised across Laurel Canyon toward his Beverly Hills office, reflecting on when I lived in the house near the Canyon Store with Crystal, back when my plan was to become a film actress. Those were innocent, fun times. Look at me now? *Here I am, going to meet a lawyer on a Sunday night because I'm in extremely deep shit because of a scam that involved more than two thousand people, and funneled more than **400 million dollars** through its doors over a twenty-year period.* The SEC said it was the longest running Ponzi scheme in California's history, and quite possibly the largest.

Madison was an older, more slender version of himself, but his basic good looks and warm personality were still intact. We hugged and gave each other a kiss on the cheek. Memories of my lawsuit against Tops flooded my brain as we walked down the hall past the deposition room. I paused and looked inside, strangely pleased to see that the mural depicting a large raven hovering overhead was still there. Once inside Madison's office, he phoned the FBI and left a message saying that all future correspondence regarding my case was to come through him. I breathed a sigh of release. I felt protected.

In the quiet, dimly lit restaurant, I told Madison the whole story. He had a lot of questions about my finances. I wasn't destitute but he knew far better than I the nature of the beast that was headed my way, not to mention his own fees that, while less than eight hundred an hour, were still considerable.

"You'll get through this and you won't go to jail," he assured me. "But it will be stressful for a few months and you may have to file bankruptcy." The notion that jail was even a talking point made the bankruptcy option attractive by comparison—and I hated that idea.

By the time we arrived back from dinner the FBI had already returned Madison's call. Madison called him back while I sat nearby listening. "We're available to come and talk to you any time this week, but being that it's already Sunday night, I don't think there's a reasonable amount of time for her to be prepared to appear before a Grand Jury on Tuesday. The fact is that she had nothing but a positive experience with both principals for over seventeen years. She lost her life savings in the deal—over five-hundred thousand dollars. She brought her family and friends into it. She's a victim."

They obviously believed him for they never did subpoena me for the Grand Jury, nor did they call me in for an interview. I did, however, receive a subpoena for all of my records, emails, notebooks, bank statements, trust deeds etc. I knew they wouldn't find anything incriminating but I cringed when I imagined them reading some of my overly enthusiastic emails to investors, announcing the availability of machines.

I would have loved to detach from the world and become a cloistered nun at that point, but I knew I had to be brave and walk through the hell that I had somehow co-created. I also had to figure out what I was going to do for income once this saga passed. My first thought was to start up Treasure Candle again. So, I typed *treasurecandle.com* into the web address bar and nearly gagged when it took me to Tops Malibu's website. Yep, they're still in business, though based in Maui now (oh, the irony).

The webpage boasted of her creativity since childhood and implied that she dreamt up the clever concept. And there you have it—after all those years, the wicked witch of the west had her dream life firmly in place, while I was trying to figure out what the next gig would be. Though tough to swallow, it is what it is. The Treasure Candle, **my baby**, gave me eleven years of personal and financial expansion, joy, and love—all of which are untouchable. The poet, Edna St. Vincent Millay, sums up my feelings in her poem titled, "Figs from Thistles: First Fig".

"My candle burns at both ends It will not last the night; But ah, my foes, and oh, my friends - It gives a lovely light."

I secured the domain *theoriginaltreasurecandle.com*—just in case.

Because a part of me died when NASI collapsed, I thought it would befit me to be of service to others as they dealt with death. *I know—I'll sell gravesites for my next gig*. I also wanted my physicality to somehow reflect the transition I was going through, so I decided to stop cutting and coloring my hair. But then the image of me with long gray hair, flipping gravesites, made me laugh and I realized it was actually a mockery of a respectable profession. In truth, I wasn't up to selling anything to anyone.

Desperate to come to an understanding of how I ended up in this nightmare so that I might heal my soul, I started writing my life's story, looking for signs and clues. I cannot overstate how valuable it's been for me to be able to get lost in the adventures of yesteryear, while the authorities screwed their claws into me. And, speaking of claws, did you ever hear the term "clawback?" I sure hadn't—but I can tell you all about it now.

"Clawback" and "disgorge" are both words that when used legally mean "to recover money that's already been disbursed." It's when the great arm of the law reaches out to retrieve all, or as much as possible, of the money an individual or corporation received, over and above the amount they invested. In my case, my investment earnings, $500,000 equaled the same as my investment. Ah, but the Receiver considered my commissions to be subject to clawback as well, so that's where I was in jeopardy.

In August, 2015, Lee was visiting when the dreaded FedEx envelope arrived. Scared to open it, I handed it to her. "1.4 million dollars is the reduced amount that we will accept, if you pay it in one lump sum within sixty days." We both started laughing our asses off. You know, that kind of painful laughter where you feel like an ulcer might be forming. It was beyond ludicrous, and it was very scary. *Will I be able to hang on to my home? Can they take everything from me?* These were the frightful unknowns, as I ventured into the ugly stressful mode of clawback.

Even though there were viable arguments that could be made on my behalf, the costs I would incur by taking it far enough to be able to make them would drag out the stressful process, and possibly wipe out my savings. For the sake of my health, I preferred to reveal everything to the authorities and try to settle as quickly as possible. I needed to get their claws out of me. Madison didn't think that was a good strategy and continued to point me down a longer road that included bankruptcy.

Meanwhile, around the same time that NASI crumbled, my brother, Billy, happened to land a consulting position in the nearby town of Culver City, and for the next two years commuted between Atlanta and L.A. His presence here was a God-send, as he always let me know that no matter what happened—he had my back. Typically, he would arrive at my place on a midweek evening with a couple bags of groceries and a few bottles of wine. It was sweet beyond words when he unpacked the gourmet cheeses, olives, berries and other delectable edibles that helped keep me from feeling deprived. Together we hosted many family gatherings. My mother once said, "There'd have to be a whole lot of dying going on, for you to be left with no family." And for that I am so grateful. Thank you, Mother.

Shortly after I'd received the Fed-Ex letter, Lee, Billy, and I, went for a walk around Lake Hollywood. I was venting my frustrations about Madison's advice when a gust of wind came and lifted my visor off my head, tossing it into the lake. Yes, I'm still that girl that looks for signs from the universe, and that one was as clear as they come—I needed to change advisors. Oh, but I dreaded the doing of it, and I had no idea who I would replace him with.

The next day, I received a call from a long-time friend, Eileen, and told her what was going on. As fate would have it, she told me that her son, who was in law school, currently had a part-time job working for a "super lawyer" who specialized in dealings with the SEC. By day's end, I had myself a new lawyer, one who believed in my approach.

In March, 2016, eight long months later, the new attorney and I got the Receiver down to a hundred thousand dollars. I had to borrow the money from a line of credit, knowing I had no sure means by which to pay it back. I felt good about bringing the matter to a close, and about contributing towards the pot which would ultimately be distributed to "net losers." One thing I've learned through my spiritual studies is to say "yes" when Spirit prompts you and let the how be revealed in time. In other words, a spiritual warrior must be willing to take leaps of faith.

Between social security payments and pulling some from savings each month, I'd be able to get by long enough to write this book. Meanwhile, I also committed to being there in any way possible to support other investors as the heavy hand of government descended upon them—for every net-winner would be victimized a second time through the clawback process. That's how big wheel turns when pertaining to Ponzi schemes.

JUDGEMENT DAY
January 2015

Thirty plus victims filled Judge Otero's courtroom. Joel and Ed sat up front with their respective attorneys while their wives and family members occupied the first two rows. The first order of business was to confirm that the partners-in-crime understood their rights and had both the physical and mental stamina to make a sound decision. Once that was satisfied, the judge asked the two men to stand while he clarified the four counts of mail fraud and wire transfer that they had plead guilty to, noting that the maximum sentence was eighty years, a fine of one million dollars, and the requirement to pay restitution.

After reading seven pages of the claims against them, Joel's attorney objected to one claim that referred to Joel as being "in charge" of the business. The objection gave way to a discussion that culminated in an agreement that the partners had held equal control. An amendment would be added to the complaint. Then, suddenly, Joel collapsed and fell to the floor. Everyone in the room gasped, and I thought *wishful thinking, Joel. You can't get out of this that easy*. But after his attorney listened for his breath and felt no pulse, it became evident that he wasn't faking.

From the victim's section of the room, a man stepped forward and applied chest compression, while Joel's attorney gave mouth-to-mouth resuscitation. After no success, a clerk came forward with an automatic defibrillator and that did the trick. How strange it was that both Joel and I should have our lives saved by a defibrillator. Anyway, his distraught wife knelt beside him, holding his hand until the paramedics arrived. And at that point, the physician returned to his seat, making a face expressing his disgust. Joel's wife responded with a loud "fuck you" that echoed throughout the room. Joel was carried off on a gurney and taken to a county hospital where he would recover.

On Monday, November 16, 2015, the Federal Criminal Courtroom was packed to the rim for the sentencing. I was there with my sister, Nancy, and a close friend, Dina, who had lost her family nest-egg. One of the facts that came out during the proceeding was that, even as the scheme was collapsing, Joel managed to collect over fifteen million dollars from unsuspecting investors. I realized that when he had accepted several hundred thousand dollars from Dina and her husband only six months prior to the end, he knew they would never see the money again. The same had to be true for Linda, the lady who "must've been a real looker in her day", who handed over the bulk of her inheritance from her deceased husband. He, knowingly and mercilessly, screwed them over, along with so many others. The harsh reality of their greed and heartlessness was sobering, to say the least.

We were horrified to see Ed grin with delight as his lawyer spun a tale about their initial good intentions for the business. It was galling to all of us, but especially to the woman sitting at Dina's right; this was a woman bursting with hatred toward the two of them. It made Dina sad to see the crippling effect that hatred was having on the poor woman. Dina had learned long ago how important it is to forgive. Did she hope to get her money back? Hell, yes! But was she going to allow this to ruin her life? Not a chance.

Four hours into it, after the judge had allowed several victims to share their stories, the two defendants stood to receive their sentences. Once he'd risen to his feet, I was finally able to get a glimpse of Joel's face. He looked terrible, all puffy and gray. I felt nothing. Then, the Honorable Judge Otero issued the sentences: ten years for Joel and nine for Ed—with no possibility of parole.

The judge explained that he took into consideration their age, health, early plea of guilt, and helpfulness toward the Receiver. The two crooks would be sent to different prisons. It was done… for them.

Lastly, there was the matter of the bank that proudly dealt with NASI for the entire life of the company, serving to inspire confidence in investors. Any potential investor could call the branch manager and get a rave review on Nationwide. But as was revealed in a lawsuit instigated by victims against the bank, it came to light that the branch manager was an investor himself. He had covered bad checks and turned a blind-eye to several indicators that NASI was a Ponzi scheme.

However, there would not be the satisfaction of a trial, and the corrupt manager would not be charged with any crimes. The matter was settled and the bank agreed to pay 33million dollars to the net-loser victims without admitting guilt. I can't overstate how anticlimactic an outcome that is. The bank, in my worthless opinion, should have been required to make everyone whole again, winners and losers. But that's not the way it played.

After a third of the money is paid to the attorneys, the remainder will go to the victims—eventually. In the meantime, the Receiver has collected more than 35 million dollars through clawbacks, also intended to be distributed to the net losers. Between the bank suit and the clawbacks, the total sum of money to be dispersed to them equals close to fifty percent of their loss. It'll be a day of celebration when it finally comes. However, the Receiver has been promising to disburse those funds for two years already. Every six months it seems the net losers are told to expect payment within the next six months…and on and on it drags.

I find it unconscionable that the Receiver and his team continue to hang on to that money while it collects interest and they continue to pay themselves. Clearly, I'm no lawyer, but what possible good reason could there be to withhold those funds for all this time? I view it as a kind of Ponzi scheme constructed on top of a Ponzi scheme. Anyway, the repayment is inevitable and when it does happen it will represent the end of this saga.

WHAT WISDOM GARNERED?

My like-minded friends and family, along with my Agape spiritual community, gave and continue to give me strength as I navigate my way to the other side of this. I recall one Sunday when Reverend Michael shared a metaphor about a certain seed in the forest that lays dormant for decades, possibly even centuries, until a forest fire has occurred. Then, somehow the ash and debris create just the right composition for its growth to be activated. *Could I be like one of those seeds, and was this my forest fire?*

It is true that since I started writing, I've felt the creative juices stirring once again, and that has given me fresh energy and even hope. Also, having been brought to my knees with shame and guilt, I've lost much of my ego, and no longer feel the need to protect and hide my less than perfect moments. It's very freeing in a weird way. Now, I'm one hundred percent purpose driven and am committed to utilizing whatever time I have left on the planet to share my gifts to the fullest measure. And at the moment, I believe that means sharing my story/stories.

Meanwhile, I continue to work on forgiveness with the forgiving of myself being the greatest challenge. *How could I have been such a fool?*

I see now that Joel was grooming me for his purposes as far back as 1994 when he pretended to be disappointed that he was only able to give me twenty-thousand back, rather than the sixty thousand he'd been priming me to receive. He had anticipated that I would be impressed with his honesty, and sad to see the 25% return come to an end, so he gambled that I'd play into his hands by asking if I could keep my principal invested and continue to receive the interest. I sure did like that money coming in and so timely too! It took some financial stress off and served to fire up my desire for more of the same. Eventually, when I owned several machines, I was one happy investor and my enthusiasm about it was contagious to others. He had me right where he wanted me.

The financial abundance I enjoyed for years was based on a lie—and that can never end well. But again, how could I attract this into my life? Surely, there must have been some red flags. Oh, yeah…how about that time when I was considering buying the first ATM and my dad, brother, lawyer, and CPA all said, "No. It sounds too good to be true?" But instead, I allowed the ego aspect of myself—that part of me that wanted what I wanted, when I wanted it—to sway my wiser self to take the gamble. My ego loved the notion that I was a maverick in business and had earned my place in the winner's circle. Now I recognize that it's far more admirable to be courageous enough to take risks that are backed up by solid research and understanding, than it is to simply take a leap because you believe that you'll be lucky.

So, why did they do it? I'll never know for sure, but my guess is that it was for the short-term pay-off and the glory of the ride. Hey, wait a minute…that's not so unlike my own pattern of taking risks for the sake of the story. Though I usually had good reason to hope for a positive outcome, I was often willing to gamble with my well-being, even when many unknowns were involved. Is that how I went astray with Joel? Should I have required more knowledge of his business? *Yes.* Did I deeply want his path to riches to be true? *Yes.* Did I rely too much on trust? *Yes!* Was I inexcusably naïve? *Yes.*

Getting screwed in this way is horrid. It's emotionally devastating, financially debilitating, and due to the extreme stress it causes, physically life-threatening. My diagnosis of breast cancer a year ago attests to that. Ah, yes…we're back to the topic of my breasts again. And, I must tell you, I never appreciated them more than when their very existence was threatened. I was totally shocked when I got the news, for never did I think that such a fate would befall me, and for many reasons. First and foremost—because they're so darned small, but also because I have no family history of such, and finally because I live a healthy, active lifestyle. But there you go—I'm not at the wheel after all.

"Frances, if you'd been willing to have breast implants, you would've had a career," said my friend, Stanton, who I was in *Echoes* with. I'll never know if he was right about that, but I do know that I don't regret my decision. And I'm happy to report that I still have both my breasts and I am on the other side of the whole cancer ordeal, which for me, included radiation but not chemotherapy. I was extremely fortunate in catching it early.

Obviously, I hope to never have to deal with it again, for it is a show-stopper that reduces you to your most vulnerable self... something that I've become all too familiar with. Perhaps the tumor in my physical body paralleled the disease in my body of financial affairs. Perhaps it was a manifestation of the guilt and pain I felt for everyone else's suffering. But once again, the love and support of family and friends got me through the toughest of times. No doubt about it, in that regard, I am a wealthy woman.

Something remarkable happened recently while I was reading *Brave* by Rose McGowan. I felt gratitude that my acting career didn't happen—gratitude for being spared from any further abuses of the "Me Too" nature. I never thought I'd be able to see a gift in that loss. I was only able to see what appeared to be the injustice of not being able to share my gifts. And guess what—it's never too late to return to acting.

So, where does this all leave me? Some people think I was stupid to spend all the time I have writing this book. But I will never regret my choice. First of all, I now have the book. And maybe equally significant is the fact that I fell in love with the process. I'm not going to count on it to be my financial answer, but I am excited to see where it will take me—what doors it will open. I have many options and am eagerly moving forward, one day at a time.

I love my home and I love Los Angeles, and it would be terribly difficult to leave, but having a peaceful heart and a peaceful mind mean more to me than any address. So, in that sense, home is wherever I am. Saying it is one thing—walking it quite another. But I am stronger than ever and committed to living life to the fullest measure possible, finally understanding that wisdom stems from the heart, not the mind. The apprentice once again, I will expect miracles along the way, but however it manifests, I say "yes" to a purpose driven future—and whatever I do, I'll do my damnedest to bring it all the way home.

May God bless you on your journey and remember…
                              it's the quality of the trip that counts.

Frances McCaffrey

Born in 1951, Frances grew up in Birmingham, Michigan, the fourth of six children. She joined the National Touring Company of Charles Gordone's Pulitzer Prize winning play, No Place to be Somebody, cutting short her second year at Wayne State University. The dream of becoming a film actress fueled her through four challenging years in New York City and another ten in L. A (five of which were spent as a limousine chauffeur in Hollywood), before her world was rocked by a unique idea for a candle. Flash forward and she is the CEO of The Treasure Candle, Inc. grossing more than three million in sales.

The happy family business lasted for a decade but with the saturation of the market and copycats abounding, the business wavered and was ultimately sold. Frances then entered into a business opportunity with a trusted associate who invited her to be a ground-floor investor and a sales representative for his new ATM enterprise. It worked out great and she prospered over the course of the next seventeen years, never doubting its legitimacy. However, in September of 2014, the Security

Exchange Commission was tipped off that something was amiss and soon exposed the terrible truth—it was nothing more than a Ponzi scheme; one of the longest running in U. S. history. In a single day, she lost her life savings, her entire income, and faith in herself. But what was worse than all of that was knowing that she was the channel through which most of her family members, dear friends, and many friends of friends, came into the investment—and most of them were hit hard by the collapse as well. She wanted to curl up and die…but opted to write her life story instead.

Her hope is that you might be entertained by her adventures, emboldened by her courageous choices, and enlightened by her mistakes—and that you be spared the pain of ever being scammed.

Frances currently lives in Los Angeles where she is devoting herself to a new dream—that of being a writer. Please keep an eye out for her next book, *My Limousine Memoirs & More*.

HOME, JAYNE

@homejayne
homejayne2020@gmail.com

www.ingramcontent.com/pod-product-compliance
Lightning Source LLC
Chambersburg PA
CBHW071334080526
44587CB00017B/2833